Racial Battle Fatic

Racial Battle Fatigue in Faculty examines the challenges faced by diverse faculty members in colleges and universities. Highlighting the experiences of faculty of color — including African American, Asian American, Hispanic American, and Indigenous populations — in higher education across a range of institutional types, chapter authors employ an autoethnographic approach to the telling of their stories. Chapters illustrate on-the-ground experiences, elucidating the struggles and triumphs of faculty of color as they navigate the historically White setting of higher education, and provide actionable strategies to help faculty and administrators combat these issues. This book gives voice to faculty struggles and arms graduate students, faculty, and administrators committed to diversity in higher education with the specific tools needed to reduce Racial Battle Fatigue (RBF) and make lasting and impactful change.

Nicholas D. Hartlep is the Robert Charles Billings Endowed Chair in Education and is the Chair of the Education Studies Department at Berea College, Kentucky, USA.

Daisy Ball is Assistant Professor and Coordinator of the Criminal Justice Program in the Department of Public Affairs at Roanoke College, Virginia, USA.

Diverse Faculty in the Academy
Series Editor: Fred A. Bonner II

Racial Battle Fatigue in Faculty: Perspectives and Lessons from
Higher Education
Edited by Nicholas D. Hartlep and Daisy Ball

Racial Battle Fatigue in Faculty

Perspectives and Lessons from Higher Education

Edited by Nicholas D. Hartlep and Daisy Ball

Routledge
Taylor & Francis Group

NEW YORK AND LONDON

First published 2020
by Routledge
52 Vanderbilt Avenue, New York, NY 10017

and by Routledge
2 Park Square, Milton Park, Abingdon, Oxon, OX14 4RN

Routledge is an imprint of the Taylor & Francis Group, an informa business

© 2020 Taylor & Francis

Library of Congress Cataloging-in-Publication Data
Names: Hartlep, Nicholas Daniel, editor. | Ball, Daisy, editor.
Title: Racial battle fatigue in faculty : perspectives and lessons from higher education / Edited by Nicholas D. Hartlep and Daisy Ball.
Identifiers: LCCN 2019046425 (print) | LCCN 2019046426 (ebook) | ISBN 9780367149376 (hardback) | ISBN 9780367149383 (paperback) | ISBN 9780429054013 (ebook)
Subjects: LCSH: Racism in higher education–United States. | Minority college teachers–United States–Social conditions. | Discrimination in higher education–United States. | Universities and colleges–United States–Faculty.
Classification: LCC LC212.42 .R343 2020 (print) | LCC LC212.42 (ebook) | DDC 378.1/982996073–dc23
LC record available at https://lccn.loc.gov/2019046425
LC ebook record available at https://lccn.loc.gov/2019046426

ISBN: 978-0-367-14937-6 (hbk)
ISBN: 978-0-367-14938-3 (pbk)
ISBN: 978-0-429-05401-3 (ebk)

Typeset in Perpetua and Bell Gothic
by Deanta Global Publishing Services, Chennai, India

Contents

CONTENTS

Editors

Nicholas D. Hartlep (Ph.D., University of Wisconsin, Milwaukee) holds the Robert Charles Billings Chair in Education at Berea College where he Chairs the Department of Education Studies. Before coming to Berea College Dr. Hartlep Chaired the Department of Early Childhood and Elementary Education at Metropolitan State University, an Asian American and Native American Pacific Islander-Serving Institution (AANAPISI) in St. Paul, Minnesota. While there he also served as the Graduate Program Coordinator. Dr. Hartlep has published 22 books, the most recent being (2019) *What Makes a Star Teacher? Seven Dispositions that Encourage Student Learning* which was published by the Association for Supervision and Curriculum Development. His book *The Neoliberal Agenda and the Student Debt Crisis in U.S. Higher Education*, with Lucille L. T. Eckrich and Brandon O. Hensley (2017) was named an Outstanding Book by the Society of Professors of Education. In 2018, the Association of State Colleges and Universities (AASCU) granted Dr. Hartlep the John Saltmarsh Award for Emerging Leaders in Civic Engagement Award. In 2017, Metropolitan State University presented him with both the 2017 Community Engaged Scholarship Award and the President's Circle of Engagement Award. In 2016, the University of Wisconsin, Milwaukee presented him with a Graduate of the Last Decade Award for his prolific writing. In 2015, he received the University Research Initiative Award from Illinois State University and a Distinguished Young Alumni Award from Winona State University. Follow his work on Twitter at @nhartlep or at his website, www.nicholashartlep.com

Daisy Ball (Ph.D., Virginia Tech) is an Assistant Professor of Criminal Justice and Coordinator of the Criminal Justice Program in the Department of Public Affairs at Roanoke College (Salem, Virginia). Her research focuses on the intersection of race and the criminal justice system, with an emphasis on the criminal justice contact of Asian Americans. Recent publications have appeared in journals including *Deviant Behavior* and *Sociological Spectrum*.

Contributors

Noelle W. Arnold (Ph.D., University of Alabama) is the Associate Dean for Equity, Diversity and Global Engagement in the College of Education and Human Ecology at The Ohio State University. A former administrator at the district and state level, Dr. Arnold has over 50 publications and her articles have appeared in the *Journal of Higher Education*, *Teachers College Record*, *International Journal of Qualitative Studies in Education*, and the *Journal of Educational Administration*. Dr. Arnold has 6 books including Ordinary Theologies: Religio-spirituality and the Leadership of Black Female Principals. Dr. Arnold serves as executive series editor of *New Directions in Educational Leadership: Innovation in Research, Teaching and Learning*.

Mildred Boveda (Ed.D., Florida International University) is an Assistant Professor of Special Education and Cultural and Linguistic Diversity at Arizona State University. In her scholarship, she uses the term "intersectional competence" to describe teachers' preparedness to address intersecting equity concerns. Drawing from Black feminist theory and collaborative teacher education research, she interrogates how differences are framed across education communities to influence education policy and practice. Dr. Boveda earned an Ed.D. in Exceptional Student Education at Florida International University and an Ed.M. in Education Policy and Management from Harvard Graduate School of Education. Dr. Boveda started her career as a special education teacher in Miami Dade County Public Schools. She engages in various professional activities that allow her to examine the research, practice, and policies involved with educating students with diverse needs. She is an immediate past president of the Division for Diverse and Exceptional Learners of the Council for Exceptional Children (CEC) and currently the chair of the Diversity Caucus for the Teacher Education Division of CEC.

Paula R. Buchanan (MBA, MPH, University of Alabama-Birmingham) is an Instructor at Jacksonville State University's School of Business. After graduating from Tulane University, Ms. Buchanan served as an AmeriCorps volunteer, and later completed training to become a diversity facilitator for the Corporation for National and Community Service, the federal agency that administers the AmeriCorps program. She has conducted diversity workshops throughout the Pacific Northwest and in Washington, D.C. Ms. Buchanan has also worked as a diversity co-facilitator for mandatory diversity training for State of Alabama University employees. As an Instructor, she has incorporated diversity awareness into the Principles of Management and Organizational Behavior courses that she teaches by providing students with case studies during class discussions that focused on business leaders that were female, people of color, international, or a combination of these groups. By including these diverse case study discussions, she helps to expand students' knowledge of a wide variety of business leaders. In addition, these case studies provide students from under-represented groups with more positive role models from the business sector. Currently, she consults as a Communications Specialist and diversity trainer, and can be contacted via her website at www.paularbuchanan. com and on LinkedIn at https://www.linkedin.com/in/paularbuchanan

Sayil Camacho (Ph.D., University of California, Los Angeles) is a Scholars Strategy Network Postdoctoral Fellow at Vanderbilt University's Peabody College of Education and Human Development. Sayil explores the intersections of workplace experiences, campus climate, and immigrant populations. Her article published in *The Journal of Higher Education* was the first study to explore the unionization phenomenon of the postdoctoral workforce, and the findings were framed within the broader contexts of globalization, institutional power dynamics, and racial and social hierarchies. Sayil co-founded the first student-led campus climate intervention program at the University of California, Los Angeles (UCLA)—Bruin Excellence and Student Transformation grant program, and is the recipient of the 2017 UCLA Equity, Diversity, and Inclusion award.

Anita Chikkatur (Ph.D., University of Pennsylvania) is an Associate Professor and the current Chair of the Department of Educational Studies at Carleton College, Northfield, Minnesota. Chikkatur served as the program co-chair for Division G, Section 1 for the 2016 American Educational Research Association Annual Meeting. She serves as an internal reviewer for *Anthropology & Education Quarterly*. Her research and teaching areas include student and teacher perspectives on race, gender, and sexuality in middle and high schools and issues of diversity and difference in K–16 educational institutions. In 2015, she received a grant from Youthprise and Minnesota Campus Compact to work with five Carleton students on a participatory action research project investigating the experiences of students from under-represented groups in STEM majors at Carleton. In 2018, she received a grant from Carleton's Public

Works Mellon Initiative to develop participatory research work on educational inequities in Faribault, Minnesota.

Andrew Cho (Ph.D., University of Washington) is a professor of sociology at Tacoma Community College (TCC) as well as the chair of the Anthropology, Political Science, and Sociology Department. At TCC, he has been awarded the prestigious "Faculty Excellence Award" several times and has also been recognized by the Black Student Union as the "Most Inspirational Faculty." Most recently, he published the chapter "Not in My Hood: Identity, Crime, and Policing in Seattle's International District," which appeared in the book *Asian/Americans, Education, and Crime: The Model Minority as Victim and Perpetrator*. He has also written an article on "Slavery Reparations" published in the *Encyclopedia of Race and Ethnic Relations*. As the son of Burmese refugees, he strives to empower immigrant and refugee populations. Recently, he helped conduct several basketball clinics in the country of Myanmar with former NBA and WNBA players as part of the "Unity Through Sports" program sponsored by the U.S. Department of State and the Myanmar Basketball Federation. A sports enthusiast, Dr. Cho teaches a "Sociology of Sports" class that focuses on social issues related to race, class, gender, and sexuality within sports. In his free time, he enjoys spending time with his wife, Kaidie, and his son, Darwin.

Robin R. Ford (Ph.D., New York University) is an Assistant Professor of English at Queensborough Community College, City University of New York. A queer, black woman, whose scholarship is both academic and personal, her focuses include the use of graphic genre works to teach critical literacy; intersectionality of race, gender and sexuality; social justice; and critical interrogation of the spaces we occupy. She has presented scholarship on race and space, popular culture, and the creation of identity through literacy at American Educational Research Association (AERA), Pacific Ancient and Modern Language Association (PAMLA) and Conference on College Composition & Communication (CCCC) conferences. She has published at Salon.com, in the *Kenyon Review* and *The Conversant*, and appeared on NPR's "On Point, with Tom Ashbrook." Her work can be found on www.robinrford.wordpress.com

Cleveland Hayes (Ph.D., University of Utah) is a Professor of Education Foundations and interim Associate Dean for Academic Affairs in the School of Education at Indiana University-Indianapolis. Dr. Hayes teaches elementary foundations of education, elementary science methods, and qualitative research methods. Dr. Hayes's research interests include the use of Critical Race Theory in Education, Historical and Contemporary Issues in Black Education to include the school-to-prison pipeline, Teaching and Learning in the Latino Community, Whiteness, and the Intersections of Sexuality and

Race. Dr. Hayes is an active member of AERA at the Division Level, SIG level and committee level. He currently is a program section Co-Chair for Division K and is a member of the Special Interest Group Executive Committee. He is also the President of the Critical Race Studies in Education. Dr. Hayes's research can be found in *Democracy and Education*, *Qualitative Studies in Education*, *Gender and Education*, *Urban Review*, and *Power of Education*. In addition, he is the co-editor of the books *Unhooking from Whiteness: The Key to Dismantling Racism in the United States* and *Unhooking from Whiteness: Resisting the Esprit de Corps*.

Jameson D. Lopez (Ph.D., Arizona State University) is an enrolled member of the Quechan tribe located in Fort Yuma, California. He currently serves as an Assistant Professor in the Center for the Study of Higher Education at the University of Arizona. He studies Native American education using Indigenous statistics and has expertise in the limitations of collecting and applying quantitative results to Indigenous populations. He carries unique experiences to his research that include a 2010 deployment to Iraq as a platoon leader where he received a bronze star medal for actions in a combat zone. As an Indigenous quantitative researcher, he tends to examine research through tribal critical race theory which contends governmental policies toward Native Americans focus on the problematic goal of assimilation. This challenge often results in relatively low numbers of Native American voices in comparison to dominant culture voices in quantitative research, but can be overcome through increasing Native American participation in academic and policy discourse, and including Native American voices in quantitative research through Indigenous statistics.

Nadia I. Martínez-Carrillo (Ph.D., Penn State) is an Assistant Professor of Communication Studies at Roanoke College where she teaches communication courses. Her research focuses on global media and representations of intersections of identity in popular media and across cultures. Her most recent projects seek to identify effective ways to resist narratives and media dynamics that perpetuate social inequality and the stigmatization of social groups. Her work has been published previously in *Journalism and Mass Communication Quarterly* and *The Journal of Popular Culture*.

Sopang "Pang" Men (M.F.A., University of Michigan) teaches writing and literature at Tacoma Community College (TCC). A fiction writer, his short stories have won the Hopwood Award for Short Fiction and Frederick Busch Prize in Fiction. His experiences as a refugee and first-generation Cambodian American inform much of his writing, and he is currently developing a short story collection that explores Southeast Asian diaspora in the United States. Previously, he worked as a community liaison for the Korean Women's Association, a nonprofit that connects immigrant and refugee populations to basic needs resources. An avid runner, he is training for his 25th half marathon.

Salisha A. Old Bull (M.P.A., M.I.S., University of Montana) was born, raised and educated in Montana. Her mother is a Bitterroot Salish woman from the Flathead Reservation and father, a Mountain Crow man from the Crow Nation. Her educational motivations included the advice to obtain a college degree and return home for the betterment of Indian Country. After exploring the avenues of educational opportunities she settled her academic career at The University of Montana. There she obtained four college degrees: B.A. in Psychology, B.A. in Native American Studies, Master's of Interdisciplinary Studies, and Master's of Public Administration. Her pursuits have led to careers dedicated to supporting American Indian students seeking higher education. She served as the Program Coordinator for The University of Montana's American Indian Student Services, Career Counselor/Business Liaison/Outreach/Admissions Coordinator and Equal Employment Opportunity Officer for Kicking Horse Job Corps, and Director of TRiO Student Support Services at Salish Kootenai College. She currently serves as a faculty member at Salish Kootenai College for the Tribal Governance and Administration Program. Her current research pursuits include the study of historical timelines for the Montana Tribal nations. The majority of focus is on the Confederated Salish and Kootenai Tribes, specifically related to governance and cultural aspects.

Robert T. Palmer (Ph.D., Morgan State University) is Department Chair and an associate professor in the Department of Educational Leadership and Policy Studies at Howard University. His research examines issues of access, equity, retention, persistence, and the college experience of racial and ethnic minorities, particularly within the context of historically Black colleges and universities. Dr. Palmer's work has been published in leading journals in higher education, such as *The Journal of College Student Development, Teachers College Record, Journal of Diversity in Higher Education, Journal of Negro Education, College Student Affairs Journal, Journal of College Student Retention, The Negro Educational Review, and Journal of Black Studies*, among others. Since earning his Ph.D. in 2007, Dr. Palmer has authored/co-authored well over 140 academic publications.

Shandin H. Pete (Ph.D., University of Montana) was raised in Arlee, Montana on the Flathead Indian Reservation. His mother is Salish and his father is Navajo. He completed a Bachelor of Arts in Native American Human Services and a Bachelor of Science in Environmental Science at Salish Kootenai College (SKC). He also completed a Master's of Science in Geology in 2006 at the University of Montana studying surface water-groundwater interaction in a restored river. In addition, he completed three years of coursework toward a Ph.D. in Geoscience at the University of Montana. He shifted his focus and completed a Doctorate of Education in 2018 at the University of Montana with an emphasis on post-secondary science education. His dissertation focused on the efficacy of culturally congruent instructional practices as a mediating factor to assist American Indian tribal college students' attitudes and achievements in natural resources degree programs. Dr. Pete has been working at SKC in the Natural Resources Division since 2008. During his time at SKC he has co-developed the Hydrology Department, the first B.S. in Hydrology among the Tribal College system. His approach to teaching and research at SKC seeks to harness the cultural values and knowledge of his community to generate students with foundational cultural values and applied science understandings. His research interests include interfacing technical hydrological skills with local Indigenous knowledge in experiential field environments. Dr. Pete has been developing an undergraduate science curriculum that bridges Salish culture and language learning within hydrological sciences as a model for Native student recruitment and retention.

Martel A. Pipkins (Ph.D., Texas Women's University) is currently the Mary Miles Bibb Diversity Fellow at Framingham State University teaching in the Sociology Department. His teaching/research activities include intersectionality, violence against women, state violence, and power/knowledge.

Dawn Quigley (Ph.D., University of Minnesota) is an Assistant Professor in the Education Department at St. Catherine University. She is a citizen of the Turtle Mountain Band of Ojibwe, North Dakota. She taught English and reading for 18+ years in the K–12 schools along with being an Indian Education program director. Her website http://nativereadermn.blogspot.com/ offers support for educators in finding, evaluating and implementing Native American curriculum content from an Indigenous perspective. In addition to her coming-of-age Young Adult novel, *Apple in the Middle* (North Dakota State University Press), Dawn has over 28 published articles, essays, and poems. She was awarded the St. Catherine University Denny Prize Award for Distinction in Writing and has been a finalist for both the Minnesota Loft Literary Center's Minnesota Emerging Writer Award and its Mentor Series.

Pamela Anne Quiroz (Ph.D. University of Chicago) is Executive Director of the Inter University Program on Latino Research [IUPLR] and the Director of the Center for Mexican American Studies and Professor of Sociology at the University of Houston. The IUPLR consists of 26 university-related institutes and centers whose main goal is to support and promote research on Latinos and their intellectual presence in policymaking. Professor Quiroz has been a fellow at the Center for the Advanced Study of Behavioral Sciences, Stanford University, Visiting Research Associate at the Autonomous University of Barcelona, and a research fellow at both the Institute for Research on Race and Public Policy, and the Great Cities Institute. She has received grants from the National Science Foundation, American Sociological Association, U.S.

Department of Education, and the Society for the Scientific Study of Sexuality. She served as Editor of *Social Problems*, a prominent journal in Sociology that focuses on the pursuit of social justice, and she has served as North American Editor for the interdisciplinary journal *Children's Geographies*. She was a Member of the Board of Directors for the Council on Contemporary Families [2013–2018]. Her book, *Personal Advertising: Dating, Mating, and Relating in Modern Society* (McFarland Press) is forthcoming.

Takumi C. Sato (Ph.D., Michigan State University) is a Clinical Assistant Professor in the School of Education at Virginia Tech. He teaches science education courses as well as the "diversity" course for pre-education students and a Critical Race Theory (CRT) course for graduate students. Scholarly interests include exposing racism in science learning experiences, inviting young people to join in Youth Participatory Action Research, and striving for a more equitable society. He is a co-Principal Investigator for a $1.6 million National Science Foundation (NSF) grant that examines the impact of a robotics program in the Mississippi Delta. He participates in various organizations including the *Critical Race Studies in Education Association* and *NARST* (science education research).

William A. Smith (Ph.D., University of Illinois at Urbana-Champaign) is a Professor of Ethnic Studies at the University of Utah. In 2003, Dr. Smith was awarded the Ford Foundation Postdoctoral Research Fellowship to further develop his theoretical concept of Racial Battle Fatigue (RBF). RBF is an interdisciplinary theoretical framework that provides a clearer method for understanding the race-related experiences of People of Color. In general, Racial Battle Fatigue explains how the social environment (e.g., institutions, policies, practices, traditions, groups, and individuals) perpetuates race-related stressors that adversely affect the health and academic achievement of Students of Color and the health, professional productivity, and retention among Faculty of Color. Whether it is from the constant stereotyping that Students of Color face on campus or the epistemological racism that Faculty of Color endure as they seek tenure and promotion, People of Color are chronically having race-related stress-responses in historically white institutions and environments that consume valuable time and energy. Dr. Smith's fellowship year (2003-2004) was also spent working on collaborative projects at UCLA with Dr. Walter R. Allen and Dr. Daniel Solórzano. Professor Smith's additional research interests are inter-ethnic relations, racial attitudes, racial identity and socialization, academic colonialism, affirmative action attitudes, and the impact of student diversity on university and college campuses.

Diverse Faculty in the Academy

Series Editor Introduction

For more than three decades, researchers and scholars have chronicled the experiences of diverse faculty who teach in Academe, particularly faculty members of color who have elected to teach in Predominantly White Institutions (PWIs) (Bonner, marbley, Tuitt, Robinson, Banda, & Hughes, 2014; Tuitt, Hanna, Martinez, Salazar, & Griffin, 2009; Bonner, 2004; Fries-Britt & Kelly, 2005; Heggins, 2004; Patitu & Hinton, 2003; Stanley, 2006; Thompson & Louque, 2005; Thompson, Bonner, & Lewis, 2015; Turner, Gonzalez, & Wood, 2008). Perhaps the most comprehensive scholarship on this topic has been Turner's (2008) *Faculty of Color in Academe: What 20 Years of Literature Tells Us*. From peer-reviewed journal articles to books, monographs, and op-eds, the negotiations of these faculty members have been studied and theorized in myriad ways. However, it has been the *seminal* work of scholars like Caroline Turner and Samuel Myers in their book *Faculty of Color in Academe: Bittersweet Success* who provided a holistic rendering of what it meant for these faculty members to negotiate a litany of challenges like professional and social integration; isolation and a lack of mentoring; occupational stress; racial bias; and tokenism—particularly as it related to promotion and tenure. It was also Christine Stanley in her book *Faculty of Color: Teaching in Predominantly White Colleges and Universities* who captured diverse faculty engagements in an array of different contexts. In addition to these books, a number of key articles and op-ed pieces have also underscored very clear and concise messages about how diverse faculty have navigated the American post-secondary landscape. *Teaching in the Line of Fire: Faculty of Color in the Academy*, Frank Tuitt and colleagues' provocative article that was penned in *Thought and Action*, the National Education Association's higher education journal brought a much-needed focus on the precarious positionalities that faculty of color often assumed in PWIs.

So too has the field-shifting scholarship of William A. Smith, especially his development of *Racial Battle Fatigue*, a conceptual framework illuminating the minefields (perils) that faculty of color negotiate in the classroom on a routine basis. Also, my own research and scholarship has attempted to foreground what it means to exist as a diverse faculty member at the intersection of multiple and competing identities, I have also attempted to provide a platform for other diverse faculty members to lend their "voices" in authentic ways. Hence, my tome *Black Faculty in the Academy* provided a space for Black faculty to unpack their respective narratives from a perspective that foregrounded their chosen positionality—class, gender, race, and sexual orientation. Prior to this book, the op-ed *Black Faculty on Track but Out of the Loop* was my early attempt to galvanize the cacophony of stories and voices, including my own, that I had heard over the years that were basically saying the same things about life in the Academy as a faculty member of color. Thus, it is the work of these scholars and several others (Daryl Smith, Paul Umbach, Sheila Gregory, Benjamin Baez, Gail Thompson, Angela Louque, Tuesday Cooper, Dolores Degado Bernal, Ocavia Villapando) who have paved the way for the contemporary vanguard who are taking up the mantle to speak about the extant experiences of diverse faculty in new and intriguing ways.

As a series, *Diverse Faculty in the Academy* will serve as a galvanizing space for scholars who seek a venue that will provide them with the space to advance critical topics speaking to their *emic* experiences in academe. The *purpose* of this book series is to stimulate discussions among members of the higher education community about the most critical topics in academe *impacting the success* of diverse faculty, particularly those faculty members in PWIs. Additionally, the synergy created by the powerful narratives from each series book will contribute to and provide essential information for those who seek to better understand how faculty from diverse academic, cultured, national, gendered, familial, and academic backgrounds successfully negotiate majority spaces and integrate their personal and professional selves in ways that ensure their continued professional success.

Through the power of asset-based counternarratives, series authors and editors will shed light on perspectives that are grounded in resilience and success. Perhaps the best example of how this series will depart from the marginalizing and pedestrian coverage of diverse faculty experiences in the academy is the first book commissioned for this series by Nicholas Daniel Hartlep and Daisy Ball, *Racial Battle Fatigue in Faculty*: *Perspectives and Lessons from Higher Education*.

I encourage the readers of this series to embrace the wisdom of legendary author and educator Stephen Covey who shared as one of his *Seven Habits of Highly Effective People*—seek to understand then be understood. Read the narratives, seek to understand the perspectives, and attempt to adjust your vision to look through their lenses at a world that is sometimes viewed in black and white and sometimes in Technicolor.

Yours truly,

Fred A. Bonner II

Fred A. Bonner II, Ed.D.
Series Editor, Executive Director of
Minority Achievement, Creativity and
High Ability (MACH-III) Center at the
Prairie View A&M University

REFERENCES

Bonner, F., & Fred, A. (2004). Black professors: On the track but out of the loop. *The Chronicle of Higher Education*, *50*(40), B11.

Bonner, I. I., Fred, A., Marbley, Aretha Faye, Tuitt, F., Robinson, P.A., Banda, R.M., Hughes, R. L. (2014). The critical need for faculty mentoring. *Black faculty in the academy: Narratives for negotiating identity and achieving career success* (pp. 123–135). New York: Routledge.

Fries-Britt, S., & Kelly, B. T. (2005). Retaining each other: Narratives of two African American women in the academy. *The Urban Review*, *37*(3), 221–242.

Heggins, W. J. (2004). Preparing African American males for the professoriate: Issues and challenges. *Western Journal of Black Studies*, *28*(2), 354–364.

Patitu, C. L., & Hinton, K. G. (2003). The experiences of African American women faculty and administrators in higher education: Has anything changed? *New Directions for Student Services*, *2003*(104), 79–93.

Stanley, C. A. (2006). Coloring the academic landscape: Faculty of color breaking the silence in predominantly White colleges and universities. *American Educational Research Journal*, *43*(4), 701–736.

Thompson, G. L., Bonner, F. A., & Lewis, C. W. (Eds.). (2015). *Reaching the mountaintop of the academy: Personal narratives, advice and strategies from black distinguished and endowed professors.* IAP.

Thompson, G. L., & Louque, A. (2005). *Exposing the "culture of arrogance" in the academy: A blueprint for increasing Black faculty satisfaction in higher education.* Stylus Publishing, LLC.

Tuitt, F., Hanna, M., Martinez, L. M., Salazar, M., & Griffin, R. (2009). Teaching in the line of fire: Faculty of color in the academy. *Thought & Action*, *25*, 65–74.

Turner, C. S. V., González, J. C., & Wood, J. L. (2008). Faculty of color in academe: What 20 years of literature tells us. *Journal of Diversity in Higher Education*, *1*(3), 139.

Foreword

William A. Smith

Dr. Fred A. Bonner has successfully commissioned Drs. Nicholas Hartlep and Daisy Ball as editors to pull together a very impressive collection of brave scholar-activists to write the inaugural publication for the "Diverse Faculty in the Academy" book series. *Racial Battle Fatigue in Faculty: Perspectives and Lessons from Higher Education* will not disappoint the reader if you are interested in learning about the hard realities faced by faculty of color and native faculty. With the ability to examine education, White Supremacy, and institutionalized gendered-racism in the manner which James Baldwin (1988) professed when he said, "The paradox of education is precisely this—that as one begins to become conscious one begins to examine the society in which [they are] being educated" (p. 11). To be sure, it is not the "formal" education process that made these authors "conscious" or "woke." It was their frank efforts expressed in each chapter to personally, intellectually, and emotionally struggle and then "clap back" against White Supremacy and institutionalized gendered-racism that makes this book so compelling.

The richness of this book rests primarily on the multiple perspectives and the diverse institutional contexts and racial/ethnic backgrounds that each author represents. It is impressive to read critical race auto-ethnographies from postdoctoral fellows, clinical faculty members, adjunct faculty, instructors, tenure-track faculty, and tenured faculty members. Seldom, even at professional conferences, do we get to listen and learn from this group in one sitting. Drs. Hartlep and Ball have provided us with this golden opportunity to learn from the perspectives of Asian American, African American, Latinx, and Native American academics in this one book. While we are witnessing major growth in Racial Battle Fatigue (RBF) research that focuses on people of color, we do not see a similar effort made on Native Americans. *Racial Battle Fatigue in Faculty: Perspectives and Lessons from Higher Education* has corrected that problem with several key chapters written by and on Indigenous People and/or First Nation's people. As long as those who read this book avoid the temptation toward racial academic voyeurism, as Dr. Sayil Camacho warns in her chapter, and reads it to learn from the honest experiences of faculty of color, progress can be made. It is very hard, especially early on in an academic's career to be brutally honest about their experiences in postsecondary institutions.

It is clear that for too long, most postsecondary educators of color have lived between risk and fear of speaking truth to power about their experiences on campus. We must recognize the heavy burdens and tremendous costs the authors have laid out in this book. You must have remarkable courage and a deep commitment to social justice to risk your career while often fighting in lone battles. You must come to grips with the fact that you are fighting for a cause that is bigger than yourself. As Dr. Pamela Anne Quiroz noted in her chapter, "prior to taking a stand, my days were filled with severe stress resulting in several voluntary visits to a local psychiatrist." Furthermore, Dr. Dawn Quigley wrote in her chapter about being falsely accused by a co-PI of "sharing the findings with a 'rival' institution" before the final presentation of the findings, and as a result, her "health started to decline in small ways: inability to sleep, developing high blood pressure and having to go on medication." The impact of gendered-racism is no small matter. These are the racist micro-level aggressions faculty of color face that result in RBF.

RBF is the outcome of what I have reclassified as toxic and persistent "offensive racist mechanisms." Previously, Dr. Chester M. Pierce placed racial microaggressions as a subcategory of what he classified as "offensive mechanisms." Offensive racist mechanisms are those "racistly" microaggressive practices, policies, procedures, institutional climates, symbols, expressions, language, and traditions that continue to render People of Color invisible, isolated, confined, tormented, overwhelmed, second-guessing, and physically, emotionally, and psychologically fatigued. As Dr. Paula R. Buchanan mentioned in her chapter, her Alabama relatives warned her as she started her professional career in their home state, "don't go past that blinking light into Piedmont [when coming to visit] … they don't like Black people in Piedmont, so don't go there." The "blinking light" is a constant reminder to many local Black residents that your movement is confined. "Niggers," as the decades-old signs that are now taken down reminded them, must know their place and where they cannot go.

RBF is the cumulation of these racist micro-level and macro-level aggressions and the subsequent negative health sequelae on marginalized and oppressed people. RBF is experienced at both individual and group levels simply by being a part of a racistly oppressed group. The symptoms are frequently communicable, as the pain is passed among family, racial in-group friends, and the larger racial group. Epigenetically, RBF has the potential to be spread across generations through collective group memories, racial socialization, coping processes, genetic transferal, and continuous endemic racist experiences. As an example, for Native Peoples, the pain that every postsecondary institution in the United States is sitting on stolen land is an agonizing reminder of the under-addressed torture and terrorism, past and present-day, inflicted against their group. Eventually, this issue must be addressed through a *Truth and Reconciliation Commission* that is led by Native Peoples before this country can begin to start its healing process.

Until then, we must recognize that these postsecondary institutions were not designed for Native Americans and other People of Color. As I have written, these are *Plessy*-like institutions in a Post-*Brown* era (Smith, 2008). We have to examine these *Plessy*-like institutions as Historically White Institutions (HWIs) instead of as simply PWIs. If we understand them as HWIs, it will help us to be clear that the gross numbers or percentages of White students and faculty, as the majority population, is not the most significant factor. Apartheid South Africa had a White minority population who abusively ruled as a racist colonial power over a Black African majority population.

Similarly, the historical and contemporary racist U.S. infrastructure that is in place, the current racist campus culture, racist ecology, and how these modern-day racist institutions still benefit Whites at the expense of all People of Color—irrespective of their socioeconomic background, gender(s), sexual identities, or physical abilities—is the most central feature of this White racial frame. This White racial frame is modern-day academic colonialism, and White Supremacy still rules. The chapters by Dr. Robin R. Ford (concerning a "majority-minority" community college), Dr. Mildred Boveda (regarding a Hispanic Serving Institution), and Shandin H. Pete and Salisha A. Old Bull (about a Tribal College and University system) elucidates how a White minority population of students and sometimes faculty members is enough to perform academic colonialism and institutionalized gendered-racism within a historically white institutional context. Two major themes arise throughout these chapters that are often unaddressed in the higher education scholarship. You will notice the presence of many "Beckys," a racist White female antagonist mentioned in almost every chapter (Dr. Paula R. Buchanan names her antagonist Becky in her chapter). We know that higher education is commonly understood as a hierarchical institution. Nevertheless, a second theme captures these White female antagonists terrorizing People of Color, no matter what their position is on campus. Becky was a janitor, student, junior professor, tenured professor, department chair, and the dean. There is no escape for People of Color, and the doctoral degree does not offer the class-based hierarchical protection that White colleagues receive. Institutionalized gendered-racism is a roadblock to healthy and successful career development for People of Color. According to Dr. Martel A. Pipkins' chapter, it is a racist professional delusion that "keeps a Nigger-Boy running" chasing "fake gold coins."

Dr. W. E. B. Du Bois (1920) believed "What a world this will be when human possibilities are freed, when we discover each other, when the stranger is no longer the potential criminal and the certain inferior!" (p. 103). Dr. Nicholas Hartlep and Dr. Daisy Ball have offered us an opportunity, within their comprehensive collection of essays, to see how human possibilities are restricted. Educational leaders must finally come to understand that they must discover the brilliance in *all* people, irrespective of their race, ethnicity, nationality, phenotype, sexuality, gender expressions, physical ability, family background, or language. We must finally dismantle whiteness, White Supremacy, and all forms of oppression, and then we will no longer be strangers who are seen and treated as the potential criminal and the certain inferior. Otherwise, the goals, dreams, and contributions of too many People of Color will continue to meet premature deaths.

REFERENCES

Baldwin, J. (1988). A talk to teachers. In R. Simonson & S. Walker (Eds.), *The graywolf annual five: Multi-cultural literacy* (pp. 3–12). St. Paul, MN: Graywolf.

Du Bois, W. E. B. (1920). *Darkwater: Voices within the Veil*. New York: Harcourt, Brace, and Howe, Inc.

Smith, W. A. (2008). Campus-wide climate: Implications for African American students. In L. Tillman (Ed.), *A handbook of African American education* (pp. 297–309). Thousand Oaks, CA: Sage Publications.

Preface

The purpose of this book is to highlight the experiences of faculty of color in higher education along both racial/ethnic lines and institutional type. In this book, chapter authors employ an autoethnographic approach to the telling of their stories, thereby contextualizing and bringing each chapter to life for the reader.

RBF refers to the stress and strain members of racially marginalized populations experience, tensions which emanate from coping with and fighting against the racism (Smith, 2008). While colleges and universities are often thought of as progressive, forward-thinking institutions, they are not immune from this phenomenon, for they came of age during eras of White domination.

This book takes a novel approach to the study of RBF—namely, asking faculty from a variety of different racial/ethnic backgrounds, and with a variety of academic experiences, to pen autoethnographic accounts of their experiences. While each story is unique, similar threads of pain, anger, frustration, tears, and injustice weave these chapters together into a single piece of storytelling. As a whole, this book represents both the debilitating power of racism, and the strength chapter authors have gathered to fight against systems of White-dominated racial oppression.

The audience for this book is primarily graduate students, faculty, and administrators in higher education. As each chapter ends with "Actionable Strategies," we intend this book to be not just the sharing of stories, but a toolbox of sorts with which readers can take actual, substantive steps toward change. The book will also be of interest to graduate students entering the professoriate in the near future.

The book is organized by authors' racial/ethnic and/or cultural identification, including African American, Asian American, Hispanic American, and Indigenous populations. For each racial/ethnic/cultural identity, three institutional types are represented: community college, teaching institution, and research institution. A fifth section of the book pays tribute to faculty of color who hold non-tenure-track positions, ostensibly dedicated to the celebration of "diversity."

All in all, this book both gives voice to the struggles faced by chapter authors as they've navigated the White-dominated halls of higher education, and pays tribute to them by communicating to the reader what actionable next steps can be taken to reduce the RBF experienced by faculty of color and Indigenous faculty. For all readers who claim they are committed to diversity in higher education, the book you hold in your hands gives you the specific tools needed to make change. And, as chapter authors make abundantly clear, making change is what is they expect of you. Onward!

REFERENCES

Smith, W. A. (2008). Higher education: Racial battle fatigue. In R. T. Schaefer (Ed.), *Encyclopedia of race, ethnicity, and society* (pp. 615–618). Los Angeles, CA: Sage Publications.

Chapter 1

The Battle of Racial Battle Fatigue

Nicholas D. Hartlep and Daisy Ball

Racial Battle Fatigue (RBF) has been defined by William A. Smith (2008) as encompassing "physiological, psychological, and behavioral strain exacted on racially marginalized and stigmatized groups and the amount of energy they expend coping with and fighting against racism" (p. 617). As Smith (2008) notes, as college and university campuses have been historically White-dominated, academic settings are not immune to this phenomenon. Much of the RBF scholarship has focused on "faculty members'" experiences, while not considering how faculty members' experiences are shaped by their institutional context. Higher education takes place in many different contexts, not all of which are Predominantly White Institutions (PWIs).

Racial Battle Fatigue in Faculty: Perspectives and Lessons from Higher Education examines faculty of color's experiences in higher education, but does so in three salient ways that are different from previously published books:

1. It takes into consideration faculty who work at different institutional types, including community colleges, teaching-focused colleges and universities, and research universities. Institutions also vary in terms of the populations they serve, including PWIs, Historically Black Colleges and Universities (HBCUs), Hispanic Serving Institutions (HSIs), Minority-Serving Institutions (MSIs), and Tribal Colleges and Universities (TCUs).
2. It shares the experiences of tenured, tenure-track, and non-tenure-track faculty members' experiences, including faculty who occupy "diversity" focused fellowship positions.
3. It explores faculty from a variety of disciplinary backgrounds, including Criminology, Geology, Education, English/Communication Studies, and Sociology.

We are honored to be the first edited collection to appear in Dr. Fred Bonner's new series *Diverse Faculty in the Academy*. We organized *Racial Battle Fatigue in*

Faculty along the lines of racial/ethnic/tribal political identification of chapter contributors, thereby allowing the reader to make in-group comparisons, although we acknowledge these groups are not monolithic. We are honored that Professor William A. Smith, the RBF pioneer, has written the book's foreword. Dr. Noelle Arnold penned the afterword, for which we are equally grateful. As an Associate Dean of Diversity at The Ohio State University, an R1 and PWI, her perspective is highly relevant for readers of this book.

Who Is the Audience?

We edited this book for a higher education audience, including graduate students and faculty in Education, Sociology, Psychology, African American Studies, Latinx Studies, Asian American Studies, and Native American Studies. We hope the book piques the interest of graduate students and junior faculty of color. We believe those who lead departments, colleges, and universities will also find value in the book. We hope that the recommendations that contributors share are not only read, but that they are adopted and practiced on higher education campuses nationwide.

As higher education is in an ongoing pursuit to diversify its faculties (Watson, 2019), this book illustrates the struggles faced by the faculty members who represent that diversity. This book puts a human face and voice to positions held by faculty of color and Native Americans. Oftentimes, colleges and universities create diversity initiatives (including creating special positions specifically for faculty of color) without thinking through the "on-the-ground" experiences of minority faculty in higher education. Our intention is for this book to elucidate the struggles, survivance, and triumphs of faculty of color and Native Americans as they navigate Historically White Colleges and Universities (HWCUs) or Predominantly White Institutions (PWIs), Historically Black Colleges and Universities (HBCUs), Hispanic Serving Institutions (HSIs), Minority-Serving Institutions (MSIs), and Tribal Colleges and Universities (TCUs), as well as other institutional types, such as community colleges, teaching-focused colleges and universities, and research universities.

THIS BOOK ...

How do an Asian American (Korean transracial adoptee) male professor of urban education and a White female professor of criminal justice come together to edit a book on Racial Battle Fatigue (RBF)? The short answer is that *Racial Battle Fatigue in Faculty: Perspectives and Lessons from Higher Education* is an example of continued editorial partnership. We have edited books together before on topics of mutual interest. For instance, in 2016 we collaborated on *Asian/Americans, Education, and Crime: The Model Minority as Victim and Perpetrator* and in 2018 we collaborated and coedited *Asian/American Scholars of Education: 21st Century Pedagogies, Perspectives, and Experiences*. While initially thinking about a book on RBF, Nicholas wanted to edit a book entirely devoted to Asian American experiences of RBF; however, upon further reflection and advice from Routledge's editorial team, the foci and scope changed from being only a book on Asian Americans to one that included a broader population. This book is more inclusive in terms of the ethnic and racial groups it encompasses, including the racialized and politicized experiences of African Americans, Latinx, Native Americans, and other marginalized people, such non-tenured or non-tenure-track academics. The chapter authors include academics who do not work at Predominantly White Institutions (PWIs) or research-intensive (R1) institutions, which we believe is important. Faculty who work at these institutions have many of the same qualifications and expertise that faculty who work at R1s have: They are Ph.D.-trained, conduct research, and teach (under)graduate curricula. The context of their work is that their institutions are different. The outcome of these revisions is a book that will appeal to a broader audience than what was originally brainstormed, and will hopefully reach the desks and nightstands of higher education leaders at a range of institutions.

How to Read this Introduction and the Book

In this introduction to the book the editors share their own stories regarding RBF on their campuses. Nicholas shares his story first, followed by Daisy. We conclude the introduction by sharing our thoughts regarding the salient themes that emerged from reading, editing, and revising chapters contained in this book. We share a framework of those distillations and interactions and conclude with recommendations for higher education administrators and leaders to reduce RBF. We hope the readers of the book (who are also leaders at their institution of higher education) implement many of the suggestions that are made for policy and practice. The stories contained in the chapters are the heart of the book, and they serve as reminders that RBF is pervasive not only at those Predominantly White Institutions (PWIs) whose primary foci are research, but also at PWI teaching-intensive colleges and universities, Minority-Serving Institutions (MSIs), and community colleges. Moreover, RBF impacts not only tenured and tenure-track professors, but it also impacts graduate students and non-tenured but tenure-track faculty and contingent faculty or those who hold fellow positions. RBF also impacts more than people of color, but also Native Americans.

NICHOLAS: EXPERIENCING WHITE SPACES IN A MINORITY-SERVING INSTITUTION

I have a story to tell you. I work at a Minority-Serving Institution (MSI), where I served as a convener for our faculty union. The union, as I perceive it, is a

White space. The union president is a White man, and many of the unit con-veners are White too. The union secretary is also White. One day, during the spring semester of 2019, during my second year serving as my unit's convener, I was publicly recalled from being convener. The recall occurred unannounced. The union president and union secretary attended my unit's scheduled meeting. Their presence was unannounced to me, although based on their interactions with my colleagues, it is possible that some in the room that day knew or were at least prepared for what was about to transpire. If they alerted my colleagues of the recall privately, but not me, it made me extremely unprepared emotionally for what was going to happen.

The reason for the recall, as they told me that day, was that I was thought to have advocated breaking the union contract. Not sure what that meant, I asked them specifically what I had advocated for. They replied, "You requested a fac-ulty member to revise her dossier for which she was going up for tenure and promotion." This is true, I did, but it was part of the process and my role as the Department Chair. I encouraged a faculty member to revise her dossier in order to strengthen it and so it reflected the documents she had added after I had reviewed her initial submission. I am not sure if my request was a microaggres-sion. It may have been. But how was encouraging or requesting someone revise his/her dossier breaking the union contract? As of writing this introduction, I have gained no explanation. Nevertheless, I did not see a basis for their pub-lic recall, which was humiliating, and from my perspective, passive-aggressive. Once the vote was tallied, they left. I was recalled and a replacement was found. Who was my replacement? A faculty member who was known to be a bully in the department, and about whom people talked behind closed doors frequently.

Unions and the Bullying of People of Color

Research by Hollis (2016)

> considered a sample of 142 community colleges through a correlation analysis to reveal that 67% of those who belong to unions are subject to workplace bullying, 3% higher than the general population reporting their experiences in relationship to workplace bullying at community colleges. Further, 76% of people of color in unions also are affected by workplace bullying in com-munity colleges. In contrast, 68% of people of color not in unions are affected by bullying.
>
> (pp. 83–84)

First, let me say that I am very much pro-union. As a millennial (35 years old at the time of writing this introduction), I am quite aware of the epiphenom-enon of unions: Unions not only help their members, but their positive effects spillover and positively impact communities. According to Draut (2005), in her book *Strapped: Why America's 20- and 30-somethings cannot get ahead*, "Young adults understand the benefit a union could have on their pocketbooks. Over half of nonunionized workers under 34 say they would join a union tomorrow if given the chance" (pp. 20–21). Indeed, as a millennial I understand the importance unions play.

I will state again, so readers are clear, I am pro-union. Research confirms the many benefits of unions, not only for workers' rights, but also the surrounding communities. Unions help all workers (Mishel & Walters, 2003). However, if a union is an institution, can it express institutional racism? I believe it can. I have another story to tell.

In my eyes, the union president and secretary's unannounced visitation to our union meeting was an example of workplace bullying. My interpretation is as follows: Although I carried out the duties required of me as my unit's union convener, I believe that the union's senior leadership thought I was dangerous because I was not a sycophant to the union. Ironically, earlier in the year, the union requested that I defend another faculty of color who was being investigated for workplace bullying. For anonymity, I cannot share more details. By refusing to speak to and cooperate with the union, I was being deliberate and direct. The union was protecting this professor of color who was a bully. Why would I want to help the union defend this professor? I didn't. He personally bullied me from the first day I arrived at Metropolitan State University.

When the union requested I speak with them I emailed my Dean, Chief Diversity Officer, and also the union leadership about my experience with this professor. I informed the union leadership and grievance officer that I would *not* attend their invited meeting and had *no* desire to talk about my experiences being bullied by this professor. My unwillingness to speak to them was my way of saying that this professor had a long track record of bullying that should have been addressed years ago.

The truth of the matter, I could claim that the union retaliated against me. The first retaliation was when they "recalled" me from being the unit's union "convener." The next act of retaliation was that the union came to my department meeting and held a "recall" vote regarding my position as Department Chair. How did I respond to this second recall, of a different position? I did not reply. Since I felt as though it was baseless, since I was voted by my colleagues for a three-year term, I did nothing. However, my Dean and the university Provost responded by hiring a consultant to interview faculty about the "climate" of the School of Urban Education. This investigation is happening—so I have been told—as I write this book's introduction.

My experiences, and my interrelated stories above, illustrate to me that higher education, even at MSIs, can be hostile for people of color to work. It also is clear to me that faculty unions can inadvertently preserve White Supremacy.

5

The tragic irony of a White union abiding by such orthodoxy and dogma is similar to the pigs in George Orwell's (1945) *Animal farm* who proclaim: "All animals are equal, but some animals are more equal than others." MSIs support and serve students of color and Native American students, yet they at times may not be serving their faculty of color or Native American faculty. Something must be done!

DAISY: WITNESSING RACIAL BATTLE FATIGUE BUT NOT EXPERIENCING IT PERSONALLY

As a White female, I have not experienced RBF directly. However, as a trained sociologist, I am highly attuned to this phenomenon, and I have both witnessed and heard from students and colleagues as to the RBF they have experienced in higher education. From the Asian American undergraduate whose professor asked her if she liked "egg rolls" on the first day of class her freshman year, to the African American colleague who was asked by his chair to lead a year-long series of diversity workshops (he had no training in holding such workshops, and was still expected to teach a full course load, maintain an active research agenda, and fulfill more formal types of service, such as serving on university-wide committees), RBF is part of the fabric of higher education. I once served on a hiring committee to fill a tenure-track position in my home department when a fellow committee member voted against a finalist of Asian descent, stating "We've already got enough people in that category." He wasn't referring to the candidate's area of specialization, or teaching style—rather, he was referring to the fact that in the past year, we had hired someone of Asian descent, and thus did not "need another." Of note, this person was a White male, one member of a department consisting of 15 White tenure-line faculty, and only two non-White tenure-line faculty, including the recent hire of Asian descent. He did not, however, point to our pattern of hiring White people when discussing the remaining White candidates.

A personal challenge I have encountered relates to my gender. As a female in higher education, early on, I grew accustomed to gender stigma, for example being taken less seriously than my male colleagues, and being given unsolicited advice about my appearance. Erving Goffman (1963) defines stigma as the "situation of the individual who is disqualified from full social acceptance" (p. i). While we typically associate stigma as tied to negative characteristics, being a female whose presentation of self (Goffman 1959/1973) is feminine in a larger culture in which femininity is viewed positively can in fact be a liability. This theme is noted by several of the female authors included in this collection, including Pamela Anne Quiroz in Chapter 3: "'You Just Bark Like a Dog for Six Years, and Then ...': Stories from the Academic Career of a Recovering Sociologist," who recounts being approached by a senior male colleague who wished to discuss his wife's "personal" issues (of a sexual nature) with her. Likewise, male colleagues have often called on me to discuss their marital problems, but not to publish with them. And, I've grown accustomed to gender-based stigma from both male and female colleagues, for example female colleagues who have instructed me to "stop touching your hair" and "stop apologizing," when I had not asked them for advice in the first place.

As someone whose workplace success will be determined, in part, by student evaluations and comments, the future looks challenging, as the literature indicates being a female instructor puts one at a disadvantage in terms of students' evaluation of their courses. For example, Harris (1975) reports, based on an experimental design, that "masculine" modes of teaching result in higher ratings of performance. More recent research indicates that female instructors in higher education routinely experience negatively biased evaluations by students; this is especially the case when it comes to male student evaluations of female instructors (Mengel, Sauermann, & Zolitz, 2018; Graves, Hoshino-Browne, & Lui, 2017; MacNell, Driscoll, & Hunt, 2015).

While writing this introduction, a job ad came to my attention:

> The Department of Political Science at ACME University invites applications for a part-time Visiting Lecturer (AY 2019–2020) in the area of Racial and Ethnic Politics to begin September 4, 2019. Teaching responsibilities will also include the Introduction to American Politics course. **This is a part-time, non-benefited contract position.** This one-year appointment could be extended. **Given how few people of color we have on our faculty, we are especially interested in selecting this person from a diverse applicant pool.**

In many ways, this ad exemplifies the central problems discussed in this book: Namely, faculty of color are being targeted for a non-benefited, contract position so as to alleviate the university's problem of lack of diversity.

SALIENT THEMES FOUND IN THIS BOOK

As we reviewed and offered preliminary and final editorial feedback to chapter contributors, we noticed that the book contained several salient themes. Our call initially sought to commission chapter contributors that fell into our prescribed table of contents for the book. Besides requesting that chapter contributors storytell their experiences with RBF via autoethnographic accounting and sharing actionable next steps and implications for policy and/or practice, we did not know what their RBF experiences would be. So, the salient themes are very much informative to us as the two individuals who were the first to read, validate, support, and encourage their telling and publication.

The main themes found in the book pertain to the following five areas:

1. Hiring experiences
2. White epistemology and alternative ways of knowing and being
3. Sense of (not) belonging
4. Experiencing microaggressions
5. (In)visibility and/or being "ignored"

Higher educational leaders ought to know that White ways of knowing are valued in higher education and the epistemologies used in higher education are biased and benefit White supremacy. Furthermore, it is not good practice when faculty members of color or Native American faculty members are (t)asked with doing "diversity work." Because they may be the only or one of a few faculty member/s of color, they should not be "taxed" and asked to do more work. For example, faculty of color who serve as mentors for non-White students beyond their capacity is a form of RBF. Because students of color gravitate toward them at PWIs, it causes faculty members to expend emotional labor, which can detract from the more formal work expected of them as they pursue tenure and/or promotion. Moreover, in the chapters of this book we see that diversity-related fellowships are created by colleges and universities with good intentions, but "well-meaning" administrators may not think through the implications of these positions in terms of the grander career trajectory of fellows so appointed (see Figure 1.1).

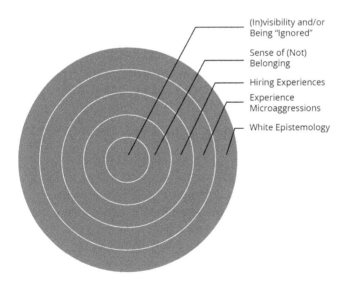

Figure 1.1. Framework of RBF.

White Epistemology and Alternative Ways of Knowing and Being

No matter what the institution type—be it a TCU, PWI, HBCU, etc.—White colonial epistemology is practiced because within these institutions of higher learning, people engage in the academic process, which relies on published documents. These documents, many times, books or articles, are part of disciplines. Academic disciplines that rely on the APA citation or style guide laid out in the *APA Manual* perpetuate Whiteness and male-domination (see Thompson, 2004). Scholarship governed by the *APA Manual* perpetuates White epistemology.

When faculty of color and indigenous faculty conduct their research, they can be made to feel unknowledgeable when attempting to collaborate with other academics. For example, we hear from a Native American faculty member, whose graduate school faculty mentor—in the course of berating his writing—reminded him: "You're going to need my recommendation to get a job." A military veteran, his response was unflinching: "I'm Native American, getting a Ph.D. with a Bronze Star Medal. I'm getting a job." (Lopez, Chapter 4, Section 4.3).

As pointed out forcefully by Quigley in Chapter 4, Section 4.2,

> In decolonizing methodologies, there may be inner and outer locations of knowledge production, with a holistic and interactive connection between the two. Using multiple forms of indigenous knowledge, outside the usual Western literature, such as data gathering and analysis methods, is a way to decolonize the designation of knowledge and the West's fragmentation of body and mind.

Higher education teaching, researching, and being is steeped in one dominant way of "knowing," but this form of epistemology, knowledge, and being can cause RBF for faculty of color and indigenous faculty members.

Hiring Experiences

Non-White scholars routinely face differential hiring practices when attempting to secure academic jobs. In some cases, they are viewed by hiring committees as little more than the "token" minority hire (Quiroz, Chapter 3, Section 3.3). This can breed confusion and/or resentment on part of students and faculty and an ill-fit in the department in the future.

Related, oftentimes the very positions created to increase diversity (i.e. diversity-related fellowships, scholars of color programs) benefit the institutions at which they are housed, but strain the careers of the people who hold these positions (Buchanan, Chapter 5, Section 5.1). For example, many such fellowships bring with them regular teaching loads, and heavier than usual service loads (i.e., advising a diversity-related club, arranging a speaker series on topics related to diversity, etc.) (Jameson, Chapter 4, Section 4.3, Pipkins, Chapter 5, Section 5.2). While this is important work, service activities in non-tenure-track positions, which many of these are, hold less weight than academic scholarship. That is, scholars of color are teaching and organizing and event planning, work which requires them to put their writing and publishing to the side. When it then comes time to apply for positions on the tenure-track, their CVs list numerous teaching and service activities, but fewer publications, which may make them less competitive on the job market. That is, the very positions that have been created to give members of underrepresented groups a leg up can have the opposite impact, ultimately becoming a hindrance to their future success.

Thus, while we, the editors of this book, support diversity-related initiatives in terms of hiring practices, they must be carefully thought out. Which members of the academic community will this position benefit? How can the institution consistently support the faculty member during their time at the institution? And, how will holding this position benefit the faculty member in terms of their career trajectory into the future? A point made so eloquently in *The Atlantic's* "The Death of an Adjunct," and also by several chapter contributors to this book, is that non-tenured positions bring with them all sorts of uncertainties which compound one another: concerns regarding health coverage, financial security, housing, social and family relationships, etc. (Hayes, Chapter 1, Section 1.3, Pipkins, Chapter 5, Section 5.2).

Faculty of color who work at PWIs often are hired and yet not invited by their White colleagues to collaborate to write articles and grants (Palmer, Chapter 1, Section 1.2). However, other services may be requested of them, for example the female Latina new to a tenure-track job, invited to play tennis by a senior colleague. During their play, he asked for her advice about his wife's "sexual dysfunction," to which the junior faculty member replied, "Since I don't have a wife I don't have to worry about it." Sadly, but not surprisingly, he did not get the hint, and continued to pursue her until met with a flat-out rejection (Quiroz, Chapter 3, Section 3.3).

Moreover, PWIs ought to be more explicit with their faculty of color and indigenous faculty members regarding how they are valued and how their work is respected. It shouldn't take a faculty member of color getting a job offer from another university for their home school to make a counteroffer and at that point express how valued the faculty member is. Colleges and universities need to have ongoing discussions with their non-White faculty and perhaps engage in cluster hiring so that the experiences their diverse faculty have are healthier and it is clear to them they are needed and respected (Palmer, Chapter 1, Section 1.2).

Sense of (Not) Belonging

Many of the routine professional socialization opportunities afforded to new White faculty are somehow eclipsed when it comes to minority faculty. This might include the department not hosting a welcome party upon their hire, when they have done so for White hires in the past. This might also include invitations for casual socialization—drinks, golf, coffee—not being extended as enthusiastically, and in some cases, not at all. At times, cultural differences are to blame—but it takes a commitment on the part of members of the institution to reach across any cultural bounds that exist and instill on campus a sense of belonging for all. Well-designed mentorship programs can help when it comes to feelings of belonging—but they must be well-thought out, and must have a proven record of success (that is, just "having" a mentorship program is not enough—the program must be effective).

Experiencing Microaggressions

A disgruntled White male student meets with his Black male professor and expresses his displeasure that the professor deducted points from an assignment. A student comments he is a similar age as the professor and thus doesn't respect the professor. A White student asks a professor, Do I really need to call you "Doctor ____?" Microaggressions around age, academic titles, and whether or not a faculty member actually is a faculty member are just some of the challenges that faculty of color and indigenous faculty members experience as they do their work. As chapter contributors point out, institutions of higher education ought to require faculty, staff, and students take courses on microaggressions (Palmer, Chapter 1, Section 1.2). Chapters note that police or campus security are called on people of color for eating lunch in a common space, for sleeping in the student lounge, or for walking across campus. To a new African American female professor, a female janitor snarled "How did *you* get this office?" as she made her nightly cleaning rounds (Buchanan, Chapter 5, Section 5.1). RBF is the outcome of this reality (Ford, Chapter 1, Section 1.1).

An Asian American faculty member begins his first day on the job at a community college. He takes a campus tour, as recommended by a colleague, so he can become familiar with the campus. While touring the Student Center, which is directly across from his office building, he introduces himself to a White male staff member by saying, "Pleasure to meet you. My name is Andrew and I'm looking forward to teaching Sociology and being your colleague." Instead of shaking his extended hand and introducing himself, the staff member merely stares at him for a few unsettling moments. Then, he breaks into a wide grin and exclaims, "Hey buddy! My wife is Asian!" (Cho and Pang, Chapter 2, Section 2.1).

(In)visibility and/or Being "Ignored"

Minority faculty are called upon for their "expertise" when it comes to diversity, but their voices are still seldom heard. For example, they are asked to collect data on the experiences of faculty of color, to make recommendations to support faculty of color, and so forth, yet nothing comes of their findings and/or recommendations (Sato, Chapter 2, Section 2.3). Having to be the diversity guru is tiring (Palmer, Chapter 1, Section 1.2). Ultimately, one wonders if this work is really just busy work to make the institution appear as though they care, and to keep the faculty member busy/distracted/feeling useful.

An Asian American faculty member is in his class and a maintenance worker enters to check on sound equipment—some speakers are not working properly. The maintenance worker tells a White student that the speakers would be fixed by tomorrow. Uncomfortably, the student replies that he is not the professor, but the Asian American standing next to him is (Cho and Pang, Chapter 2, Section 2.1). When faculty of color do speak out and reflect upon their experiences regarding race and ethnicity, such as on a blog devoted to the experience of being a person of color at an H/PWI who is tasked with teaching courses focused on identity, power, and privilege, they are often silenced, excluded, and even complained about to the administration by White colleagues who feel threatened (Chikkatur, Chapter 2, Section 2.2). While faculty experience not being seen by White colleagues, and even by some colleagues of color occurs, students of color often attempt to console, or recognize, their plight, for example a student referring to the work of a Mexican junior scholar as her "superpower," and another student suggesting to a female Asian American faculty member that a final category be added to Cross's (1971) Nigrescence model that they're studying in class: "burned out and tired" (Chikkatur, Chapter 2, Section 2.2).

REFERENCES

Draut, T. (2005). *Strapped: Why America's 20- and 30-somethings cannot get ahead*. New York: Anchor Books.

Goffman, E. (1959/1973). *The presentation of self in everyday life*. Woodstock, NY: Overlook Press.

Goffman, E. (1963). *Stigma: Notes on the management of spoiled identity*. London, UK: Penguin.

Graves, A., Hoshino-Browne, E., & Lui, K. (2017). Swimming against the tide: Gender bias in the physics classroom. *Journal of Women and Minorities in Science and Engineering*, 15–36. doi:10.1615/JWomenMinorScienEng.2017013584

Harris, M. B. (1975). Sex role stereotypes and teacher evaluations. *Journal of Educational Psychology*, 67(6), 751–756. doi:10.1037/0022-0663.67.6.751H

Hollis, L. P. (2016). Labor intensive: Workplace bullying, union membership, and unrealized civil rights for people of color. *Diversity in Higher Education*, 18, 83–101.

MacNell, L., Driscoll, A., & Hunt, A. N. (2015). What's in a name: Exposing gender bias in student ratings of teaching. *Innovative Higher Education*, 40(4), 291–303. doi:10.1007/s10755-014-9313-4

Mengel, F., Sauermann, J., & Zolitz, U. (2018). Gender bias in teaching evaluations. *Journal of the European Economic Association*, *16*, 64.

Mishel, L., & Walters, M. (2003, August 26). *How unions help all workers* (Briefing Paper #143). Washington, DC: Economic Policy Institute. Retrieved from https://www.epi.org/files/page/-/old/briefingpapers/143/bp143.pdf

Orwell, G. (1945). *Animal farm*. New York: Signetic Classics.

Smith, W. A. (2008). Higher education: Racial battle fatigue. In R. T. Schaefer (Ed.), *Encyclopedia of race, ethnicity, and society* (pp. 615–618). Los Angeles, CA: Sage Publications.

Thompson, A. (2004). Gentlemanly orthodoxy: Critical race feminism, whiteness theory, and the *APA Manual*. *Educational Theory*, *54*(1), 27–57.

Watson, J. (2019, June 3). OSU's College of Education is making diverse faculty hiring a top priority. *Diverse: Issues in Higher Education*. Retrieved from https://diverseeducation.com/article/146999/

Part I

The Racialized Experiences of African Americans in U.S. Higher Education

Chapter 2

Double Consciousness and Racial Battle Fatigue at a Community College

A Peculiar Sensation

Robin R. Ford

Every day there is another incident. Another headline, Tweet, post. I wrote an essay in the aftermath of Eric Garner's death by police, in which I questioned what I, a middle-class, well-educated, college professor, could say to my Black and Brown students who face this country's increasingly unchecked racism regularly to ease their pain. What would give my students strength to keep going as it becomes more and more difficult to live in America while non-White? They are harassed when they are on public transit, as they walk down the street, drive to school, shop for a new outfit … while just living their lives. What could I, in my role as their English professor, possibly do to help? How can I help myself?

Today's constant barrage of images, texts, and sound bites reinforce how treacherous life is in this country for African Americans and other Intersectional People of Color (IPOC). Each day a new incident comes through my Twitter feed with the hashtag #LivingWhileBlack. Incidents with #CornerstoreCaroline, #BBQBecky, #PermitPatty, and countless other women (and a few men) who feel it their duty to call 9-1-1 on Black people living their lives have become so ubiquitous that they are not even news anymore. These enter our minds as mundane incidents, "just another racist White woman" *sigh* but the psycho-emotional injury resulting lasts much longer than the monikers will.

For me, particularly troubling is that many of these incidents have taken place on college campuses, places where one might expect (slightly more) intelligent and civil interactions. Yet, cops or security are called on people of color ad nauseum for just eating lunch in a common space, for sleeping in the student lounge, for walking across campus. When will someone call security on me for being on campus too late (I teach until 10:00 PM), eating in the faculty cafeteria, or God forbid, being mistaken for a student? How long, I wonder, before I find myself having to justify my existence as an African American woman? For that is what this is: Blacks being forced to explain our simple presence in a "White" space. It is exhausting.

When I began to write this chapter, I had a difficult time pinpointing the source of my Racial Battle Fatigue (RBF). The student body at the college where I teach is highly diverse: Students from 127 countries are represented and only 15.4% of the enrolled students in fall 2017 were White. Over half of our students are Black or Latinx (City University of New York, 2017). As an African American I see myself reflected in the students across campus and in every classroom. My particular department has been proactive in hiring faculty of color, so I am not the only person of color, and I am supported by my chair and other senior faculty. I have a cohort of junior faculty with whom I have developed close friendships. I truly enjoy my job and where I work.

And yet, with such a diverse student body, the faculty does not come close to reflecting that diversity. Although the administration appears to be making an effort to increase diversity among the faculty, today approximately 64% of the full-time faculty are White, and only 25 Blacks are tenured or tenure-track in a faculty of almost 400 (City University of New York, 2016). Throughout my career I have gotten used to often being the only Black woman in a room, or on a committee, or in a department. It is something that I make note of and then put aside. But while contemplating this book I've looked at my situation, and I realize that I have placed quite a lot into the "it's no big deal" box. How much can that box hold?

DOUBLE CONSCIOUSNESS

No matter how "woke" a college tries to be, it can still be a minefield for IPOC negotiating the path to tenure and promotion. All junior faculty constantly worry about doing what is required to get tenure but for faculty of color there is an extra issue with which our White colleagues are not concerned, the question: How do others see me? "Faculty of color have to deal with both how they view themselves and how the institution and its constituents view them, affecting self-definitions and understandings of personal and professional identities" (Levin, Walker, Haberler, & Jackson-Boothby, 2013, p. 312). Over a hundred years ago W. E. B. Du Bois (1903) discussed the "peculiar sensation" experienced by Black Americans who were required to view themselves "through the eyes of others":

> It is a peculiar sensation, this double-consciousness, this sense of always look-ing at one's self through the eyes of others, of measuring one's soul by the tape of a world that looks on in amused contempt and pity. One ever feels his two-ness, an American, a Negro; two souls, two thoughts, two unreconciled strivings; two warring ideals in one dark body, whose dogged strength alone keeps it from being torn asunder.

(p. 3)

Much like code-switching—which most Blacks do instinctively based on who they are speaking to—double consciousness is subconscious, a simple reflex for most people of color. It is even more ingrained for those of us who make our living being observed. Every time an instructor enters a classroom, they become the center of attention. For Black professors, the scrutiny is doubled for we must prove our worth not just as an instructor, but as a *Black* instructor. Add any additional characteristic—queer, female, disabled—and the subconscious awareness of being "seen" increases. When a big part of our job is performative, how can we help but wonder how others see us? And, at many colleges, the data used to evaluate us is based largely on student perception (i.e. course evaluations), which exacerbates this sensation further.

I spoke to several of my colleagues who are people of color to see how they view the college and how they handle their own RBF. Every person I spoke with experienced some form of racism at the college, and most were incidents of unwitting comments from colleagues who consider themselves "progressive" and "inclusive." Yet, as well-meaning as the person may be, when you are told that you were the "diversity hire" it cannot help but sting. The knowledge that even one person in your department sees you that way can ignite suspicion and mistrust of others. To be clear, "double consciousness"—constantly being aware of being seen as a Black first and then as a person second—leads to a form of paranoia. Yet, this paranoia has proven over and over again to be warranted (Hartlep, 2016). We are not wrong to think that we are seen differently or to be on high alert for the dangers this brings. According to Elijah Anderson, the William K. Lanman professor of Sociology at Yale University, due to the recent increase in highly publicized racial incidents, "[B]lack people everywhere take note and manage themselves in a largely White-dominated society, learning and sharing the peculiar rules of a White-dominated society in which expressions of White racism are becoming increasingly explicit" (Anderson, 2018, para. 2). As overt racism becomes more prevalent, so do racial microaggressions, which according to Sue et al. (2007) are:

> Brief and commonplace daily verbal, behavioral, or environmental indignities, whether intentional or unintentional, that communicate hostile, derogatory, or negative racial slights and insults toward people of color. Perpetrators of microaggressions are often unaware that they engage in such communications when they interact with racial/ethnic minorities.
>
> (p. 271)

Microaggressions increase our cautiousness in how we present ourselves. There is often more of a need to demonstrate our credibility and belongingness, through dress, speech, and affect, on a college or university campus compared to other spaces, because historically Blacks have been viewed as "not belonging" in academic spaces. A study of racial microaggressions on college campuses shows that for many Black students, the college is far from being a welcoming place (Solórzano, Ceja, & Yosso, 2000). I know of several incidents of Black faculty being mistaken for being students and being treated quite differently from White students or White faculty. In addition to being questioned as to whether we belonged in certain spaces, interactions with White faculty, staff, and administrators are often patronizing or demeaning until they discover we are professors. Not being seen as a Black professor is problematic in two ways. First, I should not need to demonstrate that I belong in a space that my White colleagues would not be questioned in. Second, it should not matter if I am a professor or not; Black students should not be made to feel that they do not belong on their own campus, or "that their very presence [is] unwanted and assumed to be inappropriate" (Solórzano, et al., 2000, p. 68). If I, with my Ph.D. and years of experience, am made to feel that I am out-of-place, imagine how undergraduate students of color feel?

That said, overt racism is in a separate category from the covert or unacknowledged prejudices we face daily. It is the relentlessness of microaggressions that ultimately causes me and others to experience RBF. The natural reaction to RBF is either anger, numbness, dysphoria, or a combination of the three. These work against us if we are seen, stereotypically, as either the angry, lazy, or disinterested. However, these reactions are actually forms of resistance and techniques for survival. My colleagues and I experienced these reactions as I was writing this chapter.

A recent departmental meeting on grammar pedagogy took a turn toward the political. A faculty member (I use pseudonyms for all faculty members) stated that our students do not have examples of writing excellence to emulate, which explains why their writing is so bad. The racial implication of this comment was too much for one Black professor.

Theresa states that she is the "youngest, loudest, and Blackest" person in the department and on many committees, and that her very presence challenges those who do not think women of color should be in academia. She questioned what "excellence" is, because grammar *is* political. From the ability to codeswitch, to the complex grammar of African American Vernacular, to which variety of the many world Englishes is valued, composition is certainly not apolitical. How can we discuss teaching Black and Brown students grammar without addressing race and the politics of composition standards? After Theresa's question, like so many discussions that involve race, there was an awkward silence, and then the leaders moved onto noncontroversial topics. I expected the discussion to end there. This is what happens. IPOC try to address race, but if the people in charge are not ready for the discussion, it is either sidelined or completely ignored. And we are left to fume and fuss about it among ourselves. This would have gone that way too if not for René, a self-proclaimed "salty Asian professor," who was so incensed that she Tweeted about it:

All this talk about diversity and inclusion in the academy and within departments, yet no one wants to talk about race. ... I wondered, at first, if faculty members are worried about looking 'uncivil,' but my colleague made an important, but unsavory point: When we talk about Standard Written English, we are really talking about Privileged White English. ... But the conversation steered towards 'practical methods' that ignored this assertion.

This was the start of a Tweet thread that called out the faculty at the meeting for being unwilling to discuss what is so clearly part of teaching writing. In publicly drawing attention to this pedagogical and political issue both Theresa and René were willing to "reclaim the figure of the angry [feminist of color ...] willing to cause trouble and being prepared to stay as sore as our points" (Ahmed, 2009, p. 41). I, however, was not.

RESISTANCE AND DISASSOCIATION DUE TO TRAUMA

I have been contemplating the RBF I have experienced as a Black woman. Constant racial microaggressions cause many faculty of color to seek professional help, although the manifestations of this stress vary from emotional to physical (Arnold, Crawford, & Khalifa, 2016). I am fortunate to have a great therapist, and that she, a Jewish woman, my age, regularly educates herself on prejudice, racism, and social justice. She is aware of her White privilege and acknowledges that she probably commits her share of microaggressions. But, she is a supportive therapist, and positive White ally, one who tries to stay conscious and informed. When I mentioned the prior faculty meeting, I prefaced it with, "I wasn't really paying attention ... ." As annoying as it was, she did what a good therapist does, and forced me to examine my actions, asking me over and over again what I was thinking when this happened. After several instances of me saying "I wasn't really thinking anything" in different forms, I realized that I had mentally checked out when race came up. I perceived this as a form of laziness, but what I thought was simple avoidance my therapist named: Disassociation or a "detachment from immediate surroundings." She also mentioned that disassociation happens when people are traumatized.[11] Rather than become angry, which takes psychic and physical energy, I disassociated. When confronted with yet another incidence of White people being willfully ignorant, I could have spoken up. My area of scholarship is composition, specifically students of color in college composition classes, so I know what I am talking about. I considered speaking up, but then actually became too physically exhausted to form a coherent response. I could have cited scholars, studies, and texts, but why should I have to? It was obvious that no one was interested in taking the conversation in that direction, and I was not going to be the one to educate them on a topic they had no interest in. It was willful resistance. It was a reaction to trauma. It was survival.

I was very shy growing up, and still am. I learned to blend in, to never stand out or be noticed for anything other than something positive. I was born during some of the most violent years of the Civil Rights Movement, when being outspoken and visible could have deadly consequences. My father participated in the sit-ins in North Carolina to integrate lunch counters, and both parents called out racist behavior. I learned to be proud of who I was at an early age but I also learned how to fit into White society. Fresno, California in the early 1970s, was not called the "Bible belt of California" for nothing. The community was conservative and White. Although I was never the only Black girl in school, I could count the few of us on my hands. Believing in Dr. King's Dream, where everyone is judged by the content of their character, not the color of their skin, my parents taught my brother and me to treat everyone equally, and to expect the same treatment in return. We most certainly would not give anyone the opportunity to attach any racial stereotype to us. Assimilation was a survival tactic while growing up and became my default behavior as I went to college and then began my career. That is not to say that I would ignore racist behavior but I picked my battles judiciously. I knew that if I took on everyone who did or said something racist in my presence, I would not have the energy to take care of myself. I also always assumed that things would get better. And they did.

In the past decade, women, the LGBTQ community, and religious and ethnic minorities began to win legal battles and gain civil rights, and I felt pretty good about the direction the country was moving. As a queer, Black woman, I had dogs in several races, and they all looked to be winning. I was not afraid to be out at work; I did not worry about being the only Black in a room. In the back of my mind I was always aware that I was being looked at as "other," but I did not travel in places or with people who would have made me uncomfortable, and no one dared to say certain things aloud. But, then, Trayvon Martin was murdered. And Michael Brown. And Eric Garner. And Sandra Bland. Michelle Obama was called a monkey. Valerie Jarrett compared to an ape. And ... when the Black Lives Matter movement was founded, I thought positive changes would follow. Then, a new administration took office, and racists everywhere were given free rein to say and do what they had kept hidden previously.

Now, each day is an effort to dampen my fury. I suppress my emotions, anger, grief, and betrayal so I can get through the day, so I survive. I had been the proverbial "Angry Black Woman" at another college and it did not serve me well. I now have a tenure-track position at a college where I like the students and get along well with my colleagues. There is no one I have ever had an out-and-out racist, sexist, or homophobic encounter with. I am pretty damn lucky.

So perhaps my willingness to let the smaller slights slide is a way of appreciating that I now work in an environment with many allies. Levin et al. (2013) suggested that in "response to the 'double-consciousness' that faculty of color experience, faculty search for ways to adopt and project a professional identity as a community college faculty member" (p. 319). The person I am in front of my students and in academic meetings is not always the same person I am outside of work. Where I disassociate, others depersonalize, leaving the personal part of themselves at home and donning the professional persona (Levin et al., 2013). As Audre Lorde (1988) said, "Caring for myself is not self-indulgence, it is self-preservation, and that is an act of political warfare." We each find the coping mechanism that allows us to keep going. My colleague René listened to *Jesus Christ Superstar* on the commute home to get centered before picking up her children, I listen to horror podcasts. Fictional horror is very cathartic. For 30–40 minutes on the drive home I can immerse myself in someone else's horrific situation and forget all about the real world.

I am not the only one at my college to ignore some microaggressions in order to address larger more overt attacks. Richie is a 6'5" Black man. He is well aware of his stature and how the world sees him. He is also one of the sweetest, most collegial, men on campus. One of the few Black males on the tenure track, he is in high demand on service and academic committees. Recently, during a meeting regarding campus activities someone suggested showing Jordan Peele's Academy Award winning film *Get Out*. The movie is part horror film, part social commentary on Black and White race relations in this country. Due to its box office success and status as a pop culture phenomenon, this seemed to me to be an obvious yes. However, someone was uneasy with this suggestion. They thought that the film "might offend some." In the end, the college decided to show Marvel's *The Avengers*, a completely inoffensive action flick. Richie did not argue that the reason it might offend someone is the very reason it should be shown. Rather, he elected to let it go. "I can't get upset by every stupid comment. There's no point in arguing with some people, you won't change how they think." He knows that it's a small jump from voicing disagreement to becoming the "Big, Angry Black Man." He could easily be intimidating if he wanted, but instead Richie is known for his sartorial choices, like wearing bowties to class. It's much better to stand out for dressing well than for being the scary Black man.

JOHN HENRYISM

For myself and each of my colleagues I have mentioned, the specter of tenure and promotion is like Pig-Pen's dirt cloud,[22] ever-present and unpleasant. Of course, IPOC are not alone in worrying about job security, but there are extra factors we have to consider that my White colleagues do not. If we do or say the wrong thing, will it hurt us later? Are we being given the same opportunities to distinguish ourselves as scholars? Does our service to the college count as much as that of others? Is there information out there that we need but do not have access to? Each semester our class is observed by a senior faculty member who then reports on our pedagogy and skills, and at the end of the academic year we meet with a

23

member of the department's Personnel and Budget (P&B) committee to review what we have accomplished that year. These meetings are usually routine:

Did all of the boxes get checked?
Were the benchmarks met?
What is your plan for the next year?

I always had some nervousness before these meetings, more or less depending on who was doing the review. I am always prepared and I have never had anyone comment negatively on my teaching, so I assumed my interactions were the same as the rest of the department members. Until one year when it came time for my annual report and the person preparing the report spent significantly more time talking with me and getting my feedback before writing the report. They then sent it to me to proofread and add anything they might have left out. What I saw was literally shocking. They had done so much more than check off boxes. My work and contributions were described and cataloged in detail—full sentences! This was the first time in all the years I had been here that someone had taken the time to complete the report as if it was theirs. As thankful as I was to this faculty member, I realized that they were simply doing their job. This is how the previous reports should have been completed. Why were they not? Did the faculty who prepared the previous reports do only the minimum required? Was it because I am Black? Should I be happy just to get a satisfactory report? Maybe the previous faculty members were just busy. My problem is that I will never know the reason for the difference, and my double consciousness will not let me forget.

Black faculty have reason to worry about promotions and tenure. We are not privy to many of the discussions about promotion and tenure that would help us navigate the process. We get the basic facts, but it can be the minor nuances that make or break a promotion attempt. Faculty will do their job and stay quiet to ensure that no one has a reason to question their promotion. Requirements for tenure are fairly cut and dry, but promotion, (and the salary increase) is much more subjective. What is and is not valuable for tenure and promotion depends very much on who is serving on the P&B committees and what they value. "Opportunities for greater job security, advancement, and perceived equity in [promotion and tenure] are often determined by subjective processes that do not rely on policy-bound formal evaluation" (Arnold, Crawford, & Khalifa, 2016, p. 906).

My colleagues and I also worry about how we are perceived by our students because it can result in real consequences. Theresa worries that a comment on the website Rate My Professor will hurt her tenure because one student wrote "She hates White people." Although no one charged with evaluating faculty for tenure and promotion processes would admit to using Rate My Professor as a measure, this remains a real concern for Theresa. Student evaluations and classroom observations may cause faculty of color to be labeled as difficult or problematic, when in reality they are doing the work of addressing racism, sexism, or other isms (Arnold, Crawford, & Khalifa, 2016). René believes that the chair of her department supports her tenure and promotion, but fears that her Tweet may be used against her on the larger college-wide P&B committee. The worry that we have to do "twice as much to be half as good" is not hyperbole. We see how the standard changes depending on who is being measured or doing the measuring, and so naturally faculty of color learn to view themselves twice, first as a person of color, then as a faculty member. This double consciousness is draining and can be life-threatening. There is a term for Blacks who succeed, but at the cost of their health. "John Henryism," coined for both the Black folktale legend who died immediately after winning a steel-driving race against a machine, and John Henry Martin, a Black farmer who,

> against tremendous odds–freed himself and his offspring from the debt bondage of the sharecropper system, [but at the cost of] hypertension, arthritis, and a case of peptic ulcer disease so severe that 40% of his stomach had to be removed.
>
> (James, 1994, p. 167)

Claudia Rankine (2014), in her award-winning book *Citizen*, says we "achieve [ourselves] to death trying to dodge the buildup of erasure" (p. 11). I am a full-time college professor with a Ph.D. from one of the best universities in the country. I consistently receive exemplary student evaluations, and faculty observations, and yet, I still wonder if my efforts will be recognized when I come up for promotion to Associate Professor. Double consciousness causes me to constantly try and do more: Be friendlier, volunteer for more committees, respond to email quicker, and provide more support for students. But, I try to put limits on when and how I respond. I take care of myself. I am not going out like John Henry!

At the community college where I work the majority of students are IPOC, and faculty of color serve as role models for how to deal with racism. But, we faculty members cannot do this alone; there are not enough of us. I was a bit surprised and pained when teaching *Citizen* to my African American Literature class to find so many of the students relaying numerous incidents of microaggressions on campus. From "old White" professors using the word "Negro" in class, to staff rudely telling Black students sitting in the library that they "cannot sit there–get out!" to being mistaken for janitorial staff.

I was *not* surprised that incidences like these were happening; but I *was* surprised at the number of incidents they cited. For every incident of microaggression Rankine (2014) mentions in her book, the students had their own; it was heartbreaking. I could give up, stop caring, just do my job and nothing more, but these students are the reason I teach. Odds are that I am the only Black professor that my students will take. They look to me to see how I respond to microaggressions and institutional racism. If I remain silent, I am complicit, even though sometimes I am so angry I cannot think straight. So, I do speak up, but at the times of my choosing, because taking care of myself, emotionally, physically, and mentally means that I will still be here to continue to fight. Ahmed (2009) maintains,

> Angry Black women need to stay angry: even though speaking anger involves risks and costs, even when we fail to get through other people's defenses. This is not to say that we can only be angry—anger is creative, and it gives us room to do other things. And nor is it our duty; I am not obliged to keep hitting that wall, sometimes I will, and sometimes I won't.
>
> (p. 51)

I cannot be angry all the time, it is not how I work, but I know when I can no longer hit the wall there will be others to pick up the bat and bash the hell out of it. This is what colleagues who want to help make changes can do—join us.

Though the current sociopolitical climate has emboldened a startlingly large number of people to do and say racist things, thanks to movements like Black Lives Matter, #MeToo and Women's March, and of course social media, there is increasing pushback. Although it does not seem to have stopped anyone yet, perhaps the fear of being the next #BBQBecky will make people think twice before doing something racist. Although it appears that many people are now encouraged to act on their racist thoughts, there are many others who are joining together to make positive changes. IPOC, the LGBTQ community, women, Jews, Muslims … are working together to eradicate all forms of hate. But many potential allies do not know how to start or are afraid that they will add to the pile of microaggressions we already deal with so they remain silent.

ACTIONABLE STRATEGIES

Here are some things anyone can do who wants to help lessen our RBF:

1. **Educate yourself.** There is no excuse for being ignorant with Google. If a Google search leaves you feeling overwhelmed, ask us where to start. I know my colleagues and I can list books or scholars off the top of our heads to get you started. Below are just a few:
   Applying Indigenous Research Methods: Storying with Peoples and Communities edited by Sweeney Windchief and Timothy San Pedro (2019) Routledge.
   Eloquent Rage: A Black Feminist Discovers Her Superpower written by Brittney Cooper (2018) St. Martin's Press.
   Nobody: Casualties of America's War on the Vulnerable, from Ferguson to Flint and Beyond written by Marc Lamont Hill (2016) Atria Books.

The What, the So What, and the Now What of Social Justice Education written by
Warren Blumenfeld (2019) Peter Lang.

2. **Support junior faculty of color.** Just knowing that a senior colleague
has our back can reduce a lot of our anxiety. Give us whatever tools you
used to get where you are: Mentorship, co-authoring papers, nominat-
ing us for teaching and research awards, and talking us up so our names
are known.

3. **Increase the authors of color that you teach.** Seriously, just do it.
Here are helpful websites that can help people locate diverse authors for
a host of different types of books ranging from children's to young adult
to nonfiction:

   https://socialjusticebooks.org/

   www.teachthought.com/literacy/teaching-social-justice-25-books-st
   udents-change-world/

   www.goodreads.com/list/show/96191._ReadPOC_List_of_Nonfictio
   n_Books_by_Authors_of_Color

4. **Speak up.** It gets tiring being the one who constantly has to point out
racism. Step up and speak its name—racism cannot be addressed if it is
never mentioned.

5. **Tell it like it is.** It's not doing us any favors if you censor honest feedback
because you are afraid of being racist. We know if you are actually racist.
We want to know where we actually stand.

6. **Become comfortable with being uncomfortable.** All change is difficult, and racial ideologies are so entrenched in us that even looking at them
can be painful.

CONCLUSION

Writing this chapter has been both challenging and cathartic. It has forced me to
unearth issues and emotions that I have chosen to overlook or ignore in order
to get through each day. I now realize that the best thing I can do is to be seen.
Seen as a successful, strong, intelligent, quiet, fashionable, Black, queer woman.
Being invisible is damaging. Reaching out to my colleagues for this chapter has
started valuable conversations and these need to extend beyond IPOC to include
our White colleagues. We need their support and their voices. If each White
colleague who considers themselves an ally would be willing to have the uncomfortable conversations on race, to engage in dialogues without being defensive,
to admit to their own racism and unintended microaggressions, to recognize the
work of IPOC, we could start to change the climate on campus. Unless White
allies also engage in the work of anti-racism, and use the tools offered to them,
nothing will ever change. This very book will do no good if people in positions
of power—department chairs, provosts, presidents—read it but fail to act. But,

I remain hopeful. Doing the work has always been the job of the oppressed and marginalized. So, we talk, and we teach, and we write, and we hope, and we love ourselves.

NOTES

1 According to Polanco-Roman, Danies, and Anglin (2016), "Passive approaches to coping with racial discrimination such as keeping it to yourself or accepting it as a fact of life may exacerbate the effects of the resulting stress and promote harmful adaptations such as those exhibited in dissociative symptoms" (p. 611).
2 https://en.wikipedia.org/wiki/Pig-Pen.

REFERENCES

Ahmed, S. (2009). Embodying diversity: Problems and paradoxes for Black feminists. *Race Ethnicity and Education*, *12*(1), 41–52. doi:10.1080/13613320802650931

Anderson, E. (2018, June 9). This is what it feels like to be black in white spaces. *The Guardian*. Retrieved from https://www.theguardian.com/commentisfree/201 8/jun/09/everyday-racism-america-black-white-spaces

Arnold, N. W., Crawford, E. R., & Khalifa, M. A. (2016). Psychological heuristics and faculty of color: Racial battle fatigue and tenure/promotion. *The Journal of Higher Education*, *87*(6), 890–919. doi:10.1353/jhe.2016.0033

City University of New York. (2016). *Workforce demographics by college, ethnicity and gender*. Retrieved from http://www2.cuny.edu/wp-content/uploads/sites/4/pa geassets/about/Administration/offices/hr/diversity-and-recruitment/Fall-201 6-CUNY-Workforce-Demographics_02062017.pdf

City University of New York. (2017). *Current student data book by subject: Race/ethnicity*. Retrieved from http://www2.cuny.edu/about/administration/offices/oira/ institutional/data/current-student-data-book-by-subject/#Race

Du Bois, W. E. B. (1903). *The souls of Black folk* (Chapter 1 & 2). Retrieved from https:// faculty.uml.edu/sgallagher/WEBDuBois-Souls_of_Black_Folk-1-14.pdf

Hartlep, N. D. (2016). The paranoid professor. In N. D. Hartlep & C. Hayes (Eds.), *Unhooking from whiteness: Resisting the spirit de corps* (pp. 27–33). Rotterdam, The Netherlands: Sense. doi:10.1007/978-94-6300-527-2_3

James, S. A. (1994). John Henryism and the health of African-Americans. *Culture, Medicine and Psychiatry*, *18*(2), 163–182. doi:10.1007/BF01379448

Levin, J. S., Walker, L., Haberler, Z., & Jackson-Boothby, A. (2013). The divided self: The double consciousness of faculty of color in community colleges. *Community College Review*, *41*(4), 311–329. doi:10.1177/0091552113504454

Lorde, A. (1988). *A burst of light and other essays*. New York: IXIA Press.

Rankine, C. (2014). *Citizen: An American lyric*. Minneapolis, MN: Graywolf Press.

Solórzano, D., Ceja, M., & Yosso, T. (2000). Critical race theory, racial microaggressions, and campus racial climate: The experiences of African American college students. *The Journal of Negro Education, 69*(1/2), 60–73.

Sue, D. W., Capodilupo, C. M., Torino, G. C., Bucceri, J. M., Holder, A. M. B., Nadal, K., & Esquilin, M. (2007). Racial microaggressions in everyday life. *American Psychologist, 62*(4), 271–286. doi:10.1037/0003-066X.62.4.271

Chapter 3

Teaching While Black

My Experience as a Faculty Member at a Predominantly White Institution

Robert T. Palmer

INTRODUCTION

In 2004, I was accepted into a Ph.D. program in Higher Education Administration at Morgan State University, a research-intensive Historically Black University, in Baltimore, Maryland. While I intentionally chose to apply to a Historically Black College and University (HBCU) for my doctoral work, I did apply to a variety of other schools. Nonetheless, I ended up being resolute to attend an HBCU for my Ph.D. for several reasons. First, ever since I was a kid, I was intrigued by HBCUs; I viewed them as cultural oases for Black Americans, such as myself, because I was never taught about Black history beyond slavery in the K–12 system. The second, and perhaps most critical reason I strongly desired to attend an HBCU for my doctoral studies stemmed from the racial microaggressions I experienced both as an undergraduate and as a graduate student at the two different Predominantly White Institutions (PWIs) I attended. Because the Ph.D. is a terminal degree, attending an HBCU for this degree would be my last opportunity to experience all of the great things I read about HBCUs in the scholarly literature as a master's student.

Interestingly, while pursuing my doctoral studies at Morgan State University, I came across a few articles that focused on the experiences of Black faculty at PWIs. Much of this scholarship described the racism, tokenism, and other forms of oppression faculty of color endured at these institutions. Foolishly, and being quite naïve, I questioned the accuracy of this literature. For some reason, respectfully, I thought the literature was outdated and that some authors or study participants had exaggerated their results or experiences. Introspectively, I realized my perception of the literature on faculty of color was tainted by my experiences of attending an HBCU—where I was sheltered, albeit briefly, from racism. For once in my life, my race was the majority on Morgan State University's campus, and encountering racism was the furthest thing on my mind. Nevertheless, when I graduated and landed my first tenure-track faculty job at a PWI, I realized quickly my perception was partial.

30

Drawing upon the tenets of Critical Race Theory (CRT), the purpose of this chapter is to discuss my experiences as a Black male professor at a mid-size research-intensive PWI. This chapter seeks to provide implications in order to help institutions, particularly PWIs, be more intentional in their creation of welcoming, supportive, and inclusive environments for faculty of color. Before focusing on my experiences as a Black faculty member at a PWI, I find it important to give an overview of CRT and the tenets of CRT that will be of focus in this chapter.

CRITICAL RACE THEORY IN EDUCATION

The premise of CRT is that racism is deeply ingrained into the legal and cultural fabric of the United States to the point where it looks normal (Ladson-Billings & Tate, 1995). In fact, one CRT tenet—permanence of racism—denotes that racism is at the center of the political, economic, and social aspects of U.S. society, which privileges Whites at the expense of indigenous people and people of color. The objective of CRT is not only to expose institutional and systemic racism, but also to eradicate it while promoting social justice in society and empowering minoritized populations (Hiraldo, 2010). Other tenets of CRT include counterstory or narrative, interest convergence, intersectionality, and Whiteness as property (DeCuir & Dixson, 2004). More specifically, a counternarrative is an authentic narrative about minoritized demographic groups that often runs counter to the dominant narrative which tends to be undergirded by a deficit perspective about underrepresented populations. Interest convergence underscores the reality that the dominant culture only has an interest in advancing or improving the conditions of minoritized groups if it benefits the majority culture. Meanwhile, intersectionality, coined by Kimberlé Crenshaw (1989), to better understand the experiences of Black women, provides perspective on how two oppressive identities—such as race and gender or race and class of a person of color—interact to shape and form the experiences of minoritized individuals. When discussing Whiteness as property, Hiraldo (2010), citing other CRT theorists and pedagogues, posits the following:

> Due to the embedded racism in American society, Whiteness can be considered a property interest (DeCuir & Dixson, 2004). As a result, this notion operates on different levels. These include the right of possession, the right to use and enjoyment, the right to disposition, and the right of exclusion (DeCuir & Dixson; Ladson-Billings & Tate, 1995; Ladson-Billings, 1998). Historically, the idea of Whiteness as property has been perpetuated as an asset that only White individuals can possess (Ladson-Billings & Tate). During enslavement, African men, women, and children were objectified as property (Ladson-Billings). This historic system of ownership and the reverberations from it

further reinforce and perpetuate the system of White supremacy because only White individuals can benefit from it.

(p. 55)

As it relates to my experience as a Black faculty member at a PWI, I would like to frame my chapter in the following tenets of CRT: (1) permanence of racism, (2) interest convergence, and (3) counternarrative.

Permanence of Racism

In the fall of 2008, I started my first faculty position at a university in upstate New York as a tenure-track faculty member in their master's-based Student Affairs Administration program. While the normal teaching load for faculty at this institution was a "2-2" (two courses per semester), my department chair, an African American female, worked with the dean of the school to help me get a course release. Thus, during my first semester, I was only required to teach one course—"Counseling in Student Affairs"—a master's level course in the Student Affairs program. As I went about prepping for this course I had some conversations with some academic friends about requiring students to call me Dr. Palmer. Quite frankly, I was against the notion of having my students refer to me as Dr. Palmer. However, my colleagues made it clear that as an African American professor at a PWI, it was critical that I require my students to call me Dr. Palmer. With their advice in mind, when I introduced myself to the students on the first day of class, I did so using my professional title, and I politely asked the students, all of whom were White, with the exception of two students, to do the same. Nevertheless, that day after class, a middle-aged White male approached me and asked if he really needed to call me Dr. Palmer. I simply said, yes, and he walked away.

While this very same student decided to drop my Counseling in Student Affairs course, for reasons that were not clear to me, later during the fall semester, he was assigned to me as my academic advisee. After this advisee assignment was made, he reached out to schedule an appointment with me to discuss options for graduate assistantships or other funding opportunities to help support his pursuit of his master's degree. About a week later, we met in my office, with the door closed. I proceeded to discuss graduate assistantships that might be available for the spring semester. As he listened, out of nowhere, and totally off the course of our conversation, he shared that he once worked at a bar as a bouncer, and in that capacity he would prevent his White friends from calling Black people "Niggers." Naturally, I was totally shocked by his revelation and admittedly I did not know how to respond. In fact, I pretended as if I did not hear the word he uttered and refocused the conversation back to the reason for his visit to my office—discussing funding opportunities. After the student left my office, I alerted my department chair about the incident, who in turn, informed the dean. While the student was subsequently removed from my advising list and eventually dismissed from the academic program in which I taught (for a different reason), my interactions with this student helped me to realize that no matter how much I achieved or education I attained, some people would choose to look at me, not as a Black man, but as a "Nigger." Malcolm X asked the question, "What do you call a Black man with a Ph.D.?" To which he replied, "A Nigger." Malcolm X remains correct.

Unfortunately, this was not the only experience I encountered with racism or racial microaggressions from students at this university. Another incident, though not as drastic as the previous one, occurred the spring semester of my first academic year in my course, "Theories of Retention and Persistence for College Students." Similar to the last encounter, the student, a White male, who was a second-year master's student in Student Affairs Administration, had an issue with some points I deducted from a paper he submitted. Specifically, this assignment was worth 20 points and I deducted two points for grammatical errors. While I viewed a deduction of two points as very minor, that was not the case to the student. He was extremely upset and exhibited a disrespectful tone over email when he informed me of how displeased he was with having two points removed from the total grade of his paper. Later, when we met in my office to discuss the issue, he asked me if I would consider giving him the full 20 points for the assignment. When I declined, before storming out of my office, he told me he did not respect me because I was only a few years older than him. He also warned me that his uncle worked as a central administrator for the State of New York's Higher Education Commission, and that I should be careful how I treated him.

Students also took issue with the materials that I taught in my classes generally. I must point out here that I was not the only faculty of color to experience this; several of my minority colleagues at this university had experienced this as well. Specifically, some of the students openly complained that my classes focused too much on minoritized populations, and they suggested that we should spend more time in class talking about issues encumbering poor White students in society in general and on college campus nationally.

Aside from students who displayed overt forms of racism, I also experienced racism in various ways from my White colleagues. For example, while so often is the case for faculty of color who work at PWIs, my colleagues of color were the only faculty to reach out to me when I started my tenure at the institution. Not only did they play a pivotal role in helping me transition to the university and the town in which the college is situated, many of my minority colleagues made me feel welcomed, valued, and important. They supported me and gave me an opportunity to normalize my racist encounters through talking and sharing similar experiences. My White colleagues, however, did not put in the effort to get to know me or my research when I first arrived at the university as an assistant professor. There were no invitations to lunch or discussions over coffee or tea about how we could collaborate when it came to our research interests to write journal articles, books, or submit grants. There were many instances when my White colleagues would walk by my office, and make eye contact with me, and not speak to me at all. Because of their behavior, I started to feel like an invisible man.

The dean of the college certainly was not a source of support when I finally confided in her about my experiences. I remember waiting until after I earned tenure and promotion—at which point I felt empowered and able to speak up for myself—to tell her about my experiences. When I shared with the dean some of the challenges I experienced involving racism, she was somewhat sympathetic, but she was shocked and made it seem like I was the only faculty member having such experiences at the university. To this end, she asked that I do research about what she could do in her position to make the environment more supportive and inclusive for minoritized faculty. Once I completed the research, she asked that I share it with her and hold a workshop for other faculty in the college. Needless to say, I never engaged in this task for several reasons, and I never followed back up with her to arrange another meeting. She had made it abundantly clear to me how she felt, and in so many ways, she indicated that fostering a more inclusive climate for faculty of color and addressing issues of racism was not her priority. She made the victims educate the perpetrators. Unfortunately, this is a common occurrence for minoritized faculty at PWIs and it is deeply problematic. Stipulating faculty of color to educate White faculty about practices of inclusivity on campus is a blatant form of racism because it puts the onus on minoritized faculty to communicate to White folks how they ought to be treated. The very notion of doing this signals that White faculty think faculty of color are so remotely different that only they have a specialized body of knowledge to communicate how they should be treated.

Another experience that illustrates CRT's tenet of the permanence of racism is my placement on the faculty senate committee for the university to represent my college. To be honest, I was conflicted about my appointment to this committee. On the one hand, I was excited because I thought it would help me to get to know more about the university and make connections with other faculty. On the other hand, however, I was concerned because this committee routinely met with the president, provost, and other high-ranking university officials. As a faculty member, who had yet to earn tenure at that time, I was not comfortable using my voice to represent the faculty in my college and I felt as though I was the token minority on the committee.

Because of these contingencies and contexts, oftentimes I was very quiet during the convenings of this committee, which led the faculty senate chair to email me one Saturday to explain that he intentionally selected me for the committee because he wanted me to be the voice for all minority faculty on campus. Having shared this with me in confidence, he encouraged me to speak up during subsequent meetings. In my response to his email, I politely shared with him that it is a lot of weight to be the spokesperson for the minority faculty on campus because I was limited to my experiences as an individual. Also, I sought to educate him by informing him that contradictory to popular belief, faculty of color are not a homogenous group, and that his encouragement that I provide the voice for all minority faculty on campus was a "racial microaggression" (Sue et al., 2007). I concluded my email response by denouncing my obligation to serve on the faculty senate committee. While he responded a day or so later, he simply indicated that he was sorry to learn about my decision and he asked if I knew of another minoritized faculty at the university who might be interested in serving on the faculty senate committee.

Interest Convergence

As mentioned earlier, when I first arrived at the university and throughout my time as a professor there, I experienced racism, which opened my eyes to the realities of Black faculty who work at PWIs. And while I continued to feel invisible to my White colleagues—as I became more successful in my area of research and as my reputation as a scholar grew in the academy—I felt I became increasingly important to the college and university as a whole. In fact, one of my colleagues, who eventually became chair of the faculty senate committee, did not reach out or really speak to me until I started to add luster to the college and university through my research; at which point, he deemed me a "rising star." Others have written about their similar experiences (Hartlep & Antrop-Gonzalez, 2019).

Moreover, another colleague, who was appointed to my third-year review committee, shared the only reason he was supporting my contract renewal for tenure and promotion was because of my research. He confessed that he did not think I was there to serve the students, which deeply hurt me because I have always presented myself as an engaged and student-centered professor. When I confided in a senior colleague, who was a person of color, about this professor's remark, I was advised not to focus on his comments, because other people on the committee did not share his sentiment.

In addition, while I received merit raises and was recognized with a prestigious award for my research from the university system, I did not really know or understand how much I was appreciated and valued until I informed the dean that I was offered a faculty position at a different university. Suddenly then, I had the full attention of the dean, who worked with the provost to extend a counteroffer. I truly respected the dean for her efforts and for letting me know that seemingly, despite remaining invisible to my White colleagues, I had become important to the college and the wider university. Despite the attractive counteroffer, I ultimately decided to leave the university for the opportunity that presented itself.

Several reasons undergirded my decision; chief among them was that while I felt my productivity mattered, I did not feel as if I belonged at that PWI. In many ways, metaphorically, I felt like a stranger inside my own house, which is not a pleasant feeling when you are pondering an establishment at which to forge your professional future.

Counternarrative

My counternarrative is that I was successful despite the expectation that I would not succeed. In 2014, a year before leaving the university, I was tenured and promoted to associate professor. At that time, I was the second Black man in the college's history, which was founded in 2007, to achieve this rank and tenure. Moreover, of the university community at large, I was one of a very small number of Black men who held the rank of associate professor with tenure. Indeed, I was elated when this happened, but honestly, I did not think that I would achieve tenure and promotion at the university because of my feelings of invisibility, and aside from my minoritized colleagues, who became my rock and provided a safe space, I did not feel supported when I started at the college. Honestly, if it had not been for my colleagues of color—two of whom became close friends—I would have left the college within a year of arriving there. When I started at the college, I felt so alone. Not only was I in a new town with no family, I also was tasked with learning how to navigate the academy, particularly its White spaces, as a new faculty member of color.

I cannot really say enough about how my colleagues of color were critical to my success. When I thought I was going crazy or thought I was hypersensitive about the racial microaggressions I was experiencing, not only did they help to normalize my experiences, but they encouraged me to stay focused on my research, teaching, and service. They also instilled in me early on that I had to work twice as hard as my White counterparts to be successful and achieve tenure. In this sense, I had to have double the peer-reviewed publications in top tier journals while displaying grant activity, and maintaining high-quality instructional activity in the classroom. Not only did my colleagues provide a safe and cathartic space to process and discuss how we were treated as minoritized faculty, they also provided a family-oriented environment and we engaged in discussions that transcended oppression and marginalization stemming from the hegemonic culture within the college and the university at large. We became each other's support system and took an active interest in each other's well-being, personal and professional development, and family relationships. As the African proverb notes, *it takes a whole village to raise a child*, my two colleagues, along with other mentors in my field, became the village that raised, mentored, nurtured, and supported a scholar, which helped to combat the sentiment that I felt upon arriving at the college—that I was not wanted nor was I expected to be successful.

DISCUSSION AND IMPLICATIONS

My story is atypical in some ways. Despite experiencing racial microaggressions as a student at the PWIs I attended, I questioned the veracity of the literature's characterization of faculty of color at PWIs that I read as a doctoral student. My experiences as a Black faculty member in a White space, however, not only validated the challenges faculty of color encounter at PWIs, but also helped to open my eyes to the perpetual problems of racism in the United States. It also made me realize, perhaps for the first time in my life, that Dr. Martin Luther King Jr.'s dream of desiring minoritized individuals to be judged on the content of their character, but not on the color of their skin, has not yet been fully realized. Unfortunately, most White people, and perhaps some people of color, make stereotypical assumptions about me (and other Black men) simply because of the color of my skin. And knowing that I do not have the power to change or do anything about their perception of me, until they get to know me as an individual, hurts like hell!

My encounters with racism, tokenism, alienation, and disrespect from White students are commonly cited in the literature on minoritized faculty (McGowan, 2000; Patton, 2009; Turner, Gonzalez, & Wood, 2008). Despite the fact that the literature has clearly explained the benefits students receive from interacting with diverse peer and faculty, most PWIs give lip service to increasing the representation of minoritized faculty and fostering a more inclusive campus environment to support them once there (Gasman, 2016). Similar to my narrative, faculty of color at PWIs often feel less supported and valued than their White counterparts and are often expected to be the "diversity guru."

In April 2019, *The Chronicle of Higher Education* published a series of essays entitled *Being a Black Academic in America*. These heart-wrenching stories, penned by graduate students, and tenured and untenured faculty of color, provided a humanistic perspective to the realities of being Black in the academy. Michael Javen Fortner, a professor at the Graduate Center of the City University of New York, whose story was chronicled in *Being a Black Academic in America* is similar to my experience, and perhaps to other minoritized faculty at PWIs. Specifically, he noted the following:

> Being a black professor, however, is fraught with a distinct set of challenges and indignities. Imagine having a lurking feeling that a student is testing you more than he would a white male professor. … I've witnessed otherwise open-minded white colleagues take umbrage at sincere calls for equity, viewing such requests as personal indictments. I've also seen faculty members of color dismissed or disparaged for agitating for diversity. I've seen them warned against airing 'grievances' at the risk of losing critical allies. I've seen them get labeled as 'difficult' and 'uncooperative' for recognizing their own

value and guarding their interests and voice. For minority faculty members, 'good' citizenship often means adhering to norms and procedures that can limit diversity and freedom of thought.

Unfortunately, given that the Trump Presidency has emboldened people to be more explicit and confident in expressing acts of White racism, resulting in increasing acts of hate crimes on college campus (Bauman, 2018), the plight of Black faculty at PWIs may worsen before it gets better.

With this chapter, I am glad that I chose to frame my counternarrative within the context of CRT because it really has helped me to understand my experience from a multidimensional perspective. Specifically, using the tenets of permanence of racism, interest convergence, and counternarrative has aided me to have a more well-rounded view of not only the challenges Black faculty face when working at PWIs, but also the tremendous fortitude they must exhibit to be successful in the academy. Based upon my story, I offer the following recommendations to predominantly White colleges and universities interested in not merely recruiting faculty of color but encouraging them to stay with the institutional community.

ACTIONABLE STRATEGIES

Faculty Cluster Hiring

Pioneered by the University of Wisconsin, Madison in the 1990s, cluster hiring is the practice of hiring faculty into multiple departments or schools based on sharing common characteristics, such as race, ethnicity, gender, perspective, ideology, and/or methodology (Urban Universities for Health, 2015). Specifically, the Cluster Hiring Initiative (CHI) was designed to help maintain University of Wisconsin, Madison's prominence in research, to help mitigate institutional barriers to interdisciplinary research, and to keep the university at the forefront of helping to advance the state's economy (Urban Universities for Health, 2015). According to Urban Universities for Health (2015), since the program's inception, "149 faculty lines were created and faculty were hired into 48 interdisciplinary clusters with topics ranging from African languages to zebrafish biology" (p. 5). University of Wisconsin, Madison's CHI was evaluated in 2003 and 2008, and has demonstrated positive outcomes in terms of faculty retention and satisfaction.

Though faculty cluster hiring was originally intended to increase interdisciplinary research at the university of University of Wisconsin, Madison, it has become a prominent practice that other universities are using to increase faculty diversity and improve institutional climate (Flaherty, 2015). Moreover, "faculty cluster hiring programs have the potential to improve institutional excellence overall by breaking down silos, reallocating resources to benefit the whole institution, and attracting innovative, nontraditional scholars" (Urban Universities for Health, 2015, p. 4).

Campus Climate Survey

While evidence has shown cluster hiring to be critical in facilitating the diversification of faculty, it is not the "be-all-end-all" panacea for improving the institutional climate for minoritized faculty. Indeed, cluster hiring will help to attract faculty of color and Native American faculty to the university and provide a supportive community once they are there. However, I believe it is fundamentally important for colleges and universities to focus on improving the university climate so when faculty of color interact with other individuals of the university community (e.g., students, faculty, administrators) not included in their cluster, they will at least be treated with respect and dignity when it comes to working with their White colleagues who may or may not have similar life/professional experiences. One of the ways that institutions of higher education can work to ensure their work environment is inclusive, equitable, and safe is by conducting regular campus climate surveys. Research shows that campus climate surveys are best conducted by an entity that is external to the university (McCarthy, 2016), and when every constituent of the campus has the opportunity to participate in the survey.

When the results of the survey are made known to the executive leaders of the university, it is important that they exercise a sense of transparency, and not only share the findings with the university community, but also use the findings as a guide to improve the climate of the campus community. In higher education, it has often been my experience that while colleges and universities will engage in assessments and other surveys for accreditation purposes, these results are not shared with the institutional stakeholders, nor are they used to provide an action plan of change. If higher education institutions, PWIs, in particular, are seriously dedicated to recruiting faculty of color instead of a facile and token approach to making the campus inclusive to diverse faculty, they *must* be intentional in using climate survey results to change how their campus operates so that everyone on campus—students, staff, and faculty—can experience a safe, inclusive, and tolerant institutional community.

Mandatory Training on Racial Microaggressions

Tightly coupled with implementing a campus climate survey is instituting mandatory and ongoing trainings on racial microaggressions. Deans, provosts, and presidents will mandate faculty and other administrators to attend active shooter training because they see the relevance and importance of it. However,

39

institutional leaders must also emphasize training on racial microaggressions. Trainings on racial microaggressions is important for reducing Racial Battle Fatigue because not everyone is aware, particularly many White individuals, of what racial microaggressions are and how they create a hostile place for faculty of color and Native American faculty. Mandating faculty, staff, and other university administrators to attend ongoing trainings on racial microaggression is beneficial because it communicates to the campus community that it is not the responsibility of individuals of color to educate the community about issues pertaining to diversity and other -isms, which is unfortunately often the case in the academy (Palmer, 2010). The onus of educating the university community about racial microaggressions and other -isms is a responsibility that must be shared equally by all members of the university. Given that cultural competency is an ongoing process (Pope, Reynolds, & Mueller, 2019), training of this nature should occur regularly, and more than once a year.

Finally, institutional leaders at PWIs frequently use the banal excuse of the "leaky pipeline" as the reason they cannot diversify their faculty. At my previous institution, the provost attributed the university's lack of faculty diversity to a leaky pipeline. But if a homeowner had a leaky pipe in their home, they'd call a plumber and fix the leak; the same needs to be done in higher education. The "leaky pipeline" has become a convenient and hackneyed excuse for higher educational leaders to not respond to the need for more diverse faculty.

Meanwhile, a university about 50 miles from my college was engaging in action (*and not excuses*) to recruit and diversify the faculty. One of the practices this university engaged in was reaching out to Minority-Serving Institutions (MSIs) because there are a number of MSIs with doctoral programs, and they produce the lion's share of Ph.Ds of color in the STEM fields (Palmer, Maramba, & Gasman, 2012). Forming connections and proactively outreaching to MSIs for hiring newly minted Ph.D.s could be one strategy to increase the racial and ethnic diversification of an institution's faculty. I must say, however, since serving as interim department chair for two years, and now as chair of an academic unit at an HBCU that regularly produces Black doctoral recipients in education, rarely do I receive faculty announcements from PWIs to share with students and recent alumni in my department.

CONCLUSION

Using CRT to frame my counternarrative, in this chapter I have discussed my experiences as a Black male faculty member at a PWI. I would be naïve to think that my narrative, or the book in which it is published, will result in monumental change for a problem that has long plagued the United States. It is sad that in the year 2019 society continues to grapple with issues of the color line. I hope that sharing my experiences in this book will spark conversation and lead to action on college campuses across the country. I hope that leaders of and within institutions of higher learning will read and learn from this chapter and this book. Hopefully in the future, as the population of color increases, as predicted by the U.S. Census, and the faculty of America's colleges and universities continue to diversify, postsecondary institutions will merely go beyond lip service to engage in serious action to provide a more supportive and inclusive campus environment for their faculty members of color and indigenous faculty members.

REFERENCES

Bauman, D. (2018). After 2016 election, campus hate crimes seemed to jump. Here's what the data tell us. *The Chronicle of Higher Education*. Retrieved from https://www.chronicle.com/article/After-2016-Election-Campus/242577

Crenshaw, K. (1989). Demarginalizing the intersection of race and sex: A Black feminist critique of antidiscrimination doctrine, feminist theory and antiracist politics. *University of Chicago Legal Forum, 1*, 139–167. Retrieved from http://chicagounbound.uchicago.edu/uclf/vol1989/iss1/8

DeCuir, J. T., & Dixson, A. D. (2004). So when it comes out, they aren't that surprised that it is there: Using critical race theory as a tool of analysis of race and racism in education. *Educational Researcher, 33*(5), 26–31.

Flaherty, C. (2015). New report says cluster hiring can lead to increased faculty diversity. *Inside Higher Ed*. Retrieved from https://www.washington.edu/diversity/files/2016/08/New-report.pdf

Gasman, M. (2016). An Ivy league professor on why colleges don't hire more faculty of color: 'We don't want them.' *The Washington Post*. Retrieved from https://www.washingtonpost.com/news/grade-point/wp/2016/09/26/an-ivy-league-professor-on-why-colleges-dont-hire-more-faculty-of-color-we-dont-want-them/?utm_term=.d5695cc00b36

Hartlep, N. D., & Antrop-Gonzalez, R. F. (2019). An effective model of mentorship and capacity building: Lessons learned and lived out at a Midwest AANAPISI. In R. T. Palmer, D. Preston, & A. Assalone (Eds.), *Effective leadership practices for minority-serving institutions: Beyond the deficit framing of leadership* (pp. 179–197). New York: Palgrave Macmillan.

Hiraldo, P. (2010). The role of critical race theory in higher education. *The Vermont Connection, 31*, 53–59.

Ladson-Billings, G. (1998). Just what is critical race theory and what's it doing in a nice field like education? *International Journal of Qualitative Studies in Education, 2*(1), 7–24. doi:10.1080/095183998236863

Ladson-Billings, G., & Tate, W. F. (1995). Toward a critical race theory of education. *Teachers College Record, 97*(1), 47–68.

McCarthy, C. (2016). Conduct an effective campus climate survey in 10 steps. *Dean and Provost, 17*(12), 1–12.

McGowan, J. M. (2000). Multicultural teaching: African-American faculty class-room teaching experiences in predominantly White colleges and universities. *Multicultural Education*, *8*(2), 19–22.

Palmer, R. T. (2010). The impact of social capital on promoting the success of African American faculty. In S. E. Moore, R. Alexander, & A. J. Lemelle (Eds.), *Dilemmas of Black of faculty at U.S. predominantly White institutions: Issues in the post-multicultural era* (pp. 117–134). New York: Edwin Mellen Press.

Palmer, R. T., Maramba, D. C., & Gasman, M. (Eds.). (2012). *Fostering success of ethnic and racial minorities in STEM: The role of minority serving institutions*. New York: Routledge.

Patton, L. D. (2009). My sister's keeper: A qualitative examination of mentoring experiences among African American women in graduate and professional schools. *The Journal of Higher Education*, *80*(5), 510–537. doi:10.1353/jhe.0.0062

Pope, R., Reynolds, A., & Mueller, J. (2019). *Multicultural competence in student affairs: Advancing social justice and inclusion* (2nd ed.). San Francisco, CA: Jossey-Bass.

Sue, D. W., Capodilupo, C. M., Torino, G. C., Bucceri, J. M., Holder, A. M. B., Nadal, K. L., & Esquilin, M. (2007). Racial microaggressions in everyday life: Implications for clinical practice. *American Psychologist*, *62*(4), 271–286.

Turner, C. S., González, J. C., & Wood, J. L. (2008). Faculty of color in academe: What 20 years of literature tells us. *Journal of Diversity in Higher Education*, *1*(3), 139–167. doi:10.1037/a0012837

Urban Universities for Health. (2015). Faculty cluster hiring for diversity and institutional climate. Retrieved from http://urbanuniversitiesforhealth.org/media/documents/Faculty_Cluster_Hiring_Report.pdf

Chapter 4

I Feel No Ways Tired

The Exhaustion from Battling the Pathology of Whiteness

Cleveland Hayes

INTRODUCTION

In 2015, I wrote a book chapter in the form of a composite story whereby I illustrated the experiences one Black male faculty member was having in his work as a teacher educator (Hayes, 2015). His narrative illustrates how he agitated and disrupted the seemingly calm and peaceful normativity of Whiteness in the academy sufficiently and frequently enough to have brought down upon his own head a form of domestic violence. Moving forward to 2019, I am a Black faculty member who works in a school of education where the minoritized faculty are the majority. However, what is different in this new space is that the pathology of Whiteness is not coming from White people, but other faculty of color, who are complicit in maintaining White supremacy. There is still a placating of Whiteness that I argue is a "showstopper" for any progression of social justice, and puts the school at risk of losing gains toward an anti-racist agenda for the betterment of school children specifically and society in general.

The Indiana University (IU) School of Education at Indianapolis, in my opinion, is a rarity, and one of the best places I have worked as there is somewhat of a cap on Whiteness. However, at the time of writing this chapter, the ugliness of Whiteness has surfaced once again, and now, many of the faculty, including myself, are working to the point of exhaustion to make sure it does not become even more magnified. Many of the faculty in the School of Education are well-known critical scholars whose work is aimed at dismantling Whiteness and White supremacy. By design, the students in the teacher education program are gaining exposure to critical discourses preparing them to teach in any urban space in Indiana. In the Ph.D. program—Urban Education Studies—the majority of students are *not* White. This is almost unheard of at most Predominantly White Institutions (PWIs) in this country. Before I arrived, the faculty worked hard to ensure that the faculty body was critically diverse. It is important to make a distinction between being critically diverse compared to "diverse" for the sake of diversity. Through this autoethnography, I will share my battle with the complicity and pathology of Whiteness, and what I perceive to be an attempt to dismantle the anti-racist work being done in the School of Education. Many Schools and Colleges of Education claim to do anti-racist work, but in the School of Education at IU the work is actually being done via development of a critical mass of scholars who are willing to challenge Whiteness and White supremacy not only on campus but also in Indianapolis. The faculty assembled at IU Indianapolis is why I came and why I stay.

RACIAL BATTLE FATIGUE: SAME STRUGGLE, DIFFERENT FACES

When we think about Whiteness, many still think it has to do with White people. During the numerous presentations that I have given as an academic, I am clear that Whiteness has nothing to do with the way a person looks, but rather an affect or a mindset that keeps White racial domination alive. People of color can be complicit in Whiteness just as White people can be. However, the effect on the body is different. The way it is handled and talked about is different; as Malcolm X states, as paraphrased in Gaskin (2006), racism [and therefore lynching], is like a Cadillac—a new model is produced every year (p.142). Except this time Stephen[1] is driving the Cadillac. The point I am making here, is there is always conversation about White racism but very little conversation about how people of color are complicit in keeping White supremacy alive and well.

Reed-Danahay (1997) argues that an autoethnography enlists a rewriting of the social self. Quicke (2010) argues that autoethnographic work often involves, as is the case in this book project, looking back and analyzing personal memoirs, and is often focused on the self as participant in the social process. Autoethnographic accounts of experiences, by virtue of being self-reflective, are deeply personal; researchers using this methodological approach must produce highly personalized, revealing texts in which they share stories about their own lived experiences. I attempt to do this here for the reader.

Real Talk: Anti-Blackness and the Re-Centering of Whiteness

There has not been one major incident of what I would classify as a macroaggression at IU, but rather a series of small microaggressions that over time manifest into that "yuck" feeling when it comes to dealing with my colleagues who are not White but espouse anti-Blackness and at the same time perform Whiteness. The mere fact that I am writing this chapter, even in my position as a tenured full professor, brings up negative emotions and raises my anxiety. While I have reached the pinnacle in the academy, tenured and full, I am still an openly gay Black male in the academy. A space that upholds and maintains White supremacy, which does not protect me from Whiteness when my Black and Brown colleagues perform Whiteness and expect everyone else to be "well-behaved" minorities.

These "well-behaved minorities" have become the leaders in the School, which means they now have institutional power to carry out anti-Blackness policies with the hopes of being rewarded. These same Black, Brown, and Asian faculty members consider themselves liberals and believe in equality to a certain point. However, through their actions, they are still carrying out anti-Black microaggressions.

In my current role as associate dean, I am responsible for the master schedule of classes. I have to ensure that classes have faculty coverage and decide when a section of a class needs to be canceled. At the end of the fall 2018 semester, there was a class that only had three enrolled students for the upcoming term. I didn't want to leave for the holidays with a class without an instructor, or leave before canceling classes with low enrollment. In this case, there was a class that needed an instructor, and therefore, I decided to cancel the class with three students and move the instructor to a class that met enrollment.

I had talked to all of the necessary people before I approached the faculty member whose section would be canceled, and it appeared that everything was a go. Later that day, I received an email from the professor whose course I canceled; he told me that he had talked it over with his program chair, and she felt that the class should stay open. In the vein of Racial Battle Fatigue (RBF), this faculty member (who is not White), felt it was appropriate to circle back so as to question my authority as the Associate Dean for Academic Affairs. One can imagine the emotions that arose when I received this email, which implied both that my decisions do not matter, and that there needs to be validation from Whiteness before final decisions can be made. In this case the Chair is not White but performs Whiteness. This chapter is about those people of color who are complicit in Whiteness and contribute to anti-Blackness.

The two faculty members that I mention above are faculty in Education Leadership and Policy. When they come to meetings they are really big on protocol and following the chain of command and following "orders," and when other faculty members have done something similar to them, the non-White faculty members want to claim it was because of their ethnic background. What they fail to realize is that there is a mistrust in the hallway toward them because they pull stunts like this.

I am thinking now, what do I do with this? Because while I feel this faculty member was wrong for challenging my authority, the question that comes to mind is, had I been White, would he have done the same thing? As I have learned from my many years in higher education, faculty of color need allies and support when racist macroaggressions rear their ugly head, and now, I cannot trust this person. There are emotions that take over the body when people are in spaces where there is no trust at the end of the day.

45

The Trauma of "Fake Drama:" No One Is Being Mean to You

I was recently having a conversation with a colleague of mine concerning why individual scholars of color with impressive credentials are not elected to high profile positions within our research association. My response to him was, "Real talk, there is mistrust from some folk of color toward other folk of color who phenotypically are people of color but perform Whiteness. That is why some folk of color don't get elected to high profile positions."

This colleague, I think, was a little taken aback by my position on this issue. As I have illustrated in this chapter, it is tiring and exhaustive to battle people of color who perform Whiteness and how these same folk rally other folk of color who perform. Recently, as the associate dean that manages graduate programs, a question came through email as to why the Ph.D. program coordinator does not assign courses in the Ph.D. program. My response to this person was, "I don't know but let me find out some information, but I think it is time we change that."

I sent out an email and made a decision that the Ph.D. program coordinator, in collaboration with the faculty, will begin to assign courses. The former program coordinator gets busy creating the narrative that people are not being kind to them. Any time decisions are made that don't fit with this person's "agenda," then the narrative of being unkind comes up as in this case when I made the decision that we need to have another conversation about who assigns courses within the Ph.D. program.

Later in the day, this email came out from School Administration: The former coordinator of the Ph.D. program had convinced them that I was being unkind to them. Which was not the case. This is only a portion of the email, as I want to illustrate once again how people of color contribute to Whiteness:

> With so many challenges facing us as a school and the pressures of making ends meet, let's be kind to one another in developing solutions … hard choices are on the horizon, folks, and we need to be more supportive of one another.

This was the response to the email that I sent out about how decisions were going to be made. In previous emails, there was nothing mean to anyone, many of us are very matter of fact but not mean. This particular faculty member has been problematic, pulling the "folk are being mean to me" card in past situations, and now this faculty member has an audience that will listen to "people are being mean to me." This faculty member likes to use policy and "law and order" as their mechanism of control and stopping conversations they don't like or don't fit with how they think things should go.

Later in the day, the email below was sent from a faculty member of color in response to the email from School Administration, emphasizing how problematic the words "kind" and "being kind" are in these situations:

I am troubled by the language of your response. Twice you used the language of 'kind.' This obviously implies that you perceive that someone was not being kind. I find this accusation problematic and indicative of a lack of awareness regarding your positionality when you choose to enter a discussion. I believe there is a much-needed conversation regarding your choice of language connected to the campus-wide discussion for the White Racial Literacy Project and how people of color can (often unknowingly and unintentionally) appropriate the tools and language of white supremacy.

This was one of my colleagues' responses to this "madness." As folk of color, it is hard enough to work, and energy draining, when these "fights" come from White folk, but it is even worse when it comes from folk of color. My colleague and I then spent the rest of the day deconstructing this email and these responses because of which I am sure if I went to the doctor and had my blood pressure checked it would be elevated. This while I am a full professor, my colleague is not, and this took away from their writing. This is another conversation for another project, but higher administration wonders why there are so few professors of color in the academy. This kind of "crap" doesn't end, and the fact that I am having to relive it as I write this chapter contributes to the RBF.

Refusing to Talk about Race: The Pathology of Whiteness

I have to admit there is an honest attempt to talk openly about race, racism, and White supremacy at the School of Education in which I work. However, depending upon the phenotype of the individual doing the talking, one can see there is a visible discomfort when it comes to talking about race. There is a narrative on the larger campus that the faculty in the School of Education are difficult. The narrative stems from the fact that collectively as a school we challenge notions of Whiteness and do not subscribe to the neoliberal agenda that is causing harm to Black and Brown children in the local school district. The neoliberal agenda in our context is being forced to partner with charter schools or organizations that want to dismantle public school and to privatize the school district with which the IU School of Education—Indianapolis has community ties.

I often wonder why there isn't a narrative about the White faculty in my school and other schools I would consider "difficult" when it comes to conversations around equity and access. Do these White men mostly challenge their White male colleagues about being difficult? My guess is that they do not. What is worse is people of color sign off on this Whiteness and while I know the answer why, I am still wondering, why? Now, these persons cannot be trusted. This pathology of Whiteness is preventing the advancement of others because Whiteness has deemed them well-behaved minorities.

47

According to Harris, Hayes, and Smith (2016), "well-behaved minorities" exhibit some combination of the following two behaviors:

1. They never make White people feel uncomfortable and often provide support to White people when faculty of color challenge their racist discourses. What this looks like is when White fragility and White tears show up, the difficult conversation stops and we spend the rest of the time trying to make the White faculty member feel better and the situation never resolves itself.

2. Well-behaved minorities don't blow things out of proportion or get too pushy. For example, I was on the committee charged with finding a new dean for the School of Education and there was a candidate for the position who was very matter of fact about their positions on social justice and equity. To be clear, the candidate did not characterize things as "his way or the highway," but spoke very openly about his position on this topic. After the candidate finished his interview, a narrative about him developed concerning how aggressive he was, and how he made the search committee feel, and could he turn it down a bit? This enraged me (this rage is one of the effects of RBF); the conversation that followed was even more exhaustive as everyone in the room—Whites and the well-behaved minorities—claimed that the candidate's color was not a factor in why they did not like him, on which I called bullshit. I have sat in too many meetings in which White men have behaved similarly and the narrative about that White person is not the same. After the committee's discussion of this candidate—he was the last one for the day—I had to go home and lie down. I was mentally and physically exhausted, as the folk of color in the room who claimed to be committed to social justice just sat on the sidelines and let this candidate's character be attacked.

In the context of RBF, the notion of trauma comes to mind. Recently, I had a graduate student in the Ph.D. program come and speak to my pre-service teacher education students about trauma-informed schools and how in many cases, students' behaviors in class are manifested by long-term trauma outside of school. As educators, we have to rethink how we engage with students who have experienced and may continue to live in horrific environments. This graduate student explained that when students are constantly in "fight or flight" mode, specific hormones are released into the body. Release of these fight or flight hormones is good when there is a bear chasing you in the woods but experiencing this release on a regular basis in the course of one's everyday life results in decidedly negative health outcomes.

In 2015, I was diagnosed with a hormone-based cancer. Since then, I keep wondering, why I can never get my numbers where they need to be to stay cancer-free? I have had friends and colleagues who have had the same procedure, but they do not work in the sometimes very toxic and hostile world of academia where people are always jockeying for positions as if on Darwin's scale of evolution. While I am not saying that other work spaces are not toxic and/or hostile, I am arguing that the hostility in academia has its own brand. In short, I am making the case that my friends' recovery has been better because they are not in this fight mode all of the time. I am not speaking for all here, just my friends who have had the same procedure.

While I was sitting in class, as the professor, I got to thinking about my own trauma as an openly gay Black male in a space where Black women are the majority of the faculty, and how I continue to experience trauma from those who are not White. There are times that I get ready to go into a meeting with these colleagues and I have to go into "fight" mode. I enter fight mode to battle these faculty of color who are tied to Whiteness in ways that do not promote growth of the school and definitely do not help children in schools, but rather further their own agenda. This is what many would call "kingdom building" for themselves. I am placed in opposition to these faculty who question my authority when I make a decision, or worse go behind my back to higher authority and my decision is overturned. Having to fight processes that uphold hegemonic structures that again build kingdoms but do not help build the school. Fighting delays in decision making that has caused the school to miss out on opportunities for growth because these decisions do not fit into their kingdom building. Fighting behind closed doors, meeting before the meeting conversations and then pretending they did not know the meeting was happening. Fighting the pathology of Whiteness that shows up in the form of fragility because one of the duos is White or there is a performance of Whiteness from the other. This duo is married—one White and the other a person of color. Having to fight the worship of the written word, where there is no value in other forms of communication. Fighting to believe that the politics that go along with certain agendas and politics get valued over others which is framed as there are racial divides in the hallway. No, there are no racial divides in the hallways. There is an illusion created that there are racial divides in the hallway because these persons have alienated allies and no one wants to stand up to them. The victimhood actually makes me sick literally and figuratively. I would describe this fake creation of racial issues as trying to hoard power.

As a Critical Race Theorist, one of the tenets of this framework is the permanence of racism and the property of Whiteness. Racism is embedded in our thought processes and social structures with the business in our society of keeping people of color in subordinate positions. This is done through daily interactions and practices typically enacted by the very nice, morally good liberal humanists who are always quick on their feet and ready to help others different from themselves. I do not mean to convey sarcasm here, yet hope to underscore the fact that oppression is realized through processes of domination that individuals

49

and groups choose to enact and therefore could choose to act differently and then dismantle—usually the nice helpers, the good liberals, not the closet or out-ed openly hateful members of groups and society who still keep their white bedsheets ready for a midnight run of terror. Pointedly, I do realize that those targeted by oppression can and sometimes do participate in their own subjugation. Accordingly, it is only through the explicit, aggressive, intentional, very color-conscious efforts of all of us to change the way things are done. This will do much to ameliorate misery inflicted on people of color and others by White racism. This also includes other forms of oppression: Sexism, heterosexism, and ableism (Delgado & Stefancic, 2001; Tate, 2012), to name just a few.

This pathology of Whiteness must be eradicated not only for the health of individuals but for the health of the School of Education. This pathology of Whiteness performed by non-White people makes them complicit in keeping racist discourses alive and well, and in a space where the minoritized faculty are the majority, their fragility shows up even though they themselves are not White; this in turn prevents those who are about social justice from doing the work they/we need to do. This pathology of Whiteness is real and I never fully realized it until it came out of Black and Brown bodies with no clear understanding of why. So, now I am back in this fight mode with Blacks and people of color that causes internal conflict because we should be about the business of dismantling Whiteness collectively but instead, I am battling those who are minoritized who are keeping the pillars of White supremacy intact. This White supremacist culture is more than just White people; non-White people are continuing in very subtle and nuanced ways to keep Whiteness and White supremacy in full operation.

IMPLICATIONS FOR PRACTICE

Writing this section on implications for practice is in and of itself RBF. Checklists and theories to practice only serve one purpose and that purpose is to put the blame, and responsibility of success, on the persons who did not create the mess. For me this creates anger and resentment. Why is the burden of this work being placed on me and others who acquiesce and create a checklist when we know they do not work and then when the checklist fails or the items are written in ways so others can hear then the academic lynching begins? The academic lynching where the faculty member is labeled as "rude," "hostile," "needs to be right," and a whole host of other adjectives that have the potential to cause a lot of grief for the faculty member creating the list. So, against my better judgment and drawing on my experiential knowledge of checklist development and execution, here are my implications. I am providing steps that higher education administration can take to mitigate the experiences that faculty of color may be having because of the manifestation of Whiteness through people who are not White.

With all the challenges of being a Black male in the academy, the last thing any of us needs is to battle other faculty of color. The exhaustion of anger, fear, being accused of being argumentative, deliberate silence and withdrawal from stress-inducing situations takes away from the work that needs to be done to improve the educational experiences of children in general, and Black and Brown students in particular. In this section of the chapter, I will provide some critical suggestions to undo some of this in the vein of "unhooking from Whiteness" (Hayes & Hartlep, 2013). Unhooking from Whiteness is something that people of color have to do as well if we are to dismantle racist discourses. It is my understanding and belief there are no practical applications to dismantling Whiteness. Meaning it is not something that you do, it is something that you become. Again, this is why I struggle with checklists in these types of situations, but here are things that could be considered.

ACTIONABLE STRATEGIES

1. Do not allow the faculty member of color who is complicit in Whiteness to circumvent decisions after they are made. What that does is tell the faculty member who is complicit that their behavior is acceptable and the original person making the decision really doesn't have any decision-making authority. Those faculty of color who employ Whiteness are usually unwilling to recognize this question of authority, and getting permission from the White faculty whose status is lower is an example of the brutality of Whiteness (Stanley, 2006).

2. Stop the negative labeling of Black faculty who challenge inequities or inconsistent behaviors. Allowing the assigning of negative characteristics are acts of power used by the institutional agents to define us as outside of Whiteness and these faculty of color as inside Whiteness and therefore entitled to the benefits associated with Whiteness. Indeed, the negative framing of our personality and character are used as a control mechanism by the institution to shift attention away from these faculty and toward us and our apparent inability to get along with others, particularly those of us who fail to conform more perfectly with the standards of Whiteness in ways of interacting and acting in the department and institution. The Whiteness of the context, at the same time as these faculty members of color are complicit in Whiteness, remains undisturbed and thus protected with the focus shifted toward others who are attempting to dismantle Whiteness. This causes the Whiteness of the institution to be [re]secured.

3. Do not be afraid of the critical faculty who are doing the work, and stop empowering these non-critical faculty of color who are undermining the mission of the school because they make things comfortable. In the vein

of RBF, not only are the critical faculty having to battle White supremacy from White folk, now we are having to do it from the faculty of color.

4. Recognize when there is a deliberate attempt to undermine those who make people uncomfortable. This means the person who is leading the unit must be in tune with their Whiteness. Whiteness enacted by people of color still silences any discussion of race outside of niceties of liking people and what makes it worse is the tiring effect it has on our persons having to combat Whiteness on two fronts. Whiteness from White folk and Whiteness from people of color. What people of color complicit in Whiteness fail to understand is how they can and/or do embody White supremacist values even though they themselves may not embrace racism; it is through this lack of their own awareness that they support the racist domination they say that they wish to eradicate (Gillborn, 2005; hooks, 1989; Jones & Okun, 2001).

5. Be intentional about building a base for activism at the workplace even for folks whose privilege doesn't require them to think about having to be an activist. Create a culture of co-conspirators and not allies (Love, 2019; Smith, 2007).

6. Take a survey of your inner-circle. Are you having experiences that will help you see the experiential knowledge of people who may be experiencing these passive-aggressive hostilities simply because you yourself want to control the narrative of these faculty members (Jones & Okun, 2001)?

7. Following Smith (2007), pay attention to group dynamics: Who are these faculty of color complicit in Whiteness "rolling" with and why are they "rolling," especially if the unit has a very social culture? When they are in the office, what are they telling you, and what are you listening to? Are you listening to these faculty because what they are saying aligns with your beliefs, even though it offers no merit to the growth of the unit and value added to the unit and it is only creating a divide in the unit?

8. Lastly, as a higher education leader, to paraphrase Malcolm X here—if you aren't posing a very serious threat to Whiteness and saying something that seriously threatens Whiteness, regardless of your phenotype, then you are probably not saying much anyway; Whiteness only responds to threats deemed serious enough to challenge its dominance.

FINAL THOUGHTS

White supremacy is never fully secured and must be continually re-established; as I have illustrated in this chapter, people of color play a role in that re-establishment of Whiteness. Defined "as a racialized social system that upholds, reifies, and reinforces the superiority of whites" (Leonardo, 2005, p. 127), White supremacy is daily, perhaps hourly, remade through processes of race-based domination. Individuals and groups on their own and collectively draw on institutional authority to justify and make decisions, act, and interact with others in ways that further the historical privileging of characteristics, values, histories, accomplishments, and more associated with Whites (Bonilla-Silva, 2003; Gillborn, 2005; Lipsitz, 2006). The faculty of color that I make mention of in this chapter should strive toward an inclusive, integrated community blind to race-, class-, gender-, sexuality-, or creed-based differences, but as individuals and collectively they are approaching their work guided by universal, difference-neutral democratic, egalitarian-based ideals that, unfortunately, typically result in the buttressing of Whiteness and continued White racial dominance.

NOTE

1 The name Stephen is taken from the movie *Django Unchained*. Stephen, played by Samuel L. Jackson, is the house slave in the movie who helps maintain Whiteness and, in this case, instead of a White person driving the Whiteness car, a person of color is.

REFERENCES

Bonilla-Silva, E. (2003). *Racism without racists: Colorblind racism and the persistence of racial inequality in the United States*. Boulder, CO: Rowman & Littlefield Publishers.

Delgado, R., & Stefancic, J. (2001). *Critical race theory: An introduction*. New York: Temple University Press.

Gaskins, A. (2006). Putting the color in Colorado: On being Black and teaching ethnic studies at the University of Colorado-Boulder. In C.E. Stanley (Ed.), *Faculty of color: Teaching in predominantly White college and universities* (pp. 139–152). Bolton, MA: Anker Publishing Company.

Gillborn, D. (2005). Education policy as an act of White supremacy: Whiteness, critical race theory and education reform. *Journal of Education Policy*, *20*(4), 485–505.

Harris, B. G., Hayes, C., & Smith, D.T. (2016). Just do what we tell you: White rules for well-behaved minorities. In N. D Hartlep & C. Hayes (Eds), *Unhooking from whiteness: Resisting the esprit de corp* (pp. 123–146). Boston, MA: Sense Publishers.

Hayes, C. (2015). Assault in the academy: When it becomes more than racial battle fatigue. In K. Fasching-Varner, K. Albert, R. Mitchell, & C. Allen (Eds.), *Racial battle fatigue: Difference and division in higher education* (pp. 10–25). Lanham, MD: Rowman & Littlefield.

Hayes, C., & Hartlep, N. D. (Eds.). (2013). *Unhooking from whiteness: The key to dismantling racism in the United States*. Rotterdam, The Netherlands: Sense Publishers.

hooks, b. (1989). *Talking back: Thinking feminist, thinking black*. Boston, MA: South End Press.

Jones, K., & Okun, T. (2001). From dismantling racism: A workbook for social change groups. Retrieved from http://www.cwsworkshop.org

Leonardo, Z. (2005). *Race, whiteness, and education*. New York: Routledge.

Lipsitz, G. (2006). *The possessive investment in whiteness: How White people profit from identity politics*. (Expanded ed.). Philadelphia, PA: Temple University Press.

Love, B. (2019). *We want to do more than survive: Abolitionist teaching and the pursuit of educational freedom*. Boston, MA: Beacon Press.

Quicke, J. (2010). Narrative strategies in educational research: Reflections on a critical autoethnography. *Educational Action Research, 18*(2), 239–254.

Reed-Danahy, D. E. (1997). *Auto/ethnography: rewriting the self and the social*. New York: Oxford University Press.

Smith, C. (2007). *The cost of privilege: Taking on the system of White supremacy and racism*. Fayetteville, NC: Camino Press.

Stanley, C. A. (2006). Walking between two cultures: The often misunderstood Jamaican woman. In C. A. Stanley (Ed.), *Faculty of color: Teaching in predominantly White college and universities* (pp. 328–343). Bolton, MA: Anker Publishing Company.

Tate, W. F. (Ed.). (2012). *Research on schools, neighborhoods, and communities: Toward civic responsibility*. Lanham, MD: Rowman & Littlefield.

Part II

The Racialized Experiences of Asian Americans in U.S. Higher Education

Navigating Weird Comments, Stereotypes, and Microaggressions as Southeast Asian American Faculty at a Predominantly White Community College

Andrew Cho and Sopang "Pang" Men

INTRODUCTION

An article entitled "Everything Wrong with Asian Privilege" appeared in the April edition of *The Challenge*, Tacoma Community College's (TCC) online student newspaper. The article, written under the pseudonym "An Asian Person" and published with a picture of a stereotypical Japanese "Dragon Lady," claimed that Asian Americans enjoy entitlements not given to other minority groups. According to the author of the article, Asian immigrants are not expected to learn English or asked to become Americanized or to go back to their countries. *The Challenge* is only available to TCC students, so the article remained online without receiving much attention from TCC staff and/or faculty. TCC students, however, battled with one another in the article's comments section. The majority of the comments were in support of the article's claim about Asian privilege. Only a few students chose to point out the article's misinformation and generalizations.

One of the students opposed to the article forwarded it to Dr. Andrew Cho, an Associate Professor of Sociology at TCC, who then sent the article to other faculty members. As a preface to the article, Dr. Cho described the Racial Battle Fatigue (RBF) he has experienced at the institution:

> I am also feeling overwhelmed and exhausted by the TCC culture—it seems that for the past 12 years, students of color experiencing issues regarding racism and prejudice often find their way to me [...]. On one hand, I am humbled

that the students seek my guidance due to my sociological expertise in race and ethnicity and I do my best to support them. On the other hand, I'm struggling with all these incidents that occur outside of my classroom.

This incident brought to the surface many persistent issues for Asian TCC faculty such as microaggressions and inequitable labor. This autoethnography shares the experiences of two Southeast Asian male faculty members at TCC, a Predominantly White Institution (PWI) in Washington state. Dr. Andrew Cho is a tenured Sociology professor and Sopang "Pang" Men is a tenure-track English and Literature professor. Although they are at different points in their careers, they both have experienced RBF as Asian male faculty.

WEIRD COMMENTS AND MICROAGGRESSIONS WE HAVE EXPERIENCED AS ASIAN AMERICAN MALES

Andrew: I was excited to begin my first day on the job at TCC. A staff member suggested that a campus tour would be the ideal way to begin my career at the institution. As a sociologist, I tend to constantly analyze the race, ethnicity, gender, and age demographics in my immediate social setting. I had heard whispers that one of the main reasons my predecessor, a Black sociologist also around his early 30s, left the school was because he felt isolated and marginalized. However, I was not overly concerned because I had previous experience as an adjunct instructor at other local community colleges that were also PWIs. As I was led to my office, I quickly noticed that all the faculty members I saw were White and considerably older than me. I shrugged it off until I toured the Student Center across from my office building. I introduced myself to a White male staff member by saying, "Pleasure to meet you. My name is Andrew and I'm looking forward to teaching Sociology and being your colleague."

Instead of shaking my extended hand and introducing himself, he merely stared at me for a few unsettling moments. Then, he broke into a wide grin and exclaimed, "Hey buddy! My wife is Asian!" This interaction occurred on the first day that I stepped onto the TCC campus; other such incidences would follow that would contribute to the RBF that I have continued to experience as an Asian male faculty member.

Pang: Last spring during the first week of my "Argument and Persuasion" course, a student in the front row raised his hand near the end of my introductory lecture on rhetoric. The student, a young man, wearing a pair of glasses, and a puzzled expression on his face, asked me, "What class is this?"

I replied that he was in English 102.

"This isn't Sociology of Asian Americans with Dr. Cho?" he asked me. The class giggled, and I said that no, I am not Dr. Cho and that Dr. Cho's class was across campus.

The student remarked, "The teacher in the other room said that you were Dr. Cho, and she told me to come here."

As the class and the student continued in their lighthearted laughter, I felt a wave of frustration burst out of me and toward the other instructor who conflated Dr. Cho ("Andrew") and me ("Pang").

To be clear, Andrew and I do not look alike. We have marked differences in height, build, and complexion. Andrew is Burmese. I am Cambodian. Andrew teaches Sociology. I teach English. The only explanation for mixing us up is that the other instructor attached an Asian-sounding name to the first Asian-looking professor she saw—as if there could only be one Asian male faculty member at TCC. The next day I approached the instructor and politely told her what had happened in my class the day before. She offered a curt apology and went on her way.

Andrew: My wife, son, and I attended a school reception last year when an administrator asked us if we are "teaching our son Korean." I answered "no" because my wife is Vietnamese American and I am Burmese American.

He was perplexed and commented, "Oh, I thought you were Korean." This irritated me because I had recently presented at a professional development event that he had attended on basketball camps that I helped facilitate in Burma[1] during my travel there since Burma is my country of ancestry. He even asked me after that presentation about my relatives that still live in Burma. Other colleagues have assumed that I am Chinese, Filipino, or Cambodian, despite the fact that I constantly refer to myself as Burmese American and that a huge Burmese flag hangs in my office.

Pang: New colleagues have been surprised to hear that I teach English and Literature, not Mathematics or a Social Science subject. One faculty member responded by asking me, "English, like ESL?" the implication being that I am best suited to teach basic English skills to non-native speakers and immigrant students because I do not fit the image of someone who teaches writing classes: I am not White. These minor but pervasive assumptions can be viewed as a form of *identity denial*, the threat that one is not seen as a member of a group because of his or her non-prototypical features (Cheryan & Monin, 2005). Identity denial manifests itself through seemingly innocuous questions such as, "Where are you from?" or "What languages do you speak?" Fielding these queries can be belittling, embarrassing, and infuriating. I understand that "Sopang" is not as common a name as Jason or Adam, but my name should not be an invitation to ask where I am originally from or to imply I am not truly American.[2]

Andrew: My Burmese name is "San Aung." All my siblings have traditional Burmese names as well. However, my parents realized that in order to secure jobs in the United States, having a mainstream "American" name would be beneficial. Thus, even though she is Buddhist, my mom chose Catholic names for me and my three brothers: I was named Andrew and my brothers were called

Christopher and Patrick. Our oldest brother was named Richard, after "Richard the Lionheart" (Richard I of England), who they learned about after Great Britain colonized Burma. Given the fact that one's name is such a critical element of self-identity, having to adopt a different name in order to avoid discrimination in the labor market is an element of RBF that begins before we even start our professorships. Social scientific research in other communities has suggested that racial or ethnic-sounding names can dramatically decrease job and apartment rental chances (Bertrand & Mullainathan, 2004; Carpusor, & Loges, 2006; Widner & Chicoine, 2011). Along the same lines, an Asian American colleague named Wendy has been asked multiple times, "What is your Chinese name? I want to call you by your 'real name.'" Her response has always been, "Call me Wendy. That is my real name." This incident relates to the idea of Asian Americans being "Forever Foreigners" (Tuan, 1998), not truly Americans.

Pang: According to Cheryan and Monin (2005), *identity assertion* is an over-compensation of American characteristics or knowledge when threatened by *identity denial*. For me, I have read the American literary canon widely and voraciously: From James Fenimore Cooper to John Updike. Many of these novelists are White males who write about lifestyles and problems that I have not experienced myself as a Southeast Asian refugee, but I find it necessary to broaden the scope of my literary knowledge beyond minority writers who may speak more authentically to me. In a way, I want to prove—at a moment's notice—that I am as credible a literature instructor as any other older White male faculty member.

Andrew: Issues regarding Asian American curriculum have also manifested at TCC. One former Dean of Arts, Humanities, and Social Sciences held a meeting with myself and another Sociology professor. The Dean asked why we offer both a "Sociology of Asian Americans" course and a "Sociology of African Americans" course. We were puzzled. She then stated that the "course learning outcomes are the same for both classes." We were even more befuddled, and responded that "one course focuses on the sociological experiences and issues of African Americans and the other course focuses on the sociological experiences and issues of Asian Americans." After approximately an hour, she still did not understand how the two courses were different, which perplexed us, but is yet another example of a frustrating situation contributing to our RBF. The simplest situations that should be non-issues inexplicably become stressful circumstances for faculty of color.

THE MODEL MINORITY STEREOTYPE AND THE "INVISIBLE MINORITY"

Pang: The *model minority stereotype* presumes that all members of a group possess the same positive characteristics (Hartlep, 2014; Hartlep & Porfilio, 2015; Kiang, Huynh, Cheah, Wang, & Yoshikawa, 2017; Wing, 2007). Positive stereotypes of Asian Americans include studiousness, docility, and excellence in math and sciences (Hartlep, 2013). Although often stated with good intentions, these stereotypes can limit potential and perception. My first five years at TCC were spent as an adjunct instructor who aspired to become a full-time professor. Frustratingly, there was no clear path to achieving that goal, at least not for part-time instructors. The school had no professional development program for contingent faculty and openings for full-time positions were rare. Full-time faculty of color were rarer. One time I approached a tenured English instructor at the office photocopier and inquired about potential full-time positions. Instead of advice, she replied, "You don't look like an instructor!"

Asian males are stereotyped as weaker, quieter, and less masculine compared to White males (Shek, 2006). These generalizations, no matter how incorrect, can affect how Asian male professors are perceived as leaders on campus, and how Asian male professors perceive themselves (Hartlep & Antrop-González, 2019).

I was in conversation with an older, taller White male student one day before class when a member of the facilities staff came in to check on a pair of malfunctioning classroom speakers. Instead of looking at me, the facilities staff member addressed the White male student and told him that the speakers would be fixed by tomorrow. Graciously, the student was able to pivot the conversation to me, but it was an awkward moment nonetheless, one that made me reconsider how I physically present myself on campus. I now make small sartorial choices like wearing an official school lanyard, which can implicitly communicate that I have an official position at the school, or at least that I am not a student.

Negative stereotypes also affect how Asian male professors see themselves. By nature, I am a reserved person who prefers to process ideas. I would rather come to conclusions slowly than to have to backpedal a poorly conceived comment. In committee or faculty meetings, however, I can see how my prolonged silences could be seen as timidity or indicative of the quiet Asian male. I often leave meetings wondering if I should have made my voice heard more often, even if what I said had no actual substance.

Andrew: Scholars (Osajima, 1995; Hune & Chan, 1997) have discussed the challenge that Asian Americans face as the "invisible minority" in America. Oftentimes, many in society forget that Asian Americans are a racial minority and thus are not insulated from the racism and discrimination that affects other racial and ethnic minority groups in this country. An example of being an invisible minority occurred several years ago when our current institution had an open faculty forum for the finalists for president. During the forum, I asked the candidates how they would navigate the exodus of male faculty and staff of color who departed either voluntarily or forcibly due to a hostile campus climate. Some of my colleagues were stunned that I spoke up and asked that. Many who did not know me well had stereotyped me as "quiet." Others were surprised that I mentioned that hostile environment that Asian American male faculty and staff faced. The next day, I was called into a room by an administrator who chastised me for "scaring possible candidates away." I stated that those were exactly the questions that needed to be asked because our campus needs leadership on diversity, equity, and inclusion issues. The administrator shrugged me off and alluded to the prospect that I was "over exaggerating the situation."

Similar to Pang, this is another example of where I have to reflect on Asian male stereotypes about masculinity. We seem to lack presence within higher education spaces and are invisible compared to our White male colleagues. Pang and I have had conversations focused on how stressful it is for both of us to figure out how to dress on a daily basis so that we can "be seen" on campus in the same light as our White colleagues. We do not believe our other male colleagues on campus engage in similar discussions.

I'm almost six-feet-tall yet one White student in class remarked how I fit the stereotype of a "short Asian." When I told him to get up and come to the front of class to stand next to me, he was absolutely shocked to see that I was several inches taller than him. Having to fight Asian male stereotypes surrounding masculinity and physical appearance makes it challenging for us to possess the same presence on campus as our male counterparts of other racial and ethnic backgrounds.

INVISIBLE LABOR

Andrew: Despite negative interactions, we often volunteer for unpaid assignments such as being on a thesis committee at another institution because we are invested in the success of our students. From our observations, faculty of color often go above and beyond. *The Atlantic* published an article about the "invisible labor" that professors of color perform on college campuses that generally goes unnoticed and unappreciated (Matthew, 2016). Like our brothers and sisters of color on campus, we also constantly perform invisible labor that seems to be expected of us, and that goes unrecognized. Students of Asian ancestry often seek us out for issues that they face on campus. Many of these students have never taken a class with us but rather come find us on campus because they believe we will advocate for them and can also relate to their experiences.

For example, an international student from Vietnam showed up at my office and told me that her professor would not allow her to attend the class anymore. According to the student, she was speaking in Vietnamese to another classmate who is also from Vietnam about her weekend plans. During this exchange, another student in the course became upset and erroneously believed that the Vietnamese students were making fun of her. The odd solution to this perceived conflict was for the Vietnamese student to only see the professor during her office hours, but not attend class anymore while the other student was still allowed to attend the course. Given the high tuition that international students pay, the student was extremely upset and felt powerless and unsupported in the situation.

In another incident, a student came to me because his professor would not say his actual name but instead called him "Ching Chong Wah." When another student called the professor out on it, the professor claimed that he was just "sneezing" and did not say "Ching Chong Wah," even though it occurred on multiple occasions and several students heard it.

Pang: In my short time as a full-time instructor, I have seen how faculty of color take on invisible labor tasks. We are often pulled into offices, email threads, and hallway conversations to discuss racial matters on campus. We receive offers to join committees that we "would be right for." Often, this service work revolves around issues of equity and diversity. In a Faculty Forum meeting last year, another professor volunteered Andrew's name to work on the hiring committee for the new TCC President position. Andrew had just sat down in the meeting and was surprised when his name was mentioned. Nevertheless, he agreed to this important yet laborious role.

One reason that my tenure process has not been too unnerving is because of Andrew and his unofficial mentorship. TCC has a faculty mentorship program, but not one tailored for faculty of color. Andrew took the initiative to look out for me and clue me into the inner workings of the institution. Another Asian faculty member, Wendy, has also taken me under her wing and has candidly told me about her own RBF experiences. Not all faculty of color are so fortunate as me to have supporters like Andrew and Wendy. To be fair, the State Board has a cross-institutional faculty of color mentorship program that pairs faculty mentors and mentees from different colleges; however, there is no substitute for having an advocate within the same school who can help navigate departmental politics and act as a "sounding" board when the work becomes too burdensome.

THE "ASIAN PRIVILEGE" ARTICLE

After Andrew sent the "Asian Privilege" article from *The Challenge* to other faculty, the responses came fast. Faculty of color were the first to reply, many of whom expressed hurt for the Asian students who read the article and the misguided student who wrote it. However, the email thread deviated from a discussion about cultural awareness to one on journalistic standards.

Pang: In face-to-face conversations with Andrew and other Asian faculty, I also shared my frustrations with the article's generalizations about Asian Americans. My parents struggled to learn English, but it was not due to a lack of trying. My father studied for the citizenship test every night but never took the test because he was not confident in his English reading abilities. As a child, I was told to go back to my country and was called racist names by grown men

63

and women. The article's sentiment did not reflect my lived experience as an Asian immigrant.

In the email chain Andrew started, I did bring up my issues about Asian stereotypes, but I also echoed the comments of some of our White colleagues who thought that the school newspaper needed a legitimate faculty editor. As an English instructor, I see the benefits of guiding student writers from first to final drafts and providing more assertive suggestions when necessary. The sentiment of the faculty email thread went in that direction for a while before Andrew chimed in to remind everyone about the original issue: The article's promotion of racist stereotypes:

> [I]t seems like this went from a conversation on race and bigotry towards Asian immigrants and refugees to a directed conversation on the lack of a journalism program at TCC. It is frustrating as a person of color that we can't have open dialogues on race and when we start one, it gets moved to a more academic, non-race topic.

Andrew's message stunned me and made me reexamine my response as an Asian American faculty member. Because I went along with the call for more journalistic standards, I was complicit in muting an important discussion about race.

A few weeks later, Andrew organized a meeting with the student-writer and a dozen or so Asian American faculty and students. The session allowed Asian American students to air their grievances, the student-writer to explain his intentions, and Asian American faculty to share advice and suggestions. Ultimately, the student-writer wrote an apology article in the next edition of the newspaper.

Andrew: This was a tricky situation to navigate because the article was written by a young Asian American student, who faculty did not want to feel persecuted for publishing his perspective. On the other hand, quite a few Asian American students, staff, and faculty were extremely upset and hurt by the article, which was presented as the one, true Asian experience. When some of us questioned why the article was allowed to be printed in the first place, the answer from the student's newspaper advisor was that it seemed questionable, but it was still given the green light.

My response was, "Look at the article again. Now, replace the word 'Asian' wherever it appears in the article with 'Black,' 'Jewish,' 'Muslim,' or 'Mexican.' Would you still have approved its publication?"

After examining the article from that perspective, the answer we received from one faculty member was that "there's no way this hate speech should have been published. But we didn't think about it that way when it was about Asians."

Ultimately, this ended up being a positive educational experience for the TCC community. It raised awareness on campus of anti-Asian sentiment and stereotypes and it resulted in an augmented sense of pan-Asian identity and community among students, staff, and faculty. It provided a glimpse of how large, willing, and change-minded our Asian American community on campus could be.

ACTIONABLE STRATEGIES

We propose several recommendations for higher education policy and practice. First, educational institutions need to have Centers of Equity, Diversity, and Inclusion led by a high-ranking (ideally vice president level or above) individual with a team that can positively affect campus climate. Too often, Asian American faculty and staff voices are dampened. At our present institution, TCC, we are currently in the process of hiring a Vice President of Equity, Diversity, and Inclusion. Institutions hiring such a position should ensure that the individual hired possess expertise and knowledge regarding the Asian American issues we described above in the RBF section. Specifically, understanding the heterogeneity and diversity itself within the larger umbrella category of Asian American, the challenges Asian American faculty and staff face with the "Forever Foreigner" syndrome and other stereotypes, the invisible labor that we and other faculty and staff of color perform, and the unique microaggressions and microinvalidations that Asian Americans suffer from, should be part of that person's skillset. Moreover, since faculty and staff of color often do not have a physical space to seek out, having a Center of Equity, Diversity, and Inclusion can be a safe space refuge for healing conversations and reducing RBF rather than internalizing and fostering RBF when left to deal with it on our own.

Furthermore, cultural norms for some Asian ethnic groups dictate the importance of not making waves or challenging the system in public forums. Institutions should also create an easily accessible system in which incidences of racism, discrimination, and prejudice can be reported without fear of retribution. Presently, TCC has a Bias Incident Report Team (BIRT) form that employees can fill out when discriminatory actions occur, but accessing the BIRT form online is not intuitive and takes multiple steps to find. Colleges need to make reporting racist, discriminatory, and prejudiced incidences as accessible as possible; otherwise, racist, discriminatory, and prejudiced actions may go unreported.

Next, we also believe that a multilayered mentoring program can be effective for interrupting RBF. At a Professional Development workshop for the campus earlier this year, survey data was introduced that asserted Asian American students felt the "least welcome" out of all the racial and ethnic groups on campus. In response, one of our esteemed English and Humanities professors, Mary Chen-Johnson, proactively organized a series of meetings between Asian American staff and faculty and the TCC President, Dr. Ivan Harrell. The purpose of the meetings was to discuss strategies to better support our Asian immigrant, international, and Asian American students. One of the recommendations was to create a mentoring program that would match Asian American faculty and staff with Asian American students. Although our institution has Support Services for students of color, our Asian American students also get lost in discussions of race on campus. For some, the term "students of color" does not include our Asian American students, another byproduct of both the model minority stereotype and the fact that we are often invisible, even when right in front of an audience. By implementing this Asian American mentoring program, we hope to increase levels of feeling welcome and connected on campus and also to provide advocacy for our Asian American students. In addition, we envision this model to include an additional layer of mentoring with some of our senior Asian American staff and faculty being assigned to mentor new hires. Building a program like this may require the help of the institution's grant writer, who can help acquire long-term funding and support.

Another recommendation is to create an anthology of Asian American staff and faculty voices. Presently, we have a popular anthology titled *Una Voce*, which highlights TCC student voices and stories.[3] Because it may be somewhat difficult, uncomfortable, and possibly intimidating to verbally share our experiences with RBF on campus, we believe a written anthology that highlights the struggles and challenges that we face in our historically White institution would be of immense value. We have had professional development workshops on campus focused on diversity but they have rarely focused on the experiences of Asian Americans. Even if they did, it seems as if those who need to attend such workshops are never in attendance. One of the unfortunate byproducts of having tenured faculty status is that some of the most egregious offenders on campus have the ability to hide behind their tenured status and continue harmful behaviors with little or no sanctions. They also are not required to attend mandatory diversity trainings. However, we believe they might actually be willing to read first person accounts of colleagues' experiences. Moreover, some of our closest allies on campus may not be aware of our experiences either. A written anthology may expose them to new information while serving as a launching pad for further campus conversations and professional development workshops about racialized experiences of Asian Americans.

Just being able to reflect and write about our experiences with RBF may be palliative for some of the Asian American employees on campus. However, the main purpose of a written anthology would be to provide a voice for Asian Americans who are traditionally silenced by the Black | White race dichotomy in America. Yet, we realize that some employees such as adjunct or non-tenured faculty as well as classified staff may be hesitant to contribute to such an anthology for fear of retribution. Even tenured faculty may be worried about repercussions from colleagues or supervisors who feel upset that their microaggressions or blatant racism are being called out. Writing in anonymity may not guarantee insulation from retribution because given the fact that due to the small number of Asian American faculty and staff, one may easily identify who wrote which piece even if their name is not attached to it. We hope though that the majority of our colleagues would be willing to truly listen to our experiences and contribute to fostering a more inclusive and welcoming campus climate for Asian American employees. When colleagues and administrators become aware of our marginalized and oppressed statuses and our constant struggle with RBF that is often triggered by their actions, perhaps change can be implemented at the individual and institutional level. *Courageous Conversations* and mandatory diversity training that focuses on the heterogeneity of the Asian American population and diversity of experiences would go a long way to reducing RBF.[4]

We also recommend identifying and placing faculty of color in positions where they can affect change. In the last year or so, administration has installed faculty of color in important campus initiatives. One of the more visible roles is Pang's role as the Faculty Tri-Chair position for TCC's Strategic Plan Steering Committee. TCC President Dr. Harrell saw a need for diverse voices on the committee and asked around for a potential Faculty Tri-Chair. TCC's strategic plan will extend from 2019 to 2024, so new equity programs and revisions to hiring practices to support faculty of color must be voiced and fought for now. When an institution decides to embark on creating systemic change, administration must seriously consider installing faculty of color in leadership positions and supporting the development of those leaders.

In addition, we cannot stress more the importance of having support from the upper administrative levels. There generally seems to be a wave of optimism among faculty and staff of color resulting from the hiring of President Dr. Harrell. As the first permanent Black president in TCC history, he has always stressed diversity, equity, and inclusion from day one. During the previous president's term, employee morale seemed to be at an all-time low. We recommend that institutions and boards of trustees be unafraid to make changes in leadership if those administrators are not championing diversity efforts.

Furthermore, as tenured and tenure-track faculty, we recognize our privileged status at our institution. We have a certain level of protection and job security that our adjunct colleagues, professional exempt, and classified staff do not share. Therefore, we recommend that tenured and tenure-track faculty take the lead in speaking out and advocating for our colleagues when called upon by those in more tenuous positions. Too often we have witnessed the silence of tenured faculty when a colleague was in need of support.

Finally, we recognize that our experiences as Southeast Asian American males may not be wholly unique and that some of our other brothers and sisters of color and indigenous brothers and sisters have similar experiences. However, we appreciate our voices included in the narrative on RBF because too often we are indeed the invisible, silent, model minority.

NOTES

1 Although the country is now officially called Myanmar, many people such as Andrew still refer to the country as Burma.
2 "What Kind of Asian Are You" https://youtu.be/DWynJkN5HbQ.
3 https://www.tacomacc.edu/tcc-life/arts-culture/unavoce.
4 https://courageousconversation.com/about/.

REFERENCES

Bertrand, M., & Mullainathan, S. (2004). Are Emily and Brendan more employable than Lakisha and Jamal? A field experiment on labor market discrimination. *The American Economic Review*, *94*(4), 991–1013.

Carpusor, A., & Loges, W. (2006). Rental discrimination and ethnicity in names. *Journal of Applied Social Psychology*, *36*(4), 934–952.

Cheryan, S., & Monin, B. (2005). "Where are you really from?": Asian Americans and identity denial. *Journal of Personality and Social Psychology*, *89*(5), 717–730.

Hartlep, N. D. (2013). *The model minority stereotype: Demystifying Asian American success*. Charlotte, NC: Information Age.

Hartlep, N. D. (2014, May/June). Lost among Caucasians: The lethal fallacy of the model minority stereotype. *Profiles in Diversity Journal*, *16*(3), 32–33.

Hartlep, N. D., & Antrop-González, R. F. (2019). An effective model of mentorship and capacity building: Lessons learned and lived out at a Midwest AANAPISI. In R. T. Palmer, D. Preston, & A. Assalone (Eds.), *Examining effective practices at minority-serving institutions: Beyond a deficit framing of leadership* (pp. 179–197). New York: Palgrave Macmillan.

Hartlep, N. D., & Porfilio, B. (Eds.). (2015). *Killing the model minority stereotype: Asian American counterstories and complicity*. Charlotte, NC: Information Age.

Hune, S., & Chan, K. (1997). Special focus: Asian Pacific American demographic and educational trends. In D. Carter & R. Wilson (Eds.), *Minorities in higher education: Fifteenth annual status report: 1996–1997* (pp. 39–67, 103–107). Washington, DC: American Council on Education.

Kiang, L., Huynh, V. W., Cheah, C. S. L., Wang, Y., & Yoshikawa, H. (2017). Moving beyond the model minority. *Asian American Journal of Psychology*, *8*(1), 1–6.

Matthew, P. (2016). The invisible labor of faculty of color on campus: What is faculty diversity worth to a university. *The Atlantic*. Retrieved from https://www.theatlantic.com/education/archive/2016/11/what-is-faculty-diversity-worth-to-a-university/508334/

Osajima, K. (1995) Racial politics and the invisibility of Asian Americans in Higher Education. *Educational Foundations*, *9*(1), 35–53.

Shek, Y. L. (2006). Asian American masculinity: A review of the literature. *Journal of Men's Studies*, *14*(3), 379–391.

Tuan, M. (1998). *Forever foreigners or honorary whites? The Asian ethnic experience today*. New Brunswick, NJ: Rutgers University Press.

Widner, D., & Chicoine, S. (2011). It's all in the name: Employment discrimination against Arab Americans. *Sociological Forum*, *26*(4), 806–823.

Wing, J. Y. (2007). Beyond black and white: The model minority myth and the invisibility of Asian American students. *The Urban Review*, *39*(4), 455–487.

Chapter 6

When You Name a Problem, You Become the Problem

(En)Countering Whiteness at a Small, Liberal Arts College as a South Asian American Tenured Professor[1]

Anita Chikkatur

INTRODUCTION

After discussing Black and White racial identity development models (Cross, 1971; Tatum, 2004) in my "Multicultural Education" course in spring 2018, I asked my students to answer this question anonymously on notecards:

> Based on whichever model of racial identity development that you feel fits you best, which stage of racial identity development would you place yourself in? Why?

One student wrote on their notecard, "I know the Cross model has five stages, but maybe there should be a sixth—'burned out and tired.'" A few days later, the student (who I assumed had written that answer) asked me how I continue to teach about race and racism at a Historically and Predominantly White Institution (H/PWI)[2] without getting to the "burned out" stage (Chen & Gorski, 2015). In other words, how do I deal with Racial Battle Fatigue (RBF) at a H/PWI liberal arts college as a person of color who teaches about identity, power, and privilege?

In this chapter, I answer that question by reflecting on colleague reactions to my blog posts on/about racialized interactions at my workplace, which explored identity, race, power, and privilege on college campuses. Two blog posts in which my co-author, Adriana Estill, and I discussed interactions with our White colleagues led to negative reactions from colleagues, including being complained about to the administration (see Chikkatur & Estill, 2017; Estill & Chikkatur, 2016a). Drawing on the framework of critical anti-racism, especially as elucidated by womxn of color (e.g., Ahmed, 2012; Alexander, 2005; Gutiérrez y

Muhs, Flores Niemann, González, & Harris, 2012; Lorde, 2007; Lowe, 2018), I reflect on how my attempts at counter-storytelling (Solórzano & Yosso, 2001) helped me gain greater clarity about my positionality and about the nature of relationships across racial and institutional power differences. I have come to appreciate the blog as one way to combat the RBF that I, like many faculty of color and Native faculty, face. I analyze my colleagues' reactions and my college administrators' responses to delineate ideas for how colleges and universities, especially small liberal arts colleges, can better support diverse faculty. I also provide suggestions for faculty of color and Native faculty on how to survive RBF at their institutions.

INSTITUTIONAL CONTEXT

I'm currently an Associate Professor at Carleton College, a Midwestern, residential, liberal arts college with approximately 2,000 undergraduate students and 200 full-time faculty. Since I began teaching at this institution in fall 2008, student and faculty demographic diversity has increased. According to data provided by the college's Office of Institutional Research and Assessment, in the 2008–2009 academic year, approximately 21% of the students were identified as U.S. resident/born students of color. By 2016–2017, that percentage had increased to 27%. Similarly, the proportion of tenure-track, tenured, and visiting faculty who identified as White decreased between 2007 (87%) and 2017 (74%) (T. Jamison, personal communication, November 11, 2018). I was the first faculty of color to earn tenure and am currently the only permanent (tenured) faculty of color in my department—Department of Educational Studies.

MY STORY

In spring 2016, my colleague, Adriana Estill, and I started a co-written blog, named *Down with Brown*,[3] spurred on by our conversations at the time about defaced posters on campus and our frustration with the limited response from college administration to the vandalism (Estill & Chikkatur, 2016b). These student-created posters featured photos of Carleton students and messages about culturally inappropriate or offensive Halloween posters. Adriana—a Latinx tenured professor in American Studies and English at Carleton College—and I had long talked about developing a public forum to discuss ideas from our private conversations about how identity, power, and privilege impact our experiences as womxn of color faculty. Over the next few months, we wrote blog posts about our racial identity development (Chikkatur & Estill, 2016b), our perspective on the debates about whether our students were "coddled" (Chikkatur & Estill, 2016a), and our take on interactions we had on campus with our White colleagues (Estill & Chikkatur, 2016a). While our blog was not something either of us would have felt comfortable starting before we earned tenure, we decided that we needed to use the security that tenure affords to speak up about our experiences, even if these posts made some of our colleagues feel uncomfortable or vulnerable. In an era when there are fewer and fewer tenure-track positions (Hurlburt & McGarrah, 2016), Harris and González (2012) note that full-time faculty with tenure "enjoy levels of autonomy, prestige, and economic reward that are unusual" (p. 2). Recognizing that we have the power and privilege of tenure, we wanted to use our RBF experiences to illustrate how "women of color faculty members [even those with tenure] are entrenched in byzantine patterns of race, gender, and class hierarchy that confound popular narratives about meritocracy" (Harris & González, 2012, p. 2). Additionally, because I am a scholar in the field of Educational Studies, in my classes, we often discuss how my students can speak up for social justice in the educational spaces they find themselves— whether in the role of teacher, tutor, counselor, parent, and so forth. It was important for me to model doing the same in the educational space where I spend most of my work life, Carleton College.

We deliberately chose to start a *public* blog to chronicle our critical counter-narratives as womxn of color faculty at a H/PWI. Our decision was anchored in Critical Race Theory's (CRT) insistence that "the experiential knowledge of people of color is legitimate, appropriate, and critical to understanding, analyzing, and teaching about racial subordination" (Smith, Yosso, & Solórzano, 2006, p. 303). For me, it has been one way to combat RBF by helping me name and analyze openly the troubling, racialized interactions that often occurred within "closed-door" meetings where it was difficult to pinpoint in the moment why a comment bothered me and to critique such comments, especially if the person had more institutional power. We realized that we were taking a risk by putting our stories out there, especially because we are at a small college where most faculty know each other across departments. However, it felt even worse to experience certain kinds of interactions over and over again without being able to say anything. As Niemann (2012) wryly notes, for womxn of color faculty, "there is a price to pay for not remaining silent *and* for remaining silent" (p. 499, my emphasis). We are damned if we do, and damned if we don't.

We have received very positive responses to the blog. Colleagues, alumni, and friends have commented—both publicly and privately—about their appreciation of our descriptions and analyses of how identities, power, and privilege play out on college campuses. However, we have also had to deal with negative reactions. In particular, two blog posts where we discussed specific interactions we had with White colleagues at Carleton led some of our colleagues to make complaints to administrators. We did not name these colleagues in our posts, and we changed some of the specific details of the interactions to protect personal identities. After we published a post discussing a frustrating exchange that

Adriana had with a White faculty member about the emotional labor undertaken by faculty of color at Carleton (Estill & Chikkatur, 2016a), we were informed by the faculty president that several colleagues complained to them about the post. As far as we could tell, they all came from tenured faculty. Based on the summary given by the faculty president, there seemed to be three categories of complaints. One set concerned the potential damage our blog post might have done to the reputation of the White colleague involved in the specific interaction discussed in the post. Other complaints were related to the fact that we had written about a faculty meeting—and whether interactions at such meetings should be kept confidential. Another set of complaints was directed at the post's "tone." Since none of the complainants expressed their objections to us directly, it is difficult to be specific about the content of the complaints.

Our colleagues' negative reactions demonstrated clearly one of the consistent themes discussed in critical anti-racist analyses by womxn of color: In speaking up about racism, we became the problem, rather than the racism being the problem. As Ahmed (2012) aptly notes in her study about "diversity workers" on college campuses, "Speaking of racism is … heard as an injury not to those who speak but to those who are spoken about" (p. 147). Faculty who had concerns about our blog posts were worried about the reputation of the White colleague we discussed, but did not share (at least with us) their concerns for us and how we are experiencing our shared collegial spaces as womxn of color. Based on principles of anti-racist activism and intergroup dialogue, we were careful to frame our analysis of the interaction as a critique of behavior, discourse, and institutional norms, and not of a person. And yet, our critique was "heard as personal attacks on reputation" (Ahmed, 2012, p. 50).

While I agree with Smooth (2008) that the "what you said or did is racist" framing is a better way to engage in a critical dialog about racism than the "you are a racist" approach (Smooth, 2008), my colleagues' reactions demonstrate that it can be challenging to make this distinction because it seems difficult to move away from a moralistic understanding of racism (Tatum, 2003). Indeed, as Ahmed (2012) explains, these reactions illustrate how "one of the biggest accusations you can make is the very accusation that you are accusing someone of racism. … *Indeed, one of the best ways you can deflect attention from racism is to hear racism as an accusation*" (p. 151, emphasis in original). In conversations Adriana and I had with college administrators about our colleagues' complaints, the administrators did not ask us many questions about the substance of the blog posts or about our experiences as womxn of color at Carleton. Instead, the foci of these conversations were on how we/they could manage our colleagues' reactions to the post. Similarly, Lowe (2018) notes that administrators on her campus—Evergreen State College—were often "more concerned that I had concretely named the behaviors and actions of a colleague as *racist* [than] with the fact that I was experiencing and being *impacted by racism*" (para. 18). Our blog posts did not use the term "racist" to describe our colleagues' words and actions; and yet, we were confronted with pushback similar to what Lowe experienced.

Approximately a year after we wrote the first blog post that led to negative reactions from colleagues, I had to decide whether to write about a particular pre-tenure experience I had with a senior colleague that illustrated well a broader point Adriana and I wanted to make about how, as womxn of color faculty, we often felt like our presence on campus was only welcomed in superficial ways. I reminded myself of Ahmed's (2012) words: "even if we use softer language, we are already sore points. We might as well do things with these points" (p. 171). I also found strength in Audre Lorde's (1978) wise reminder that my silence will not protect me. I decided to speak up about my experience, knowing that it might not be heard in the way I wanted it to be. Disappointingly, yet unsurprisingly, this blog post led to another round of negative reactions with the strongest coming from the person with whom I had had the interaction described in the post. This faculty member filed a formal complaint against me with the Dean of the College.

It took more than a year for me to be notified of the administrators' decision that this complaint had no merit, leaving me uncertain for that time period about what consequences I might face. Despite the positive outcome, the experience led me and Adriana to experience RBF. Locher and Ropers-Huilman (2015) argue that "institutions [should] consider ways in which they can support faculty members of color when their academic freedom is challenged and when they are victims of negative identity-based scrutiny or discrimination" (p. 112). In my experience, it is also essential that decisions made about complaints challenging our academic freedom and/or freedom of speech are made and communicated clearly and quickly. While I am grateful that the administrators in my college *eventually* supported my freedom of speech rights, once again, the conversations I had with administrators and some faculty about my colleagues' reactions illustrated how insisting on the truth of my racialized experience meant that I had to face a variety of delegitimizing discourses. In the next section, I examine the range of institutional and individual responses to the two blog posts about interactions with White colleagues.

INDIVIDUAL AND INSTITUTIONAL RESPONSES

First, interactions that Adriana and I intentionally described as being imbricated within racialized structures and hierarchies of institutional power were often reduced by administrators and some faculty to problems of personality:

> Both of you have strong opinions and personalities and we want you both to be yourselves.

As Hayes (2015) notes, the stories told by faculty of color about their experiences at H/PWIs "tend not only to reflect one's realities but [also] help elicit the racialized perspectives that structure, detail, and chronicle the experiences of people of color" (p. 69). I tried to bring attention in these conversations back to the realities of structural power and privilege and to challenge the idea that our White colleagues have a different and equally valid perspective on the situation. Not foregrounding these structural realities meant that the narrative that our White colleagues were the "victims" was validated. DiAngelo and Sensoy (2014) write that Whites frequently position themselves as being "victimized, slammed, blamed, having their words 'strategically pulled apart' and their 'precious time wasted,' misunderstood, silenced, and repressed" (p. 125). We heard some of the same framing and even exact phrases from our White colleagues. As DiAngelo and Sensoy (2014) further explain, "[t]hese self-defense claims work to position the speakers as both vulnerable and superior, while obscuring the true power of their racial locations" (p. 125). In discussions about our colleagues' complaints, there was never a focus on *our* (read: Adriana and my) experiences that we chronicled in the blog, which only reinforced my conviction that the blog was a necessary space to center our perspectives as womxn of color.

Second, there were attempts made by White colleagues to reframe encounters we described in the blog posts. I was asked, for example: were these not the very same senior colleagues who were kind and helpful in ensuring that I earned tenure at the institution? These attempts were patronizing at best and bullying at worst. This discursive framing invokes the kind of treatment that many faculty of color and Native faculty endure at universities, often from seemingly liberal colleagues who recruited them. As Harris and González (2012) report, many womxn of color faculty talk about how their White colleagues boasted "about how much they had done to help the women succeed, taking credit for their accomplishments, and/or publicly expressing worries about whether they could satisfy the university's promotion and tenure requirements" (p. 12). For us, our position as tenured faculty protected and allowed us to speak and write freely about racism we encountered pre- and post-tenure. For some of our White colleagues, the fact that we were tenured meant that we should be grateful and not critique them or the institution.

Viewing my/our tenured status as an indication that the institutional processes of tenure and promotion are fair glosses over the negative experiences and the emotional and psychological anguish one experiences while going through such processes as faculty of color and Native faculty at H/PWIs, regardless of the final outcome. Often, this history of negative experiences can be ignored or silenced because it can be difficult for junior faculty who leave the institution to speak up about their experiences. Many faculty sign non-disclosure agreements when they are denied tenure as part of a severance package. Even when junior faculty leave on their own accord, they are often beholden to senior faculty in their departments for recommendation letters, even if these very same senior faculty members are the reason they are leaving. Additionally, the idea that by offering unsolicited advice, senior White colleagues were only trying to "help" faculty of color navigate the treacherous waters of the tenure system implies that we need to be "saved" from ourselves and our decisions about how to navigate academia as womxn of color. As Alexander (2005) forthrightly explains, by refusing this discursive framing, "by calling for accountability, by presuming belonging, and by insisting on the right to truth and to knowledge derived from one's social historical location," I set myself up for being viewed as "ungrateful" (p. 176).

Third, in addition to dismissing our interpretations of our experiences, the silence of our senior White colleagues and the anonymity of the majority of complaints against us have been disheartening. As many scholars of color have noted in multiple ways, being a faculty member of color at a H/PWI institution often leads to a kind of racial paranoia, where you are habitually left wondering about the meaning and consequence of every interaction you have with White colleagues and students (Ahmed, 2012; Fasching-Varner, Albert, Mitchell, & Allen, 2015; Ford, 2011; Gutiérrez y Muhs, Niemann, González, & Harris, 2012; Hartlep, 2015; Sue, Bucceri, Lin, Nadal, & Torino, 2007).

The fact that most colleagues chose to complain to the administration rather than speak with me or Adriana directly has only increased that racial paranoia. Few senior colleagues have spoken up publicly in support of us, though some have expressed their solidarity with us privately. This lack of public support, and "the implicit consent conveyed through White silence, and the absence of social censure" (DiAngelo & Sensoy, 2014, p. 114) for the complaining White faculty members only reinforced the White racial frame (Feagin, 2010) that defines the contours of my position as a faculty of color at a H/PWI (Arnold, Crawford, & Khalifa, 2016).

Finally, there were the complaints that we were "airing dirty, confidential laundry" by discussing closed-door meetings and conversations. Faculty expressed concern that we were creating a "chilly climate" because of our public discussions of "private" interactions—of course, the phrase "chilly climate" has specifically been used in educational scholarship to describe how universities are often "isolating for [womxn of color] faculty [and how the] lack of institutional support subsequently affects hiring, retention, mentoring relationships, promotion, and tenure" (Ford, 2011, p. 445). Given that Carleton is generally a politically liberal space, a place where I have not encountered faculty members using explicitly racist or derogatory terms, the racist discourse is subtler and more likely to occur in such meetings. It is in closed-door meetings, for example, where I have heard White colleagues express skepticism that a professor of color with tenure had the qualifications to earn tenure or express concern that a candidate of color might not get tenure and the negative effects that denial might have on other untenured faculty of color (see Jennings, 2016).

Adriana and I decided that our right to speak honestly and openly about our experiences was more important than preserving a sense of comfort for our colleagues. In speaking about our racialized experiences and the "daily stresses caused by constant 'on guard' duty, cultural code switching, [and] exercising 'thick skin' when insulted or experiencing microaggressions," we are, in fact, asking our White colleagues to be *more* on guard about their own behaviors and words (Giles, 2015, p. 170). We hope that they think twice before they "play devil's advocate." We want to shift the balance of who does this kind of "on guard" labor, even if this demand is seen as infringing on our White colleagues' freedom to "be themselves." Being themselves as White people in a White environment often means reifying the Whiteness of the space, and in that sense, we are asking them *not* to be themselves.

The following letter written by a Black administrator expressing frustration about and to her White colleagues after attempting to disrupt Whiteness at an elementary school through professional development aptly describes our demand of our White colleagues:

> Social justice education requires us to interrupt our patterns—of teaching, of communicating, of relating to one another. We cannot do the things the same way we have in past attempts ...This is not just about you. I know you've lived your entire lives socialized to believe everything is about you; hence your continued state of fragility since these efforts began. ... The work to change patterns of thinking ... cannot be completed until you are ready to fully examine your whiteness and why it keeps you angry, fearful, and resistant. I can't do your work for you. It's your responsibility.
>
> (Patton & Jordan, 2017, p. 88)

Adriana and I wrote (and continue to write) our blog in the spirit of this Black administrator's letter, by positing that we cannot continue to operate within current frameworks and processes if we are to move toward justice-oriented institutions that minimize the RBF experienced by faculty of color and Native faculty. In that same spirit, I will now delineate recommendations for more racially just institutional practices as well as ideas for faculty of color and Native faculty on how to combat RBF in the meantime.

ACTIONABLE STRATEGIES

1. Have honest and open conversations with administrators and others who have decision-making powers in the institution (e.g., Deans, Provost, President, Board of Trustees) about whether "diversity" to the institution means representational diversity that does not challenge the institution's core principles, or whether the institution is truly committed to rethinking core institutional policies and practices. Ahmed (2012) argues that "diversity" becomes the preferred institutional term because "it does not have a necessary relation to changing organizational values" (p. 65). If institutions

want to move beyond viewing a faculty of color and Native faculty as mere "additions" to already existing structures and processes and want instead to commit to addressing "the historical legacies of institutional, epistemological, and societal racisms that pervade colleges and universities," then they need to commit to "wholesale changes in their underlying structures and day-to-day activities" (Brayboy, 2003, p. 73).

Note: The rest of the recommendations on this list will only make sense if institutions are committed to making substantial changes.

2. Institutions should hire ombudspeople trained in mediation and conflict resolution, who understand how identity, power, and privilege impact interpersonal conflict, and who are independent from the hierarchies of institutional power. These same people should conduct exit interviews with faculty and ask explicitly about their negative racialized or gendered experiences at the institution. It is important to have a more accurate accounting of such identity-based experiences so that individual faculty experiences are understood within that context. Otherwise, institutions will stay stuck thinking in terms of "individual rehabilitation and individual remuneration" that only reinforces "mythologies of race" and colorblind meritocracy (Alexander, 2005, p. 140).

3. Institutions need to acknowledge that processes developed at a time when there were far fewer faculty of color at their institutions might not be as "fair" and "objective" as they are purported to be. Do tenure and promotion processes, for example, account for the different experiences that faculty of color and Native faculty have on their campuses in terms of student evaluations, collegiality, and research trajectories? Notions of "collegiality" are often imbued with raced, classed, and gendered expectations and are among the hidden aspects of tenure and promotion processes, particularly at smaller institutions (Flores Niemann, 2012). Therefore, framing conflicts between faculty of color, Native faculty, and White faculty merely as "interpersonal" conflicts that could be resolved if everyone merely acted more "collegially" does not take into consideration the realities of differences in social and political power within and outside institutions that are tied to racial identity. As Harris and González (2012) posit, "It is important … to read even the most seemingly personal stories … as symptomatic of a larger, structural problem, rather than solely the issues of any one woman or department, college, or campus" (p. 7).

4. At the same time, institutions should work to ensure that these processes *are* fair, equitable, objective, and transparent. At private colleges, many aspects of review processes are hidden from the candidates undergoing review. For example, at Carleton, junior faculty cannot access their colleagues' evaluative letters that substantially influence third-year and tenure review decisions. Being clear and transparent about evaluation criteria should also

ensure that no one is left feeling at the end that the outcome was based on someone "lobbying" for a particular outcome. Tenure and promotion decisions should not depend on "benevolence" on the part of senior faculty members and it should be abundantly clear to everyone that a person was granted tenure or promotion because they met clear and specific criteria.

5. Administrators need to educate themselves on RBF and feminist, decolonial, Indigenous, anti-racist analyses of "diversity efforts." They should recognize the labor that faculty of color and Native faculty often have to engage in to have their voices heard and to write about their experiences, knowing that their experiences might be dismissed or misheard. There are good reasons why many womxn of color faculty and Native womxn faculty, for example, choose not to disclose their experiences, including their fear that "they would be penalized for airing their home institution's dirty laundry in public, and they were not prepared to become pariahs" (Harris & González, 2012, p. 11). If academic institutions truly value freedom of speech and academic freedom, they need to ensure that faculty are not penalized for speaking up about their experiences of racism, sexism, homophobia, and other identity-based discrimination.

RECOMMENDATIONS FOR FACULTY OF COLOR AND NATIVE FACULTY AT HISTORICALLY AND PREDOMINANTLY WHITE INSTITUTIONS

1. Develop a network of people who understand fully that academia is a racialized, gendered, and classed space. For me, this network has included other womxn of color faculty in a variety of institutions who validate my experiences and help me understand that my experiences are not unique. They have helped me understand that the kinds of interactions I have had at my institution are not about one person or one institution but instead about the larger structural and systemic issues in academia.

2. Speak up in all the ways you see as possible given your particular circumstances. Personally, I chose to be more circumspect about my experiences before tenure and more open and honest about my experiences, including those pre-tenure, once I got tenure. It is important for those of us with the protection and security of tenure to speak about the experiences we had when we were in more precarious positions. Additionally, those of us who are racially, culturally, or ethnically privileged need to take greater risks in speaking up about racialized injustices in academia. As a class-privileged, tenured, South Asian American faculty member, I wanted to use my privilege to speak up about troubling racialized moments in my experiences, knowing that many others are not in a position to do so without risking their jobs or careers. As a South Asian American woman, I can be used as an

cxample that institutional processes "worked," a discourse that then can be used to dismiss the racialized experiences of my Black, Latinx, and Native womxn colleagues.

3. Trust yourself and your experiential knowledge and wisdom.

4. Read accounts of other faculty of color and become familiar with feminist, anti-racist, decolonial, Indigenous analyses of academia. Becoming familiar with frameworks such as CRT and RBF has helped me understand my situation in ways that does not make it about me or my shortcomings.

5. If possible, don't do it alone! Writing the blog with another tenured faculty member has made me braver than I probably would have been on my own. I'd like to thank Adriana Estill, my co-writer, co-conspirator, and my sister-friend, for being an inspiration and source of support and for always listening and supporting me. I have also participated in collective responses that have challenged mainstream ways of addressing issues of racism in academia (WOC Faculty, 2018). As bell hooks tells us,

When we dare to speak in a liberatory voice, we threaten even those who may initially claim to want our words. In the act of overcoming our fear of speech, of being seen as threatening, we engage in the process of learning to undo domination. When we end our silence, when we speak in a liberated voice, our words connect us with anyone, anywhere who lives in silence.

(as quoted in Alexander, 2005, p. 137)

In her powerful essay about choosing to speak up despite severe and harrowing consequences, Lowe (2018) concludes, "For years I thought that academia's illusion of comfort was worth swallowing my anger and compromising my integrity. I'm grateful to have gotten free of that lie before it rotted me from the inside out" (para. 24). Despite the stress of having to face the negative consequences of speaking my truth out loud in a public forum, I am glad that I did. I know that my "silence will not protect me" (Lorde, 1978) and, more importantly, I know that my silence would only have perpetuated the silencing of perspectives from those of us who are bringing our different bodies, ideas, and experiences to the White supremacy of academia.

NOTES

1 Author's note: I would like to thank Adriana Estill and Christopher Geissler for providing feedback on earlier drafts of this chapter.

2 I've chosen to include both terms to describe Carleton College, reflecting both its history as a place that enrolled mostly White students and employed mostly White faculty, as well as its contemporary reality of having a majority White student body and faculty and a predominantly Eurocentric curriculum (see Brunsma, Brown, & Placier, 2013).

3 The blog site can be accessed at this address: https://downwithbrownblog.com/.

REFERENCES

Ahmed, S. (2012). *On being included: Racism and diversity in institutional life.* Durham, NC: Duke University Press.

Alexander, M. J. (2005). *Pedagogies of crossing: Meditations on feminism, sexual politics, memory, and the sacred.* Durham, NC: Duke University Press.

Arnold, N. W., Crawford, E. R., & Khalifa, M. (2016). Psychological heuristics and faculty of color: Racial battle fatigue and tenure/promotion. *The Journal of Higher Education, 87*(6), 890–919.

Brayboy, B. M. J. (2003). The implementation of diversity in predominantly White colleges and universities. *Journal of Black Studies, 34*(1), 72–86.

Brunsma, D. L., Brown, E. S., & Placier, P. (2013). Teaching race at historically White colleges and universities: Identifying and dismantling the walls of Whiteness. *Critical Sociology, 39*(5), 717–738.

Chen, C. W., & Gorski, P. (2015). Burnout in social justice and human rights activists: Symptoms, causes and implications. *Journal of Human Rights Practice, 7*(3), 366–390.

Chikkatur, A., & Estill, A. (2016a). Coddled or resilient. Retrieved from https://downwithbrownblog.com/2016/06/02/coddled-or-resilient/

Chikkatur, A., & Estill, A. (2016b). We speak of (our) glorious brownness. Retrieved from https://downwithbrownblog.com/2016/06/30/we-speak-of-our-glorious-brownness/

Chikkatur, A., & Estill, A. (2017). Feminist formations, Part III: Our friendship meets the Bechdel Test ALL THE TIME. Retrieved from https://downwithbrownblog.com/2017/04/28/feminist-formations-part-iii-our-friendship-meets-the-bechdel-test-all-the-time/

Cross, W. E. (1971). The Negro to Black conversion experience: Towards a psychology of Black liberation. *Black World, 20*(9), 13–27.

DiAngelo, R., & Sensoy, Ö. (2014). Getting slammed: White depictions of race discussions as arenas of violence. *Race Ethnicity and Education, 17*(1), 103–128.

Estill, A., & Chikkatur, A. (2016a). It's not about cookies: The politics of allyship. Retrieved from https://downwithbrownblog.com/2016/05/19/its-not-about-cookies-the-politics-of-allyship/

Estill, A., & Chikkatur, A. (2016b). The one in which we talk about defaced posters. Retrieved from https://downwithbrownblog.com/2016/05/05/first-blog-post/

Fasching-Varner, K., Albert, K., Mitchell, R., & Allen, C. (Eds.). (2015). *Racial battle fatigue in higher education: Exposing the myth of post-racial America.* Lanham, MD: Rowman & Littlefield.

Feagin, J. R. (2010). *The White racial frame: Centuries of racial framing and counter-framing.* New York: Routledge.

Flores Niemann, Y. (2012). Lessons from the experiences of women of color working in academia. In G. Gutiérrez y Muhs, Y. Flores Niemann, C. G. González, & A. P. Harris (Eds.), *Presumed incompetent: The intersections of race and class for women in academia* (pp. 446–499). Boulder, CO: University Press of Colorado.

Ford, K. A. (2011). Race, gender, and bodily (mis) recognitions: Women of color faculty experiences with White students in the college classroom. *The Journal of Higher Education, 82*(4), 444–478.

Giles, M. S. (2015). Behind enemy lines: Critical race theory, racial battle fatigue, and higher education. In K. Fasching-Varner, K. A. Albert, R. W. Mitchell, & C. A. Allen (Eds.), *Racial battle fatigue in higher education: Exposing the myth of post-racial America* (pp. 169–177). Lanham, MD: Rowman & Littlefield.

Gutiérrez y Muhs, G., Flores Niemann, Y., González, C. G., & Harris, A. P. (Eds.). (2012). *Presumed incompetent: The intersections of race and class for women in academia.* Boulder, CO: University Press of Colorado.

Harris, A. P., & González, C. G. (2012). Introduction. In G. Gutiérrez y Muhs, Y. Flores Niemann, C. G. González, & A. P. Harris (Eds.), *Presumed incompetent: The intersections of race and class for women in academia* (pp. 1–14). Boulder, CO: University Press of Colorado.

Hartlep, N. D. (2015). An adopted Korean speaks out about his racialized experiences as a faculty member at a predominantly White institution. In K. Varner, K. Albert, R. Mitchell, & C. Allen (Eds.), *Racial battle fatigue: Exposing the myth of post-racial America* (pp. 115–122). Lanham, MD: Rowman & Littlefield.

Hayes, C. (2015). Assault in the academy: When it becomes more than racial battle fatigue. In K. Fasching-Varner, K. A. Albert, R. W. Mitchell, & C. A. Allen (Eds.), *Racial battle fatigue in higher education: Exposing the myth of post-racial America* (pp. 69–76). Lanham, MD: Rowman & Littlefield.

Hurlburt, S., & McGarrah, M. (2016). *The shifting academic workforce: Where are the contingent faculty?* Washington, DC: American Institutes for Research. Retrieved from https://www.deltacostproject.org/sites/default/files/products/Shifting-Academic-Workforce-November-2016_0.pdf

Jennings, M. E. (2016). The spook who sat by the door: The challenge of unhooking from Whiteness in the African American faculty experience. In N. Hartlep & C. Hayes (Eds.), *Unhooking from Whiteness: Resisting the espirit de corps* (pp. 1–12). Rotterdam, The Netherlands: Sense Publishers.

Locher, H., & Ropers-Huilman, R. (2015). Wearing you down: The influence of racial battle fatigue on academic freedom for faculty of color. In K. Fasching-Varner, K. A. Albert, R. W. Mitchell, & C. A. Allen (Eds.), *Racial battle fatigue in higher education: Exposing the myth of post-racial America* (pp. 103–114). Lanham, MD: Rowman & Littlefield.

Lorde, A. (1978). *The Black unicorn: Poems* (1st edition. ed.). New York: Norton.

Lorde, A. (2007). *Sister outsider: Essays and speeches by Audre Lorde.* Berkeley, CA: Crossing Press.

Lowe, N. (2018). I fought academia's cult of civility and all I got was this lousy PTSD diagnosis. *Medium*. Retrieved from https://medium.com/@yourstrulynaima/aca demias-cult-of-civility-30007869d4d4

Patton, L. D., & Jordan, J. L. (2017). It's not about you, it's about us: A Black woman administrator's efforts to disrupt White fragility in an urban school. *Journal of Cases in Educational Leadership*, *20*(1), 80–91.

Smith, W. A., Yosso, T. J., & Solórzano, D. G. (2006). Challenging racial battle fatigue on historically White campuses: A critical race examination of race-related stress. In C. A. Stanley (Ed.), *Faculty of color: Teaching in predominantly White colleges and universities* (pp. 299–327). Boston, MA: Jossey-Bass.

Smooth, J. (2008). How to tell someone they sound racist. YouTube. Retrieved from https://www.youtube.com/watch?v=b0Ti-gkJiXc

Solórzano, D. G., & Yosso, T. J. (2001). Critical race and LatCrit theory and method: Counter-storytelling. *International Journal of Qualitative Studies in Education*, *14*(4), 471–495.

Sue, D. W., Bucceri, J., Lin, A. I., Nadal, K. L., & Torino, G. C. (2007). Racial microaggressions and the Asian American experience. *Cultural Diversity and Ethnic Minority Psychology*, *13*(1), 72–81. Retrieved from http://www.oregoncampusco mpact.org/uploads/1/3/0/4/13042698/racial_microaggressions_and_aa_expe rience.pdf

Tatum, B. D. (2003). *"Why are all the Black kids sitting together in the cafeteria?" and other conversations about race*. New York: Basic Books.

Tatum, B. D. (2004). Talking about race, learning about racism: The application of racial identity development theory in the classroom. In S. L. Anderson, P. F. Attwood, & L. C. Howard (Eds.), *Facing racism in education* (pp. 199–226). Cambridge, MA: Harvard Education Press.

WOC Faculty. (2018). A collective response to racism in academia. *Medium*. Retrieved from https://medium.com/@wocfaculty/a-collective-response-to-racism-in -academia-35dc725415c1?fbclid=IwAR1RK4ySz5FMGdjmldK8roORg4kN yrw6bEjYbG1MwHine-Cm4V6cPXNWxXI

Chapter 7

Ignored, Pacified, and Deflected

Racial Battle Fatigue for an Asian American Non-Tenure Track Professor

Takumi C. Sato

INTRODUCTION

The following critical autoethnography of my experiences as an Asian American, cisgender male faculty member at a Predominantly White Institution (PWI). I used AsianCrit as it draws from critical race theory (CRT) to center the experiences of Asians and Asian Americans with race and racism. AsianCrit validates my experiences with race and racism that permeate work responsibilities and interactions at a PWI. I understand that I am "afforded" some privileges as a member of the so-called "model minority" (Hartlep & Porfilio, 2015) and viewed as "problem-free" (Suzuki, 2002). Yet, AsianCrit scholars have argued that Asian Americans in higher education have been maligned due to stereotypes as achievers (Teranishi, Behringer, Grey, & Parker 2009). CRT posits that the model minority myth is used to situate Asians in the larger system of oppression (Delgado & Stefancic, 2017). The model minority myth is a tool used by the dominant group by which to maintain oppression and deny the existence of racism (Museus & Kiang, 2009). The false argument is made that racism cannot exist alongside Asians' myriad of successes in U.S. society. In fact, Asians and Asian Americans are systematically denied entry into the highest levels of the social hierarchy, particularly in leadership positions (Suzuki, 2002). My scholarly work verifies that Asian faculty must constantly combat oppressive forces in the quest for equitable outcomes for intersectional people of color (IPOC) (Delgado & Stefancic, 2017).

CRT scholars have extensively documented the challenges of doing scholarly work that exposes racism and confronts the systems of oppression within academia. Scholarship that is not considered mainstream in the field is questioned by tenure and promotion committees (Bernal & Villalpando, 2002). Manuscripts are often rejected by the top journals, and when published in journals more receptive to anti-oppressive scholarship, the legitimacy of such manuscripts are questioned (Stanley, 2007). Faculty of color (FOC) are overwhelmed with service requests when diversity is sought and often find that they have to stand up for themselves on racial equity issues (Stanley, 2007). FOC are disproportionately hired into contingent positions rather than tenure-track jobs (Bernal & Villalpando, 2002; Finkelstein, Martin, Conley, & Schuster, 2016; Rideau, 2018) and rarely hired into leadership positions in higher education (Suzuki, 2002).

Given all the ways in which FOC are taxed in their jobs, the cumulative effect of these stressors results in Racial Battle Fatigue (RBF), which according to Smith, Yosso, and Solórzano (2006) consists of constant microaggressions that inflict psychological, physiological, and emotional trauma. In sharing my experiences, I describe how situating myself as an Asian Critical Race (AsianCrit) Scholar who works at a PWI results in the constant struggle of having to seek legitimacy for my work and my existence before peers, students, and institutional leaders. The total impact of enduring constant racially laced salvos is beyond stressful and exhausting.

CRITICAL AUTOETHNOGRAPHY

Critical autoethnography is particularly useful to discuss the ways that RBF has impacted me professionally and personally. Traditionally, the voices of marginalized people have been excluded from academic work. Critical ethnography provides a tool through which voices can be heard that challenge the status quo, in particular, Western ethnocentrism (Trueba, 1993). Furthermore, critical ethnography is a means to develop agency as a member of a marginalized group (Calabrese-Barton, 2001). Delgado-Gaitin and Trueba (1985) argue that critical ethnography allows for the study of human interaction. Critical autoethnography enables me to contextualize the ways that interactions with individuals at the PWI have additively contributed to to my RBF. Finally, as an accepted approach to scholarship, critical autoethnography makes it harder to delegitimize and silence marginalized voices.

EXPERIENCES IN THE ACADEMY

In what follows, I provide examples of how the responsibilities and experiences as a racially minoritized faculty member at a PWI have real psychological, physiological, and emotional consequences. I illuminated the sources of RBF as a means to break down oppressive conditions so that we can lessen the impacts that disproportionately are experienced by FOC. To be clear, I have chosen to be vocal regarding racial equity issues at my institution rather than remain passive in self-preservation or fear of consequences. I use my scholarly expertise to professionally and firmly call attention to efforts that are limited or underinformed regarding racial equity.

I recounted several experiences in which I carried a racialized burden as a non-tenure-track faculty member within the School of Education (SOE). The SOE is comprised of 48 faculty members with 37 identified as White (Virginia Tech, 2017); I am one of two Asian faculty members in the SOE. Then, I was able to narrow my focus to two primary sources of RBF. Job expectations were the first source of RBF, which include responsibilities of faculty to engage in teaching, research, and service. In this chapter I focus on service and the committees for which I *volunteered* to serve in hopes of having a voice in the policymaking process regarding diversity and equity issues.

Interactions with superiors were the second source of RBF. My experiences with "leadership" directly and negatively impacted personal advancement as well as efforts to meet performance expectations. I intentionally placed quotation marks around leadership given that the actions I observed were not consistent with what I expect of leadership. I am highlighting the power differential invoked by "leadership" using their superior position to discredit and negate my experiences and efforts. In this chapter, I share experiences with two different Directors for the SOE, one White female and one White male. In addition, I recount my conversation with the Dean of the College, a White female.

Job Expectations

I first describe service experiences on two committees, one at the school level and one at the university level. Then, I will use AsianCrit to understand the outcomes of those experiences. The first committee was for the SOE and was assigned the task of identifying and addressing equity and inclusion across our unit. The second committee was under the auspices of the university governance structure and was charged with insuring the institution was working toward equal opportunity and diversity. The university level committee is referred to as a commission, therefore I will use the same term, *commission*, to distinguish from the school level committee. Neither entity was exclusively focused on race and racism but rather the broader spectrum of inclusion that impact marginalized populations.

The entire faculty within the SOE was *strongly encouraged to volunteer* to serve on one of four committees to examine priority areas as determined by the White male School Director. Despite my hesitation, I joined the committee tasked to evaluate and provide solutions on the issues of equity and inclusion pertaining to the student experience. In short, marginalized students had shared their stories with me and I was concerned that any outcomes of the committee would fall short of the needed systemic changes without critical perspectives, a viewpoint that I could offer.

The first meeting of the committee had an inauspicious start with the Director present to deliver our charge. He indicated that we should select a leader for the committee—but he qualified that—by suggesting it be someone with tenure so that the burden did not fall on junior faculty. In one statement, he disqualified two individuals on the committee—myself included—who do critical work to expose and examine inequity in education. Furthermore, he strongly urged us to gather data to inform the recommendations made by the committee in spite of both school and university level climate survey data that was readily available and consistent with the body of critical scholarship on how students are often marginalized in university settings. The Director had even indicated that this committee was in part a result of his meetings with students of color who had experienced marginalization within the school.

In a subsequent committee meeting, I made a case against data collection to avoid redundancy and instead use existing data and literature to develop a strategic plan to address inequity and exclusion in our school. Predictably, I was met with resistance. The committee elected to develop a survey that occupied much of the remaining time and effort. In late spring, the survey was issued electronically and had a low response rate. We had one final committee meeting with those able/willing to attend and reviewed survey data we had collected. We determined that we needed to disaggregate the data in order for it to be useful. The committee members who were present at this last meeting did not want to make any decisions without a majority present. That would become our final meeting, as faculty were largely unavailable in the summer. During the following year, the Director did not indicate that the committees would reconvene to continue the work.

The university level appointment was voluntary through a self-nomination and application process for which I served as an at-large faculty representative for a term of three years. The commission consisted of representatives for diverse faculty, staff, and student groups with vested interests in "equal opportunity, affirmative action, accessibility, compliance, diversity, and inclusion." The commission had the capacity to introduce policy and procedure resolutions into the university governance structure for consideration. During my three-year term, I developed two primary concerns regarding the operations of the commission.

First, the various issues brought forth from each interest group represented structural issues pertaining to one group rather than seeking to effectively address the systemic imbalance of power between the dominant and marginalized groups. For example, gender-inclusive bathrooms were a topic under consideration to meet the needs of transgender members of the university community rather than policies or procedures that address power of the heteronormative majority. I am not dismissive of such efforts or the interests of each group, as structural changes can positively influence climate for marginalized individuals. But failure to address the systemic issues leads to slow and only incremental changes toward equity and social justice.

My second concern arose in noticing that race and racism was seemingly secondary to the concerns brought to the commission by the various groups or did not get the same reciprocity of support. In one case, a leader of the Indigenous student organization penned a letter to the commission and spoke before the group to request a resolution asking the university to change Columbus Day to Indigenous Peoples' Day. A White commission member was quick to point out that this was a state-level issue. She argued that such a change at the institution could inadvertently create payroll issues for university employees given that Columbus Day is an official state holiday. Unfortunately, the student group's concern was sacked instantaneously and remaining commission members were reluctant to advocate for moving forward with supportive action.

I wrote a letter outlining my concerns and submitted it to the chairperson for further consideration within the commission. In response, the chairperson informed me that my letter would be shared with the commission but that there would be no time available on the agenda to engage a discussion around my concerns. My three-year term ended and to my knowledge, nothing further has come from my concerns.[1]

Interacting with Leadership

I have faced personal battles with school "leadership" that are arguably tied to my racial identity—Asian American—even if not explicitly named. For example, a former White female School Director issued a charge to faculty to increase grant activity in a school-wide meeting. Prior to the Director's arrival, I had received a major grant award for over $1 million as co-Principal Investigator. I informed the internal grant office and the Director of my intent to apply for a new grant and provided my Letter of Intent (LOI). But, the newly installed Director actively tried to disqualify me from applying because I am not a tenure-track faculty member. I made a second request for support from the Director after the request with LOI went unanswered. Finally, I received a response back from her stating the following:

> I have looked over the LOI you gave me, plus the RFP. I am wondering if you have talked with anyone at William T. Grant about your eligibility. Specifically, the requirements indicate that you must be in a career-ladder position—which they further describe as meaning a tenure-track position, if you're in the university world. If you have something from them indicating that they would consider you eligible, please forward it to me to attach to your LOI. But my interpretation of the requirements—and their description of the selection criteria on pp. 12–14 of the RFP, relative to supporting individuals in research positions—would be that you do not qualify.[2]

The Director, a White woman, had applied her own interpretation to the rules to suggest that applicants must be tenure-track. I reviewed the entire Application Guide prior to requesting the Director's support and again after receiving the response above. The words "tenure" or "career-ladder" do not appear within the document. In the eligibility statement, the document stated, "Institutions usually have their own eligibility criteria regarding who can act as Principal Investigator (PI) on a grant" (William T. Grant, 2014, p. 12). The foundation encourages broad participation indicating that graduate students may serve as Co-Principal Investigator and the foundation values projects "led by members of groups under-represented in academia" (William T. Grant, 2014, p. 9). The Director inexplicably sought to exclude me from pursuing the grant, which was inconsistent with the Foundation's openness to the rank of lead investigators and desire for a diverse pool of applicants. The Director was ultimately relieved of her duties in the wake of what became a tumultuous and contentious relationship with the faculty.

An internal replacement, a White man, was named Director and he initially made efforts to connect with each faculty in one-to-one meetings. In my meeting, I indicated that I would like to be considered for a promotion in the coming year in accordance with guidelines for clinical faculty. I was told he would look into the process given that he was unfamiliar with guidelines for non-tenure-track promotions. I also followed up via email to the Director and his administrative assistant reiterating my request to be considered for a promotion. I did not receive acknowledgment or approval and the academic year moved on with no further communication. I made another inquiry, to which I was told that the Promotion and Tenure Committee would need to meet and update the promotion guidelines for clinical faculty. In addition, my request for a multiyear contract renewal was denied in favor of a one-year contract despite the fact I was completing a five-year appointment.

One year after my first request to be considered for promotion, I was given a highly condensed timeline of one week's notice to declare my intent and one month to have my dossier submitted. Despite these abbreviated timelines, I was able to submit my materials to the Director and Promotion and Tenure Committee. Eventually, I learned that my bid for promotion was stopped by the Director himself without advancing to the college level due to student evaluation scores of my teaching. My average over 5 years and 28 sections of teaching was 5.0/6.0, which was 0.20 below the school's average. In the Clinical Faculty Promotion guidelines, given the teaching-intensive responsibility, faculty are expected to be above the school's average. To explain my score, I had purposefully written about the ways in which FOC that teach courses on diversity often receive lower scores (see Dixson & Dingus, 2007). But my concern was dismissed as the Director suggested it was the other courses I taught that were the issue, not the "diversity" course for pre-service teachers that I developed at the request of the school and taught every spring semester.

METHODS

After compiling a list of various marginalizing incidents, I purposefully selected events that were personally directed as well as those that took place with my service efforts in the campus community that still came to bear upon me as a person of color. I wrote a narrative for each incident and cross-referenced details through emails, documents, and other artifacts that serve as record of my experiences. I reviewed documents including letters I wrote to the university commission and the LOI to apply for grant funding to verify my activity. I reread additional documents including grant proposal guidelines and promotion guidelines for clinical faculty to verify rules and processes pertaining to these areas. Identifying and reviewing documentation was important to increase credibility to my narratives. I am not claiming objectivity, but rather, I verified my lived experiences seen through my eyes by thoroughly reviewing the details and records of the incidents.

ANALYSIS

In my critical analysis, I identified the ways I had been impacted by the microaggressions contained in each incident though some arguably are not always small provocations. It is the cumulative impact of the microaggressions that contributes to RBF (Smith et al., 2006). Therefore, I elected to consider the totality of these microaggressions as I experienced them rather than try to name the ways each incident added to my psychological, emotional, or physiological stress.

I used an AsianCrit lens to identify the mechanisms underlying the microaggressions to make sense of how White supremacy is maintained. I started with the responses from those I engaged with directly through concerns or inquiries. In particular, did the respondents fully engage with the racial issue at hand? And, what were the outcomes based on the responses? Then, I looked across all incidents to uncover patterns, if any, in the responses. In the next section, I report on the patterns, which I refer to as tactics or mechanisms, that caused RBF and preserved the advantages of the dominant group.

RESULTS

I was able to identify patterns in the responses and actions by individuals with whom I interacted across my experiences. The three tactics or mechanisms that emerged included efforts that: (1) ignored, (2) pacified, and/or (3) deflected my work efforts, concerns, and ideas, and as a result, caused me RBF. To be ignored is, as it sounds, the act of simply dismissing my very existence by not engaging or responding. Being pacified entails engagement but only as a means of appeasement, rather than actual efforts toward meaningful responses or action. And to be deflected is when the respondent shifts the focus to ancillary reasons as justification for decisions in order to negate possible accusations of racism. In my experiences, the individuals with whom I interacted deployed at least one of these tactics to avoid engaging with me around issues of race or racism or to actively marginalize me. These tactics are consistent with colorblind racism that is entrenched in society (Bonilla-Silva, 2006).

Being Ignored

The ability to consciously choose not to engage with and/or ignore an individual is a function of power and privilege. There is choice in having a non-response without consequences, which is generally reserved for those that enjoy positions of dominance. By ignoring, there is no further discussion to be had. The superior is blatantly indicating that the individual or concern is a not a priority. And with no discussion or engagement, there is no need to act. When FOC are ignored, the system continues to exist in the current, oppressive form.

When I formally requested consideration for promotion, the Director ignored our face-to-face conversation and follow up email by never acknowledging or honoring my request. While ignoring a request for promotion is not a racialized issue, the fact that as an FOC my request went unanswered for an extended period of time added to the RBF I experienced. My goal to be promoted and any potential salary increase was delayed for two years because it was ignored and then abruptly stopped when I was allowed to submit my dossier.

Being Pacified

Pacification, by definition, is to appease. For those with power and privilege, racism is often a touchy and difficult topic leading to reluctance to engage in dialogue. Hence, token efforts are made by those with power to create the illusion of shared concern and effort toward equity to quell further unrest and escape uncomfortable conversations. Pacification is a charade of offering support but does not require action. In my experiences, those in power, specifically the Chair of the University commission and White male Director moved with the intentionality of demonstrating effort or concern until the issue faded away over time.

My letter of concern regarding the approaches of the University commission to systemic oppression was shared by the Chair but not discussed at a meeting. My ideas were disseminated via email to the entire commission, but in not allowing for discussion, there was never intent to meaningfully engage in how the commission conducted its work. Combined with the end of my term, pacifying my concerns proved effective as I would no longer have a seat from which to push on the ways the commission addressed systemic problems.

Within the School of Education, the formation of an equity and inclusion committee was also exemplary of the pacification tactic. By forming the committee, the Director was able to publicly show that efforts were being made to address racism and other inequities across the school. Internally, the committee was never intended to deliver meaningful outcomes. The Director's push for gathering new data neutralized efforts from the outset. The committee was complicit in agreeing to develop a survey instrument rather than tackling the ways our school marginalizes students. Between the need to disaggregate the survey data, low response rate, lack of attendance by committee members, and arrival of summer, no action was taken. The Director made no further mention of reconvening the committee and continuing the work as a new academic year arrived.

Pacification does not seek to end racism or oppression. In fact, it is a tactic that upholds White supremacy because there never is intent to work toward equitable outcomes. The tactic relies on the fatigue of FOC like myself and the fact racism is never a primary concern of the majority. Keeping the committee members busy doing "busy" work, work that duplicated data that the PWI already had, serves to maintain the status quo. With the concerns of FOC pushed aside, equity issues are soon replaced by other issues that the predominantly White faculty deem important. For example, discussions of budget cuts and reduced faculty funds elicited a much more feverous response as the majority White faculty wanted to know *how does this affect me?*

Being Deflected

Deflection is often another tactic used in which the foci is shifted to an ancillary issue. I distinguish deflection from ignoring in that there is an engagement instead of outright refusal to acknowledge concerns or issues. That is, the ensuing dialogue becomes focused on something other than the core issue. The deflection tactic is also separate from being pacified. When deflected, the response is never about the concern but only about the ancillary issue.

In my request to submit for a grant program, the Director at the time made the issue about my qualifications as contingent faculty to apply for funding in accordance to grant program rules. Outwardly, it was not about being FOC. In reality, I was eligible to apply. As FOC, being disqualified from seeking a grant by the Director actively hindered my work productivity and ultimately my body of work by which I am evaluated for retention and advancement. It is conditions such as these that are sources of RBF for FOC and contributes to attrition rates from the academy (Thompson, 2008) and challenges with recruitment and retention (Turner, Myers Jr., & Creswell, 1999).

My initial appointment came with a five-year contract, which was set to expire. My request for a multiyear renewal with the White male Director was deflected as an issue at the Dean's level. The Director suggested that the Dean implemented a policy of only offering one-year contracts to contingent faculty. Yet, a newly appointed White contingent faculty member was offered a multiyear contract in the same year my contract was expiring. While not explicitly a racial issue, as FOC I was not afforded the same opportunity as a White faculty member to secure a multiyear contract. I asked to meet with the Dean who stated that she had not issued any limitations on multiyear contracts. This was a direct contradiction to the information from the Director. Then, she moved to defend the Director by suggesting that perhaps he was operating off of the previous Dean's guidelines. But the sitting Dean would have known and had to approve the multiyear offer given to the new faculty member by the Director. Rather than take up my concern as FOC, the Dean deflected my concern to old policy and worked to protect the Director, a fellow White administrator.

When I asked the Director for a reason why my bid for promotion was stopped, he quickly deflected from the point I made in my dossier that FOC teaching diversity courses is often met with resistance by White students. For me, this was a crucial point given that I work at a PWI and our student demographics in our teacher education programs are the same if not higher than national data that shows that 82% of K–12 teachers are White (U.S. Department of Education, 2016). As I tried to explain how student course evaluations from the diversity courses impacted my scores, he argued that the primary cause of my "lower" scores was the other courses I teach. I was not offered any other viable explanation as to why I could not be promoted besides the student evaluation scores. In essence, my five years of work at the PWI as a contingent FOC were negated by student evaluation scores with no other reason given to deny promotion. I had two peer evaluation letters that praised my teaching that were included in my dossier, but that could not overcome the student scores. Ironically, one of the letters was written by the Director himself, after a teaching observation, and in the meeting to explain why I was not being promoted, he stated that there was "no doubt" I could teach. The Director opted against lobbying in my favor instead choosing to stop my promotion bid despite the evidence available and firsthand account. As James Baldwin (1985) famously wrote, "I can't believe what you say, because I see what you do" (p. 594). Clearly, the Director was double speaking and this caused me great RBF.

DISCUSSION

The tactics named above—being ignored, being pacified, and being deflected— can often blur lines, but the end result is always the same: FOC experience RBF, and White supremacy is upheld. In the case of my letter written for the University commission, an argument can be made that I was ignored or the issue was deflected just as much as I was being pacified. The committee never discussed the concerns, which could be interpreted as being ignored. Likewise, the stock story was that there was a lack of room in the agenda to discuss my concerns, which would be an example of deflection. I settled on pacification as my concerns were distributed to appease me and the issue allowed to fade away.

López (2003) argues that there is a race neutral approach to politics in education that reifies racial oppression. That is, there is more context to every situation, but context is often intentionally omitted to deny that race was ever a factor. Arguably, all of the responses I described in this narrative intentionally neutralize race and racism by ignoring, pacifying, and deflecting it. In the administrators' responses, there is also an insidious effort to maintain good public relations over actually working toward equity and inclusion. The grand narratives that were told were not about the need to address issues within the PWI that perpetuate racism, but rather projecting an image that racism is a non-issue despite the evidence to the contrary. The PWI frequently cites the Principles of Community, an aspirational statement with no enforceability given it is not embedded in governance or policy. The document suggests that the campus espouses equity and inclusion when in fact it serves as a shield from consequential dialogue and transformative efforts toward change. Units across campus are charged with compliance, which leads to school level committees like the one I joined. The end result is the retention of hegemonic conditions and an unfair system of advantages for the dominant group at a PWI.

From my experiences, there is also a need to understand and *change* the rules and policies that are often engrained with either racial biases or structures that deny equal treatment or attention to issues of concern for IPOC. Harris (1995) explained this very clearly in describing *Whiteness as property* in that White is a form of property that comes with property rights and value through which privilege is embedded. Thusly, if institutional rules and policies were written by White people, then it must be understood that they were intentionally written in the interest of White people. To operate and be strategic in environments that are often outright hostile toward the interests and rights of IPOC, these rules and policies must be challenged and rewritten to be inclusive of all people. Throughout this chapter, Whiteness as property permeated the incidents described. The University commission worked within the institution's governance structures and any proposed policy change had to work through all of the other governing bodies before any possibility of adoption. A frequent question for any suggested policy change was whether the commission felt there was a chance to gain support from all the other governing bodies before drafting a resolution. This approach insured that the property rights of White people were prioritized and protected in that multiple governing bodies had to lend their support on policy that can positively impact IPOC and other marginalized groups. Rather, as in my letter, I wished for the commission to strategize how to work within the structures to gain support across the governing bodies for needed policy changes.

A troubling, but necessary point, was to name the ways in which IPOC become complicit in maintaining systemic oppression. The chairperson of the University level commission, a person of Asian descent, decided against a discussion on the issues brought to the group in my letter. While I cannot speak for the individual, their actions are consistent in fulfilling the "model minority" trope by willfully marginalizing voices of color and compounding RBF. Within the University commission, other than sharing my letter, I was silenced. My intent was to ask the commission to be more strategic in its efforts and increase awareness of the blind spots within the commission toward equity issues as we work collectively toward a truly inclusive campus community. Such denials are also a rejection of the lived experiences of IPOC in the community. In having one's experiences negated, the additional stress inflicted leads to increased fatigue.

ACTIONABLE STRATEGIES

Specific to the experiences described in this chapter, PWIs can take measures to reduce RBF for IPOC who are not on the tenure track. First, institutions must provide support and encouragement in all aspects faculty of work, especially when FOC go beyond expectations such as clinical faculty seeking grants. Second, Directors and faculty colleagues must understand FOC are often rated lower by students in course evaluations than White faculty and face even more challenges when teaching White students about White privilege and systemic oppression (Dixson & Dingus, 2007) when evaluating FOC's job performance. Third, PWIs need to hire IPOCs as Directors and across leadership roles as focus on the recruitment for diversity is most often on students and faculty. In my six years at the same PWI, I have worked under three Directors plus an additional three interim Directors and two Deans and one interim Dean that are all White. Fourth, the contributions and perspectives of FOC must be valued if PWIs and their diversity committees are truly committed to transformation of campus climate to include the well-being of IPOCs. For these recommendations to be realized, PWIs must be ready to confront White supremacy directly and follow through with sustained efforts toward systemic change.

In order to effect systemic change, efforts need to be strategic in understanding how the structures have been written into place that protect the interests of White people. The first step is a critical examination of rules and policies to uncover all the places White property is protected and the interests of IPOC omitted. Second, a comprehensive strategy needs to be developed that is proactive toward building a case for the desired changes. This includes identifying fundamental points that can be leveraged in discussion and deliberation, highlighting the benefits of the change and engaging the key constituents that can advance or end any efforts. IPOC must be the ones to author policies that seek to eliminate disparities in opportunity and strategically frame the potential outcomes. For example, diversity policies should leverage the benefits to all students, not just White students, when people of different backgrounds interact in classroom spaces and informal settings (Gurin, Dey, Hurtado, & Gurin 2002; Hurtado, 2007). In continuing to be strategic, IPOC must also anticipate the responses from those in power that will actively protect Whiteness as property through acts of pacifying, ignoring, and deflecting issues of racism, and be able to respond accordingly. That is, the strategy must not allow race to be neutralized or deeper context stripped from the lived experiences of IPOC. Engaging in racial politics in higher education is not an individual battle but requires the collective strength and voices of FOC to come together to work in solidarity. One individual wearing the burden of RBF is likely to get burned out and perceived as a nuisance by those in power and rendered a non-priority. Whereas, if multiple voices of concern are raised, it is no longer just one person's concern but a larger issue that requires a response. An inherent issue, especially at a PWI, is that FOC are underrepresented, making it more challenging to amplify their voices. The difficult nature of this work is exacerbated when IPOC are subservient to the system of White power and privilege and end up working against the needs of the marginalized.

CONCLUSION

In naming the tactics of ignoring, pacifying, and deflecting as sources of RBF in higher education, FOC must be strategic in anticipating such actions and proactive to counter these measures. Admittedly, I was on occasion inadequately prepared for the many tactics being used against me in interactions described here. In service on committees explicitly charged with addressing equity issues, I underestimated the ways systemic oppression permeated such spaces. An important point in analyzing the impact of RBF was the looming reminder of the "permanence of racism" (Bell, 1992). Through my experiences, an underlying and reoccurring theme was that those in power will continue to find ways to marginalize.

The purpose of detailing my experiences is not to be incendiary or compile a list of grievances. Rather, my hope is that laying bare the ways in which racism is a burden upon FOC can open meaningful dialogue toward equitable outcomes for those of us routinely exposed to psychological, physiological, and emotional distress. Furthermore, I am hopeful that new, effective strategies can be developed to challenge and dismantle the existing structures, including rules and policies, that historically have been written by White people for the benefit of White people.

NOTES

1 In the following year, the first commission meeting minutes indicated that a recent opinion article in a major news publication "led to a lively and informative discussion among CEOD members about our charge and how [the article] resonates with the work we each are doing" (CEOD, 2018). And the discussion led directly to revisiting and developing a resolution to recognize Indigenous Peoples' Day, which months later was successfully passed through governance (Korth, 2019).
2 Author's records.

REFERENCES

Baldwin, J. (1985). *The price of the ticket: Collected nonfiction, 1948–1985.* New York: St. Martin's Press.

Bell, D. (1992). *Faces at the bottom of the well: The permanence of racism.* New York: Basic Books.

Bernal, D. D., & Villalpando, O. (2002). An apartheid of knowledge in academia: The struggle over the "legitimate" knowledge of faculty of color. *Equity & Excellence in Education, 35*(2), 169–180.

Bonilla-Silva, E. (2006). *Racism without racists: Color-blind racism and the persistence of racial inequality in the United States.* Rowman & Littlefield Publishers.

Calabrese Barton, A. (2001). Science education in urban settings: Seeking new ways of praxis through critical ethnography. *Journal of Research in Science Teaching, 38*(8), 899–917.

Commission on Equal Opportunity and Diversity. (2018, September 17). *CEOD full committee meeting.* Virginia Tech. Retrieved from https://governance.vt.edu/assets/cms_ceod_09-17-2018.pdf

Delgado, R., & Stefancic, J. (2017). *Critical race theory an introduction,* (3rd ed.). New York: New York University Press.

Delgado-Gaitan, C., & Trueba, H. T. (1985). Ethnographic study of participant structures in task completion: Reinterpretation of "handicaps" in Mexican children. *Learning Disability Quarterly, 8*(1), 67–75.

Dixson, A. D., & Dingus, J. E. (2007). Tyranny of the majority: Re-enfranchisement of African- American teacher educators teaching for democracy. *International Journal of Qualitative Studies in Education, 20*(6), 639–654.

Finkelstein, M. J., Martin Conley, V., & Schuster, J. H. (2016). *Taking the measure of faculty diversity.* TIAA Institute Report. New York: Teachers Insurance and Annuity Association of America.

Gurin, P., Dey, E., Hurtado, S., & Gurin, G. (2002). Diversity and higher education: Theory and impact on educational outcomes. *Harvard Educational Review, 72*(3), 330–367.

Harris, C. (1995). Whiteness as property. In K. Crenshaw, N. Gotanda, G. Peller, & Thomas, K. (Eds.), (2000). *Critical race theory: The key writings that formed the movement* (pp. 276–291). New York: The New Press.

Hartlep, N. D., & Porfilio, B. J. (Eds.). (2015). *Killing the model minority stereotype: Asian American counterstories and complicity.* Charlotte, NC: Information Age.

Hurtado, S. (2007). Linking diversity with the educational and civic missions of higher education. *The Review of Higher Education, 30*(2), 185–196.

Korth, R. (2019, February 19). Virginia tech to recognize second Monday in October as Indigenous peoples' day. *The Roanoke Times.* Retrieved from https://www.roanoke.com

López, G. R. (2003). The (racially neutral) politics of education: A critical race theory perspective. *Educational Administration Quarterly, 39*(1), 68–94.

Museus, S. D., & Kiang, P. N. (2009). Deconstructing the model minority myth and how it contributes to the invisible minority reality in higher education research. *New Directions for Institutional Research, 2009*(142), 5–15.

Rideau, R. (2018). *A critical race analysis of the work experiences of non-tenure-track faculty members of color* (Doctoral dissertation, Virginia Tech).

Smith, W. A., Yosso, T. J., & Solórzano, D. G. (2006). Challenging racial battle fatigue on historically White campuses: A critical race examination of race-related stress. In C. A. Stanley (Ed.), *Faculty of color teaching in predominantly White colleges and universities* (pp. 299–327). Bolton, MA: Anker.

Stanley, C. (2007). When counter narratives meet master narratives in the journal editorial-review process. *Educational Researcher, 36*(1), 14–24.

Suzuki, B. H. (2002). Revisiting the model minority stereotype: Implications for student affairs practice and higher education. *New Directions for Student Services, 2002*(97), 21–32.

Teranishi, R. T., Behringer, L. B., Grey, E. A., & Parker, T. L. (2009). Critical race theory and research on Asian Americans and Pacific Islanders in higher education. *New Directions for Institutional Research, 142*, 57–68.

Thompson, C. Q. (2008). Recruitment, retention, and mentoring faculty of color: The chronicle continues. *New Directions for Higher Education, 2008*(143), 47–54.

Trueba, H. T. (1993). Race and ethnicity: The role of universities in healing multicultural America. *Educational Theory, 43*(1), 41–54.

Turner, C. S. V., Myers, S. L., Jr., & Creswell, J. W. (1999). Exploring underrepresentation: The case of faculty of color in the Midwest. *The Journal of Higher Education, 70*(1), 27–59.

U.S. Department of Education. (2016). *The state of racial diversity in the educator workforce.* Retrieved from https://www2.ed.gov/rschstat/eval/highered/racial-diversity/state-racial-diversity-workforce.pdf

Virginia Tech Office of Institutional Research & Effectiveness. (2017). Full-time faculty by rank, gender, race/ethnicity for liberal arts and human sciences: School of Education 2017 [Online data]. Retrieved from https://irweb.ir.vt.edu/webtest/FacultyStaffGenderEthnicity.aspx

William T. Grant Foundation. (2014). *Research grant application guide.* New York: William T. Grant Foundation.

Part III

The Racialized Experiences of Latinx in U.S. Higher Education

Chapter 8

Intersectional Competence within a Diverse Latinx Community

Conceptualizing Differences at a Hispanic Serving Institution

Mildred Boveda

INTRODUCTION

In this chapter, I revisit the reflexive journaling I maintained between February 2015 and September 2016, when I initially developed the Intersectional Competence Measure (ICM) for my dissertation study (Boveda, 2016). When I was a doctoral candidate, I was also an adjunct professor at Florida International University (FIU), a Hispanic Serving Institution (HSI) in my hometown Miami, Florida. The ICM measures pre-service teachers' understanding of intersecting sociocultural identities, and how schooling in the United States is implicated in the intersectionalities of minoritized students, including those with disabilities. At the time of my dissertation study, all of the tenure-line faculty of the doctoral program were White. A substantial number of participants in the study were undergraduates who self-identified as Hispanic or White Hispanic (Boveda & Aronson, 2019). Descriptors like Hispanic, Latinx, and People of Color are often used as essentializing terms in the United States to categorize people of multiple ethnicities, diverse colonial histories, and distinct intersectionalities (see Boveda & Bhattacharya, 2019). As such, I argue that darker-skinned Latinx[1] students and faculty—in my case, a Black, Afro-Latina at an HSI—may experience microaggressions and Racial Battle Fatigue (RBF) regardless of the significant percentages of minoritized students at the university.

I begin this chapter by exploring how all universities in the United States, including Minority Serving Institutions (MSIs), are connected to the larger history of westernized universities that devalue Black, Indigenous, and feminine/feminist onto-epistemologies.[2] I proceed by situating my embodied professional and personal understandings at the time of the reflexive journaling as I was simultaneously (a) a researcher, faculty member, and doctoral candidate, and

(b) Black, Latina, and a woman. In describing my intersecting professional and personal identities, I offer examples of microaggressions by White faculty and students with familial ties to Latin America who embraced Whiteness. I conclude this chapter by encouraging those who research or practice in HSIs to consider the anti-Black and Eurocentric ways that racialized Latinx students and faculty are socialized (and wounded) within these contexts. More specifically, I suggest that Latinx college and university faculty in the United States engage in reflexive journaling and autoethnographic tracings to examine their professional socialization, make sense of their racialized experiences, and monitor the messaging that institutional misfit is a sign of personal failure.

RBF IN THE WESTERNIZED UNIVERSITY

RBF was originally conceptualized to describe the psychologically stressful experiences that produce emotional and physiological effects in Black college students and faculty at Predominantly White Institutions (PWIs) in the United States (Smith, 2004; Smith, Allen, & Danley, 2007). RBF has since been used to examine the experiences of Latinx students (Franklin, Smith, & Young, 2014; Yosso, Smith, Ceja, & Solórzano, 2009), and Activists of Color at PWIs (Gorski, 2019). I, myself, have documented the microaggressions I confronted at PWIs as an undergraduate and graduate student at Ivy League institutions (Boveda, 2019). Furthermore, I am an Afro-Latina (i.e., a Black woman), who is a tenure-track faculty member working at a large research-focused university. I thus experience daily challenges when working with students and colleagues in a field comprised of predominantly White women. In this chapter, however, I revisit encounters I faced at a school comprised mostly of students with familial ties to Latin America and the Caribbean. In order to contextualize how RBF can occur at MSIs, I turn to Grosfoguel's (2013) description of the westernized university.

Historians, sociologists, and philosophers who trace global knowledge systems explain that the university was westernized as a result of the violence and dehumanization of those subjected to Eurocratic colonialism and patriarchy (e.g., de Oliveira Andreotti, Stein, Ahenakew, & Hunt, 2015; Grosfoguel, 2013). The sociopolitical context leading to the 16th century—such as the persecution of Muslim and Jewish people in Europe, arrival of Iberian settlers to the Americas, enslavement of Africans, and execution of women accused of witchcraft—was a defining time that continues to influence who is considered knowledgeable within the westernized university. The wealth and capital derived from exploited lands and captured people funded the expansions of Western philosophies while simultaneously perpetuating cultural imperialism in the form of genocide, linguicide, and epistemicide (i.e., the destruction and suppression of knowledge systems; de Sousa Santos, 2015). As a result of centuries of European colonial violence, today, in the social sciences and humanities, there is a privileging of the epistemologies of White men from five countries—France, Germany, Italy, the United Kingdom, and the United States (Grosfoguel, 2013).

A closer examination of the westernized university in the United States reveals the multiple colonial histories/present realities and imperial intentions of this nation (Chatterjee & Maira, 2014; Churchill, 1995; Kendi, 2016). These multiple and intersecting colonial forces influence the way race is constructed and racism enacted within universities across the country, including MSIs (e.g., García, 2018; Exkano, 2013). While Historically Black Colleges and Universities (HBCUs) and Tribal Colleges and Universities (TCUs) were established explicitly to expand educational access to minoritized people,

> HSIs evolved as sizeable numbers of Latinas and Latinos enrolled in affordable two and four-year institutions close to home, a pattern uncovered in the late 1980s, which led advocates within the Latino community to form the Hispanic Association of Colleges and Universities (HACU). (Gonzales, 2015, p. 29)

Since the 1990s, non-profit Institutions of Higher Education (IHEs) with 25 percent or more of Hispanic/Latinx undergraduate students are eligible for the HSI designation and the government support that comes with it. Although other MSIs are vulnerable to the Eurocentric effects of the westernized university (e.g., Exkano, 2013), the growing designation of PWIs as HSIs has garnered the attention of those concerned that Latinx students and faculty are underserved in these contexts. As noted by Vargas (2018), in 2016 there were 37 historically PWIs that were newly designated HSIs. Moreover, "only three HSIs actually mention Hispanics in its mission statement, vision, or history … Hostos Community College, Boricua College, and National Hispanic University" (Sanchez, 2011, p. 149). Vargas (2018) expressed concerns that Hispanic students are being recruited for the purpose of getting the funded designation but are underserved once they arrive to the campus.

To further complicate the challenges of meeting the needs of Latinx students at HSIs, there is documented colorism and anti-Black sentiments across Latin America that is further compounded when Latinxs immigrate to the United States (e.g., Murguia & Saenz, 2002). In addition to the racial stratification that exists within Latinx communities, Latinxs of conspicuous Indigenous and African heritage also contend with racism in the United States:

> Latino/a immigrants' anti-Black sentiment reflect the continued power of colonialism and White dominance, whereby Latino/a cultures are often still afflicted with colorism and darker-skinned Latino/as are accorded the lowest social statuses.
>
> (Chavez-Dueñas, Adames, & Organista, 2014, p. 479)

103

Esmieu and Terrazas (2017) thus ask whether Afro-Latinx students are adequately attended to at HSIs. In the following section, I explain how my Afro-Latinidad made me especially vulnerable to RBF, both as a doctoral student, and as an adjunct faculty member at an HSI. My recollections of tense experiences with White faculty and self-identified White Hispanic students reveal the importance of studying RBF, even within MSIs.

AFRO-LATINIDAD WITHIN UNIVERSITY-BASED TEACHER EDUCATION PROGRAMS

As a daughter and sister of immigrants from the Dominican Republic—the first in my family born in the United States—Grosfoguel's (2013) identification of the colonial settlement of the Caribbean as a catalyst for the westernized university is especially relevant (see Boveda & Bhattacharya, 2019). Although the first university established in what came to be known as the Americas was on the island of their birth, neither of my parents were formally educated when they arrived in South Florida. During my P–12 schooling, my mother worked in factories and later as a housekeeper. My father had a job in maintenance at FIU. I distinctly remember visiting the school for "Take Your Daughter to Work Day" and seeing the white uniforms he and his coworkers wore as they worked outside in sheds. Approximately two decades later, I was responsible for teaching undergraduate and graduate special education courses at this same institution, this time in air-conditioned buildings.

While serving as an adjunct professor, I also collected data for my doctoral dissertation. As a Black, Afro-Latina whose research focused on preparing teachers to work with students with disabilities, I was drawn to Black feminist theory and critical pedagogies. I thus embarked on a mixed-methods sequential exploratory research design to develop and validate an instrument that measured Intersectional Competence (i.e., the ICM). During the qualitative phase, I collected data that strengthened the theoretical basis for validating the instrument (i.e., interviews with focus groups, consulting with experts, and cognitive pre-testing). The second phase of the study involved quantitative analysis and the piloting of the items with 107 participants. I maintained a reflexivity journal throughout all phases and stages of the study.

In their call for the application of intersectionality in special education research, García and Ortiz (2013) explain the need for researcher reflexivity when conducting research in multicultural contexts. Because the communication of scientific findings is both discursively and socially mediated, a researcher's disposition inevitably influences their approach to the research process, interpretation of the outcomes, and how they report the findings. In order to actively explore subjectivities and to "manage it—to preclude it from being unwittingly burdensome" (Peshkin, 1988, p. 28), it was critical that I was transparent about the discursive and culturally mediated processes involved in the collection and interpretation of the data (Ortlipp, 2008).

The encounters I describe below are told within the context of the development of the ICM as recorded in my reflexivity journal. During the two years I maintained the journal, the two largest groups of undergraduate students at FIU were Hispanic/Latinx (64%) and Black/African American (12.5%) (from NCES Integrated Postsecondary Education Data System as cited in Data USA, n.d.). My doctoral cohort was comprised of nine educators who self-identified as Hispanic/Latinx, and three educators who self-identified as Black. Meanwhile, by the year of my graduation, all of the faculty responsible for our doctoral program were White.

In the first narrative presented below, I share an interaction that took place during the qualitative stage of the study. I reflect on the disappointment I felt when I inadvertently compromised my role as an observer-researcher during a focus group session. In addition to my journaling, I return to the focus group transcripts to make sense of my reaction to an undergraduate student who revealed her attitude toward Black boys and their families.

In the second narrative, I revisit excerpts in my journal that document my realization, over time, that all members of my dissertation committee were White. I also discuss an especially stressful day when I experienced back-to-back microaggressions. The pressures and indignities I encountered that day resulted in physiological effects that doctors suspected was broken-heart syndrome (i.e., takotsubo cardiomyopathy).

What Do You Mean by "Angry Black Boy?"

Shortly after I developed a set of guiding questions related to the Intersectional Competence construct, I conducted three focus group sessions with pre-service teachers. Overall, the focus group sessions went smoothly. My colleague, a Haitian American woman, facilitated the discussions while I served as an observer, took notes, and managed the audio-recordings. I sometimes interjected when I wanted participants to expand their answers or felt the need to redirect the discussion. As a result of these interviews, I made modifications to the indicators of the construct and developed items that reflected intragroup differences among members who shared racial/ethnic sociocultural categories.

One of the participants in the third and final focus group initially self-identified as White in a questionnaire given prior to the interview, but later revealed her Latinx heritage during the session (pseudonym Ariana). It came out as a confession of sorts after participants were asked if there were any labels ascribed to them that they were ashamed of and/or proud to claim. Ariana, a fair-skinned, blond-haired woman who grew up near the university said:

I'll admit that I use my physical [appearance] and my background to my advantage. Growing up, I got made fun of a lot for always having the light skin and light hair and light eyes … because everybody else around me was Hispanic. So, I was like the odd one out. And I would try so hard to tell them I was Hispanic too. But I grew up in a household that was so Americanized, where we did not speak Spanish in the house and if I tried to speak Spanish, I'd get made fun of too. So eventually, I kind of just like relented and said, 'No, I'm just American.'

She went on to explain the fluidity with which she claims her Latinidad, how it changes across different contexts in the United States, and how she turned it on and off for different professional purposes,

But then there have been times where I've gone away from Miami and I like to really show off that I can speak Spanish … but when it comes to being taken seriously, like for jobs, I'll go right back into saying I'm White—what I fill out for my ethnicity and my race, it depends on where I am and what it's for … because there is definitely a stigma against certain things. So, if I can take advantage of having a name that's not really ethnic, and take advantage of my look and my accent, I'm going to do it because in the end, I need to get ahead.

In response to this particular focus group session, I jotted down the following notes in my journal:

Excerpt from: Focus Group C April 6, 2015

Today's focus group was far more frustrating than the previous two. There were a couple of politically incorrect statements that stung me as a Researcher of Color. There was one point where one of the participants who identified as White stated she uses her Whiteness to get ahead. That's one of several comments made that piqued me. The moment that sort of pushed me to break the 'researcher' character was when [this] participant kept calling Black boys "angry." I pointed it out and perhaps gave them the impression that it bothered me because 10 minutes or so later (note to self: check transcripts) the participant backtracked to fix or explain her statement.

Now I'm a bit upset with myself because in this qualitative phase, I am the primary research tool. Also, the purpose of qualitative studies is to get the perspective of the participants and my obvious frustration may have altered her response. I have reached out to some friends to see if I could get resources to address researcher positionality, subjectivity, and general bias. I realize now that the concepts of intersectionality and inclusion are quite political. This is a very fascinating thing because my intersecting identities are obviously a factor in my data collection research decisions and will be in my analysis.

I wrote a note to myself to review the transcripts and to check my potential biases. Three years after the initial session, I recognize the exasperation I felt as a Black, Afro-Latina listening to a White-passing woman describe her privileges. This same participant insinuated that Black boys are overrepresented in special education due to their desire to fit in.

> **Ariana:** So maybe this child [who] is African American [thinks], "Oh, what do I see that looks like me on TV and in music and in movies? This, like, angry persona? I need to fit this." Even if this child is living in a middle-class neighborhood ... there's kind of like, "Oh, this is what I need to be."
>
> **Mildred:** Interesting. So angry keeps coming up when you talk about it. Which goes back to perceived rationale for behavior...
>
> **Another Focus Group Participant:** That maybe ... like they just need to fit into that stereotype. ...
>
> **Mildred:** The kids wants to fit into a stereotype? That's interesting.
>
> **Ariana:** That's identity.

Ariana, a high achieving undergraduate student, was perceptive and picked up on my vexation. As noted in the journal excerpt shared above, she insisted on clarifying her "angry" statement:

> And that's what I was going to add on to when you were asking before. I think that in general, we have this mentality of like, this is a cultural cycle, versus this is an isolated incident. So, you have, the White boy acting out one time or a little girl, or whatever she misbehaved, "Oh that was an isolated incident," versus the African American child or the Hispanic child. I think the reason I keep using the word, "angry," is because of a video that's going around the Internet that has been on my mind.
>
> So, it happened up in Tallahassee, there's this little boy and he's walking around a Dollar General and he's throwing everything on the ground, and this child is just upset. It's sad, he's not there with a parent. He's clearly just been abandoned there. Everyone else in the store, whatever area this is, it's clearly an African-American area because that's who's in the store. And this guy is following him around with his camera recording him, and he's like, "We got a jit going ham in the dollar store." The kid is just throwing things around and they are laughing at it, and this kid is angry and people are approaching him, and he starts like raising items to hit them. He's like, "Back away, I'm not afraid to do it." The kid's like 9 or 10. And finally, they drag him out and they

107

say, "Okay, cops are coming for you." And people are sharing this kind of like, "Oh, if that was my child, I would …"

Yeah and to me, it's like the child needs discipline, but there's also severe lack of affection there too. This is an angry child. I think that's why I keep saying this has been on my mind, just people's reaction to it. I think people see this statistic and instead of thinking, like this is an over-representation, they might think this is a cultural thing and we need to break the cycle. The way that we are going to do it is, we have the Hispanic boys in the class who's acting out, we have the Black boy in the class who's acting out, we are going to put him in this program, we are going to edit that behavior from now.

In her effort to justify herself *to me*, she described an incident captured in a viral video. She made deficit-oriented assumptions about the family of the Black boy in the video, stating he had been "abandoned," lacked discipline, and lacked affection. She imitated Black Miami slang (i.e., *jit*) to describe what the patrons of this Tallahassee, FL store said. She insisted on repeating the word "angry," despite my clear disapproval of the trope used to describe Black people. Revisiting this exchange elucidates the psychological exhaustion I felt after the focus group session.

The Faculty Are All White

For some reason, I had not noticed that most of the doctoral faculty at the HSI I attended were White until I came to the end of my dissertation project. In deciding who was to provide feedback in the development of the ICM, I selected four committee members who studied issues related to equity and cultural and linguistic diversity. They were helpful; yet despite their research interests, their Whiteness became increasingly salient as the time to defend came closer.

I had a moment of clarity about the racial composition of my committee when I was asked

about the status of my dissertation revisions hours after video footage of Philando Castille's death was released to the public. While the emerging and established Scholars of Color I knew were reeling from the images, my White committee members seemed unaffected. Proximity to People of Color did not always result in empathy because of their limited embodied experiences with intersectional oppression.

The quote above, taken from my journal, demonstrates a microaggression I experienced. But even prior to the July 6, 2016 killing of Castille that prompted the entry, I had a day that exemplified the RBF I endured at this HSI. In fact, I ended up in the emergency room and had several follow-up visits with cardiologists to determine whether I experienced a condition known as "broken heart syndrome."

On a Saturday in Spring, faculty from our program scheduled interviews with candidates for enrollment in a master's program. Participating in the admissions process revealed a lot about the faculty. There was one White man, for example, who refused to acknowledge the ethnic background of applicants and how their racialized experiences may play a factor in their application. It was especially frustrating when I tried to advocate for a Black applicant. He was a former athlete at a Division I school. His undergraduate grades were not as strong as those he received in his first master's program. He applied to a second master's program because he was interested in learning more about disabilities. Thankfully, another faculty member stood up and agreed with me, even though the White man was annoyed when I brought up the underrepresentation of Black men in our field.

During a break, I checked Qualtrics to see the participation status of the quantitative phase of my dissertation study. At that moment, I somehow lost the data of over 100 participants. Devastated, I immediately contacted Qualtrics' customer service. Those around me did not notice my distress. I "kept it together." Within two hours, I recovered the data, but later learned that the damage was already done.

Excerpt from: Valentine's Day and Broken Heart Syndrome February 13, 2016

It looks like losing my dissertation data last Saturday may have almost killed me. Well, my cardiologist suspects I have "Broken Heart Syndrome" and will be running more analyses tomorrow to see if there was any structural damage to my heart. … Happy Valentine's Day! ☺ It's all good. Apparently, even though I didn't feel it at first, and even though I was able to retrieve all of the data within hours of losing the info (thank God for Qualtrics customer service being open on the weekends), the initial shock took a lot out of me. It's a reminder that this is very personal work and that I need to stop and chill.

That Saturday was a hectic day and I was in the midst of trying to apply for jobs. At the same time, I tried to get my dissertation data in order. It was just too much to do both simultaneously. At any rate, at this point I am focused on getting better and on wrapping up the dissertation. The job hunt will have to be put on hold (because something has to give, and that something should not be my health).

What I did not disclose in this initial entry was that the same Saturday I lost my dissertation data (and was interviewing graduate applicants with White colleagues), I had a conversation with a faculty member who I previously considered an advocate. I asked her about my job prospects, and she surprised me with her response. When I asked if she thought I was competitive for the university tenure-line job market, she said no. According to her, there were far more accomplished candidates than me who had doctoral degrees from more prestigious institutions than the HSI I attended. She then said that perhaps my minoritized identities would give me a slight advantage. That final statement was especially disappointing. It was the first time I heard her make a micro-aggressive statement. Her comment, conceivably one made without much thought, had a long-lasting effect on how I viewed my doctoral experiences. It contributed just as much to my "broken heart" as the temporary dissertation setback.

As I indicated in the journal, it took a couple of days before the stress caught up with me. By the following Monday, I felt chest constrictions and it was hard for me to breathe. I first went to an urgent care facility and my heartbeats were irregular enough that they recommended I go to a larger hospital. Given my family's history with heart conditions, the doctors were concerned. After a long line of questioning, and a description of my challenging Saturday, the emergency room cardiologist surmised the source of my illness.

Broken heart syndrome, *also called stress-induced cardiomyopathy or takotsubo cardiomyopathy*, can strike even if you're healthy. ...

Women are more likely than men to experience the sudden, intense chest pain—the reaction to a surge of stress hormones—that can be caused by an emotionally stressful event. It could be the death of a loved one or even a divorce, breakup or physical separation, betrayal or romantic rejection. It could even happen after a good shock (like winning the lottery. ...).

Broken heart syndrome is usually treatable. Most people who experience it make a full recovery within weeks, and they're at low risk for it happening again (although in rare cases it can be fatal).

(American Heart Association, 2019)

After a few weeks, and several doctor visits, all was well with my health. I spoke with the offending faculty member a couple months later and she immediately apologized when she made the connection between her statement and my hospital visit. A fleeting comment had a profound effect on how I perceived her. What was especially perplexing was that she had personally recruited me to attend the same HSI she felt was not competitive with other research institutions. Thankfully, her low estimation about the status of the university was not shared by the six universities that contacted me once I finally applied for academic positions. Nonetheless, the ethical implications of her recruiting minoritized students to a university she deemed less competitive deserves a closer examination.

ACTIONABLE STRATEGIES

IHEs in the United States, including HSIs and other MSIs, are implicated in the reinforcement of westernized onto-epistemology. As higher education scholars and practitioners consider the diverse geographic locations of HSIs in the United States, each with their distinct colonial histories, it is critical to consider the diverse racialized experiences of multiethnic group categories such as Hispanic/Latinx. Doing so will also elucidate the role that IHEs have in reifying colonial dynamics, especially for Latinx faculty and students with Black and Indigenous ancestry. I share the following four implications from my autoethnographic reflection about my work at an HSI:

- HSIs must communicate their westernized history and work to de/colonize curriculum, pedagogy, and structures in ways that empower Latinx students (Garcia, 2018).
- Latinx students and faculty should be encouraged to engage in autoethnographic tracings of their educational journey to identify de/colonial tensions and racialized experiences within the westernized university (Boveda, 2019; Boveda & Bhattacharya, 2019).
- White faculty at HSIs must be careful not to recruit or advise students if they deem their program will insufficiently prepare Latinx and other People of Color to "compete" with students from the dominant group (Greene & Oesterreich, 2012).
- College and university leaders must better examine the racial and ethnic composition of faculty members working with undergraduate and graduate-level students.
- Funding agencies desiring to support HSIs must examine whether the institutions' mission and vision statements explicitly reference serving Latinx students of diverse intersectionalities before allocating resources to the institution.

CONCLUSION

Latinx and other People of Color attending HSIs have a range of embodied perspectives that are insufficiently attended to in research and practice (Esmieu & Terrazas, 2017). My journal entries captured how *I*, even while teaching or conducting interviews with students like Ariana, was in need of faculty and colleagues who enacted Intersectional Competence. Perhaps my experiences with RBF would have been diminished had the faculty at this HSI had

an understanding of the interlocking and simultaneous effects of multiple markers of difference; an understanding of the systems of oppression and marginalization that occur at the intersection of multiple markers of differ-ence … a belief of teaching as agency for social change; and evidence of high expectations for all students.

(Boveda, 2016, p. 99–100)

I did not intend to essentialize the faculty and students discussed in this chapter. Nonetheless, in revisiting my journal, I traced interactions that led to RBF and explored the resulting damage captured by my body. Failing to unpack all of the nuanced experiences within broad ethnic categorizations like "Latinx," "Black," and "Asian" renders many needs invisible within the higher education context. My physiological and psychosocial reactions helped to (a) warn me of the toxicity I was exposed to, (b) reassess my expectations of colleagues, and (c) articulate my desires for supports that were inadequately provided for me and other racial-ized members within this HSI community.

NOTES

1 When referring to people with personal and familial ties to Latin America, I will use the terms Latina/o/x unless directly quoting other texts or when an individual self-identifies differently (e.g., Hispanic).
2 I conceptualize onto-epistemology as individuals' hybridized ways of knowing and being as they navigate and make sense of the different terrains of their lived experi-ences (Boveda & Bhattacharya, 2019).

REFERENCES

American Heart Association. (2019). Is broken heart syndrome real? Retrieved from https://www.heart.org/en/health-topics/cardiomyopathy/what-is-cardiomy opathy-in-adults/is-broken-heart-syndrome-real

Boveda, M. (2016). *Beyond special and general education as identity markers: The development and validation of an instrument to measure preservice teachers' understanding of the effects of intersecting sociocultural identities* (Doctoral dissertation). Retrieved from http://digitalcommons.fiu.edu/etd/2998

Boveda, M. (2019). An Afro-Latina's navigation of the academy: Tracings of audacious departures, re-entries, and intersectional consciousness. *Feminist Formations, 31*(1), 103–123.

Boveda, M., & Aronson, B. A. (2019). Special education preservice teachers, intersec-tional diversity, and the privileging of emerging professional identities. *Remedial and Special Education*. doi: 10.1177/0741932519838621.

Boveda, M., & Bhattacharya, K. (2019). Love as de/colonial onto-epistemology: A post-oppositional approach to educational research ethics. *The Urban Review, 51*, 5–25.

Chatterjee, P., & Maira, S. (Eds.). (2014). *The imperial university: Academic repression and scholarly dissent*. Minneapolis, MN: University of Minnesota Press.

Chavez-Dueñas, N. Y., Adames, H. Y., & Organista, K. C. (2014). Skin-color prejudice and within-group racial discrimination: Historical and current impact on Latino/a populations. *Hispanic Journal of Behavioral Sciences, 36*(1), 3–26.

Churchill, W. (1995). White studies: The intellectual imperialism of US higher education. In S. Jackson & K. Solís (Eds.), *Beyond comfort zones in multiculturalism: Confronting the politics of privilege* (pp. 17–35). Westport, CT: Bergin and Garvey.

Data USA. (n.d.) Data USA Florida International University. Retrieved from https://datausa.io/profile/university/florida-international-university/

de Oliveira Andreotti, V., Stein, S., Ahenakew, C., & Hunt, D. (2015). Mapping interpretations of decolonization in the context of higher education. *Decolonization: Indigeneity, Education & Society, 4*(1), 21–40.

de Sousa Santos, B. (2015). *Epistemologies of the south: Justice against epistemicide.* New York: Routledge.

Esmieu, P. L., & Terrazas, M. (2017). Are you serving all of us? Afro-Latinos/as and Hispanic serving institutions. In M. Gasman, A. C. Samayoa, & W. C. Boland (Eds.), *Educational challenges at minority serving institutions* (pp. 64–74). New York: Routledge.

Exkano, J. (2013). Toward an African cosmology: Reframing how we think about historically Black colleges and universities. *Journal of Black Studies, 44*(1), 63–80.

Franklin, J. D., Smith, W. A., & Hung, M. (2014). Racial battle fatigue for Latina/o students: A quantitative perspective. *Journal of Hispanic Higher Education, 13*(4), 303–322.

Garcia, G. A. (2018). Decolonizing Hispanic-serving institutions: A framework for organizing. *Journal of Hispanic Higher Education, 17*(2), 132–147.

García, S. B., & Ortiz, A. A. (2013). Intersectionality as a framework for transformative research in special education. *Multiple Voices for Ethnically Diverse Exceptional Learners, 13*(2), 32–47.

Gorski, P. C. (2019).Racial battle fatigue and activist burnout in racial justice activists of color at predominately White colleges and universities. *Race Ethnicity andEducation,22*(1),1–20.

Gonzales, L. D. (2015). An acción approach to affirmative action: Hispanic-serving institutions as spaces for fostering epistemic justice. *Association of Mexican American Educators Journal, 9*(1), 28–41.

Greene, D., & Oesterreich, H. A. (2012). White profs at Hispanic-serving institutions: Radical revolutionaries or complicit colonists. *Journal of Latinos and Education, 11*(3), 168–174.

Grosfoguel, R. (2013). The structure of knowledge in westernized universities: Epistemic racism/sexism and the four genocides/epistemicides of the long 16th century. *Human Architecture: Journal of the Sociology of Self-Knowledge, 11*(1), 73–90.

Kendi, I. X. (2016). *Stamped from the beginning: The definitive history of racist ideas in America.* New York: Nation Books.

Murguia, E., & Saenz, R. (2002). An analysis of the Latin Americanization of race in the United States: A reconnaissance of color stratification among Mexicans. *Race and Society*, *5*(1), 85–101.

Ortlipp, M. (2008). Keeping and using reflective journals in the qualitative research process. *The Qualitative Report*, *13*(4), 695–705.

Peshkin, A. (1988). In search of subjectivity—one's own. *Educational Researcher*, *17*(7), 17–21.

Sanchez, B. (2011). Work-in-progress, Hispanic-serving institutions: The modern Historically Black colleges and universities? *Voices of Claremont Graduate University*, *1*, 144–166.

Smith, W. A. (2004). Black faculty coping with racial battle fatigue: The campus racial climate in a post-civil rights era. *A Long Way to Go: Conversations about Race by African American Faculty and Graduate Students*, *14*, 171–190.

Smith, W. A., Allen, W. R., & Danley, L. L. (2007). "Assume the position … you fit the description" psychosocial experiences and racial battle fatigue among African American male college students. *American Behavioral Scientist*, *51*(4), 551–578.

Vargas, N. (2018). Racial expropriation in higher education: Are Whiter Hispanic serving institutions more likely to receive minority serving institution funds? *Socius*, *4*, 1–12.

Yosso, T., Smith, W., Ceja, M., & Solórzano, D. (2009). Critical race theory, racial microaggressions, and campus racial climate for Latina/o undergraduates. *Harvard Educational Review*, *79*(4), 659–691.

Chapter 9

"Counterspaces" and Mentorship as Resources for Immigrant Faculty of Color Facing Racial Battle Fatigue[1]

Nadia I. Martínez-Carrillo

INTRODUCTION

A distinct moment of awareness of my own experience with Racial Battle Fatigue (RBF) (Smith, 2008) happened while talking with a small group of students following a class in which we had just discussed social constructions of race. A student of color asked me how I was able to manage talking about race in the classroom, a topic he said he usually avoided and was afraid to discuss. The tone of his voice—one of astonishment—when he asked me his question made me feel that my ability to discuss race was some kind of superpower. I could feel tears forming in my eyes. As I tried to articulate a response, I was thinking of my own experiences of fear, pain, tension, and anxiety when navigating and discussing racial dynamics inside and outside of academia.

This moment was memorable to me for three reasons. First, I was unexpectedly prompted to an awareness of how RBF impacted me as a pre-tenure, Mexican immigrant woman of color in predominantly White U.S. academic institutions. Second, it led me to identify and reflect on the individual and contextual factors that have been key to helping me manage RBF experiences throughout my career in higher education in the United States. Third, it was not the first time that a student of color approached me informally to look for support in finding strategies to deal with systemic racism. In fact, these "counterspaces" (Case & Hunter, 2012; Yosso, Smith, Ceja, & Solórzano, 2009) of human connection and solidarity have been helpful in my own journey in academia.

"Counterspaces" as "Borderless Spaces"

My experience is not exhaustive of the ways that people understand their immigrant identity within academia nor of how this identity impacts their lives. We all have different experiences of simultaneous oppression and privilege shaping and being shaped by the unique combination of our social identities (Crenshaw, 1991). My experiences with RBF are not the exception and are shaped by the identities that I embody. Despite the challenges of navigating academia and immigration processes as a Mexican scholar of color, I am still a highly educated, bilingual, middle class, cisgender woman. I believe that these privileged identities have in many ways facilitated the negotiation of my place in academia and my dealing with RBF. Thus, my experiences should not be used to define those of every Mexican scholar in higher education.

A discussion that addresses the complexity of the systemic reshape needed in academia to eradicate a culture of institutionalized racism and nativism (De la Luz Reyes & Halcon, 1988; Pérez Huber, 2010) is beyond the scope of this chapter. Rather, I focus on contributing my story to the body of "counternarratives" (Solórzano & Yosso, 2002) to hegemonic accounts that reinforce the exertion of Whiteness in academia (Leonardo, 2009). Through my experiences, I examine the importance of having "counterspaces" available to me during my academic journey (Yosso et al., 2009). Counterspaces can be defined as spaces that "build a sense of community" (Yosso & López, 2010, p. 84). They also develop "critical resistant navigational skills" (Solórzano & Villalpando, 1998). These spaces provided me with guidance, solidarity, and support.

The importance of "counterspaces" for helping students and faculty of color to navigate historically and contemporarily White academic institutions has been widely documented by scholars (see Yosso et al., 2009; Yosso & Lopez, 2010). However helpful informal mentoring (Bynum, 2015) is, the service and mentorship work done in these spaces relies overwhelmingly on people of color, especially women (Domingue, 2015; Gonzales & Ayers, 2018), and most of it goes largely unrecognized in formal evaluations of academic labor (Guarino & Borden, 2017). While there are calls for having this work at least recognized and valued (Guarino & Borden, 2017; Jones, Hwang, & Bustamante, 2015; Wood, Hilton, & Nevarez, 2015), the corporatization of higher education poses a challenge to the existence of these spaces.

According to Aronowitz and Giroux (2000), "as corporate culture and values shape university life, corporate planning replaces social planning, management becomes a substitute for leadership, and the private domain of individual achievement replaces the discourse of public politics and social responsibility" (p. 334). In this way, increasing faculty workloads, higher student-teacher ratios, and lower timeframes for producing larger amount of research (preferably beneficial to private corporations) leave faculty with little time to dedicate to spaces for creative research, teaching improvement, civic engagement, and the fulfillment of their community's needs and social relations. This is worrisome for marginalized scholars and allies who rely on "counterspaces" to deal with RBF in higher education given that the amount of time, trust, and community building involved in constructing these spaces can be at odds with the time needed to reach the rising standards of individual achievement and competition imposed by academia (Aronowitz & Giroux, 2000; Giroux, 2009). In other words, "counterspaces" can simultaneously be these faculty members' means for survival and a threat to their place in academia by taking away from activities that are formally required of them for promotion.

In addition to contextualizing my experiences within the growing incorporation of business models into academia, a political environment of increasing xenophobic public policies and discourse situates my immigrant identity as particularly relevant for this analysis (Macedo & Gounari, 2015). With hate crimes on the rise (Center for the Study of Hate and Extremism, 2015), enhanced immigration enforcement and discrimination have generated high levels of stress among both undocumented and documented immigrants (Collins, 2008; Hacker et al., 2011). Particularly, faculty immigrant women of color report microaggressions and discrimination that vary according to their skin color, accent, and ethnicity (Chen & Lawless, 2018). They also experience ambiguity, stress, and fear at adapting to U.S. culture and navigating U.S. academic and immigration systems (Chen & Lawless, 2018). Drawing from Moraga and Anzaldúa's (1981) "theory of the flesh," which positions brown bodies as sites of negotiation of identity and agency and Crenshaw's (1989) "theory of intersectionality," I analyze my experiences with RBF within these political and academic contexts across three different institutions: (1) a small, private, liberal arts college, (2) a public regional university, and (3) a large Research 1 (R1) university.

It is important to note that my autoethnographic analysis is focused on identifying moments and spaces that empowered me to cope with RBF. I chose this perspective to illustrate the support that worked for me with the hope that my story can add to the growing body of "counterstories," which together may generate ideas for safer institutions. Since I am centering my analysis on empowering moments, it might look like my experiences within historically White institutions are mostly positive. They are certainly shaped by the privilege of support I received from wonderful people of color and allies I met in a well-funded, social justice-oriented graduate program and in the universities I have worked for. However, my autoethnographic narrative should not be understood as a comprehensive picture of my journey. There have been intense moments of race- and immigrant-related mental, emotional, and physical tensions. I am focusing on how, peers, mentors, and staff have generously provided me with their friendship and spaces of guidance, solidarity, and support sometimes at the cost of limiting their time to work toward the individual achievements that their institutions required from them. I have also tried to pay this forward and follow their example by giving the same support to my students, peers, and friends in academia.

In the following section, I explain how the time colleagues dedicated to me, and the professional and social connections that I developed in these spaces helped me manage RBF. As a Mexican woman (in the United States), the intersection of my racial and immigrant identities is usually salient in my experiences.

Crossing Physical and Social Borders

Institutional support for international scholars, flexibility, mentoring, and "counterspaces" were essential for me while navigating immigration processes in academia. Although I do not come from a wealthy family in Mexico, I was able to attend one of the leading and most expensive colleges in the country thanks to several scholarships that I received due to good academic performance. When I arrived to the United States as a doctoral student of mass communications at a large R1 university in the Northeast, I was in one of the most diverse research-doctorate programs in the field, a documented non-immigrant student (see Travel.State.Gov, n.d.), fluent in English and funded by a doctoral grant from the Mexican government. I also had a master's degree and seven years of work experience in higher education. Despite these privileges, arriving to the United States as a "Brown" scholar meant facing a learning curve in navigating U.S. cultural and racial dynamics, a different identity construction as a person of color, and also U.S. immigration processes in general.

My learning process was exciting, but quite often stressful and required a good amount of my own time as well as that of colleagues, mentors, and administrators. In the short time after I arrived to the United States, I had to navigate systems and procedures related to transportation, housing, health care, social security, immigration, and work eligibility processes that I was not familiar with, or at least not with the way they function in this country. All of this was done without the lifelong network of support in my country of origin. I did, of course, try to figure everything out on my own, and in many cases, I did. Many other times, though, I relied on institutional resources such as orientation talks and materials and office hours from staff in the corresponding office of support for international students. However, I often found the guidance and support I needed in informal spaces and conversations with peers and mentors. The network I built during these years in graduate school has been extremely important to help me navigate my post-graduate school life in U.S. higher education.

Besides the institutional resources and mentoring that mitigated RBF as a newly arrived scholar of color, there were some contextual factors that also helped. I was thrilled to be in this doctoral program and in one of the top universities in the world. As the granddaughter of a woman who was born into poverty in a rural area of Mexico to parents who forbade her from having an education due to her gender, this accomplishment was particularly meaningful yet financially impossible for me to afford without the doctoral grant that I was awarded by the Mexican government. It was also an exciting moment to be living in the United States. There was a sense of hope that racial justice would be advanced after that year's

118

election of the first African American president (Finn & Glaser, 2010). I did have some encounters with obvious racism in the college town, such as seeing a White guy walking down the street with a shirt that read "Keep America White," or being told to "Go back to Guatemala!" while speaking Spanish downtown with some friends. However, I was excited that most of my professors and peers were invested in advancing social justice. They were as caring as humans as they were accomplished as scholars. However, my excitement also came with a sense of inadequacy, impostor syndrome, stress, and fear of failure. I was still stepping into an unfamiliar environment, far away from my longtime established network of support, and the safe "bubble" provided by people in my doctoral program was not representative of my interactions with the world outside that space.

The experience and flexibility that my R1 university had in working with international scholars was key for me during a difficult time in my life. After I graduated from my doctoral program, I went back to Mexico to comply with the two-year requirement of my non-immigrant student visa (see Travel.State. Gov, n.d.). I managed to get a waiver for that requirement and I applied for an immigrant visa to return to the United States. However, due to how uncertain the processing times for immigrant visa applications are and the limited period of time that the U.S. government gives to enter the United States once they are accepted (see Moattar, 2019), my professional career was negatively affected. I was excluded from applying for full-time jobs or attending professional development events such as conferences since I had no idea when I could start or end a job, or when, if ever, I could travel to the United States. Because the staff at my R1 university were familiar with the legal and administrative processes required to employ a foreign national, I could keep teaching online courses from my location, which kept me professionally active. During my time in Mexico, I also managed to get a few more online courses from a public regional university in the Midwest. Although the staff at the regional public university were not as familiar with the paperwork needed for me to be able to teach courses from Mexico, they were flexible and willing to help. My previous knowledge about the process also helped to smooth the paperwork and lowered my stress.

Around the time that my immigrant visa was accepted and after a little more than two years in Mexico, I was offered a visiting assistant position at the same regional public university for which I had been teaching online courses. The flexibility of my regional public university and the privilege of having a lawyer were key during the process of returning to the United States. My immigrant visa, necessary to enter the United States, arrived in the mail a few weeks after the semester started. This was only after my lawyer contacted a congressional office to intervene on my behalf. My regional public university allowed me to teach my courses online during those first few weeks and then face-to-face as soon as I arrived to the United States.

When I joined my current institution, a small, private, liberal arts college, I was in the process of applying for U.S. citizenship. I was privileged in that I was more familiar with navigating academia in the United States at that time and also still had my lawyer. Thus, I did not have to rely as much on institutional support for the process except for the employment verification letters that I needed and that my institution promptly provided me with.

The Gift of Time and Knowledge

Formal and informal mentoring and access to "counterspaces" were also valuable resources to manage RBF. Even to this day, the time and support provided to me by people at my large R1 university remains one of the most helpful gifts. Some of the negative interactions that increase my RBF happened in the classroom with students when I started teaching in the second half of my doctoral program. For instance, I received comments in my teaching evaluations stating that I had an accent. Granted, there were very few of these comments, and those that did exist were ambiguous in that they did not provide feedback about how having an accent was related to my teaching skills. The comments were usually short and asserted things along the lines of "She has an accent." However, I usually got one or a few of these comments each semester I taught. Despite the reassurance from peers and professors that this was not an issue, the recurrence of these comments made me doubt my English-speaking skills and made me self-conscious about my accent. This concern undermined my confidence as an instructor and generated more anxiety for me. I invested more time than usual in prepping lessons, rehearsing words I was planning to say, and double-checking that important concepts were clear for my students, illustrated by several examples, and written in the visual aids I used. I also spent time simply worrying about my classes every day because of the comments regarding my perceived accent.

The graduate program assigned doctoral students to teaching mentors. I was grateful for this. In a meeting with one of my mentors, a White senior female professor, I told her about my concerns regarding comments in my evaluations and how self-conscious I had become about my accent and my teaching skills. Instead of seeing my accent as a source of concern, she spent a good amount of time helping me find research on racial and gender bias in teaching evaluations as well as providing me with teaching resources to help students deconstruct and be aware of this bias in their perception of instructors (see the end of my chapter for a list of references). This was very meaningful for me. From then on, I not only walked away from these encounters armed with research that helped me understand what I was going through and practical ways to work through issues in the classroom, but I was also affirmed that my cultural identity belonged in the college classroom and I did not have to erase it. The combination of the time people, like this mentor, invested in me and the institutional support given to teaching mentorship reduced my stress.

120

I cannot recall any formal mentoring program that helped me with RBF in my regional public university. I did have an annual meeting with a committee formed by some colleagues to talk about my research production and teaching. They gave me good feedback to prepare for my annual evaluation but not much related to RBF. Even if there were formal mentoring programs, it would have been hard for me to find the time to participate due to my workload. By my third year in this institution, I had a tenure-track position, a 3-3 load, and I had prepped 14 different courses in addition to the usual research and service required. Valuable mentoring that helped me with RBF in my regional private university came usually within informal, short, unplanned conversations with a few colleagues. Although I wish I could have invested more time in these sporadic interactions, that would have come at the cost of falling behind in the sort of production that I was "formally" evaluated for in the institution.

It was hard for me to cope with RBF at my regional public university. Besides not being able to reach out for institutional support, I was teaching courses at the time on critical perspectives of race, gender, media, and politics in an increasingly polarized and xenophobic political environment (see Bobo, 2017). A day after the 2016 presidential election a White male student came to class wearing a hat featuring Donald Trump's campaign slogan, "Make America Great Again." I was heartbroken to see my student wearing a symbol of a campaign largely based on anti-immigrant policies and rhetoric. Some students excused themselves that day from class because of their peer's attire. I continued the class with the remaining students and told my committee about it in the next annual meeting hoping to be directed to institutional resources to help faculty and students with RBF. Instead, I was advised to look for helpful class management strategies and to call campus security if situations escalated, which of course was not a solution to the problem. Given the high number of new courses that I was prepping, I rarely got to teach the same course twice, which would have afforded me the chance to revise them and thus feel more confident teaching them. During this time, the informal advice, time, and support that I got from my public regional university colleagues and my R1 university mentors and peers (usually in virtual settings or at conferences) was helpful.

In my current institution, a small, private, liberal arts school, I have found formal and informal spaces of mentoring. The institution offers frequent teaching workshops led by faculty members that are voluntary and open to the whole college. The topics that they offer are not directly related to RBF but some of the teaching experiences and strategies shared in these spaces are. Through the exchange of teaching experiences and strategies in these forums by faculty members from different backgrounds and disciplines I have found guidance, support, and solidarity. I have similarly benefited from a different program in my institution that offers periodic orientation workshops for faculty throughout their whole first academic year. I also have a supportive group of colleagues in my academic department whom I enjoy working with. I consider them part of my networks of support that I explain next.

Developing (Human) Networks

Another important factor that helped me with RBF was the development of networks of support, which can be traced back to my early years as a graduate student. I am fortunate to have these networks and have been successful at expanding them. Sometimes, physical spaces encouraged the development of these networks. For instance, in graduate school, the institution assigned us to a collective office space just for graduate students that provided us with a place to work, but that we also used as a place to exchange ideas about our teaching and research, and to provide each other with emotional support. Although we were all extremely busy, it was always easy to find at least one person in this space willing to engage in thoughtful conversation.

I also found support in the conversations and social gatherings with people who I met in Women's Studies courses. Most of these interactions during graduate school developed into lifelong friendships that I treasure, and we rely on one another for emotional support related to RBF and career advice as most of us went on to pursue careers in academia. The relationships that I developed with my mentors and advisors in graduate school have been equally important. I appreciate having mentors who have invested time in me despite some of them being pre-tenure with the corresponding demands of individual achievement and related stress. They have always been there to provide me with career advice, recommendation letters, and their friendship.

These networks have expanded to include friends that I met first as colleagues at my regional public university and my small, private, liberal arts school. All of these people and the spaces where I can interact with them have been critical for my survival in academia. This is particularly true when it comes to dealing with the emotional drain that comes from teaching race-related courses and for navigating racial dynamics. I have daily interactions with a few of these friends in which we exchange teaching strategies, research ideas, career advice, words of encouragement, jokes, and practical solutions to manage RBF. I am in contact with many of them infrequently but we still keep each other informed about the conferences we plan to attend and the work we are doing, so as to look for opportunities to interact, support each other, exchange ideas, and collaborate on projects.

Escaping Dynamics of Cheap and Racialized Labor in The Corporate University

Overall, supportive peers and mentors have been key in helping me cope with RBF. These lifelong relationships that I have built in academia developed within a variety of spaces, inside and outside of the classroom, social and professional gatherings, and physical and virtual spaces. However, the increasing corporatization of higher education leaves little time for the creation and maintenance of these spaces. For example, finding these spaces became more challenging at my regional public university despite having supportive colleagues. In order to attract more students, our department created new majors for which we were understaffed in the hopes that, once more students came in, the administration would authorize more faculty lines. We did not get more lines but, since we expanded our course offerings, members of the existing faculty, usually junior, were tasked with teaching them. This helps explain why I ended up preparing 14 new courses in three years. There were also plans to increase the faculty load from a 3-3 to a 4-4, which would have had increased the already intense workload and exacerbated my RBF had I stayed at that institution. During my years there, I had little time to find spaces of support and to revise and improve my race-related courses, which were becoming more challenging under the increasingly polarized political context. Additionally, the institution decided to cut more than a dozen programs and eight majors, which only added to the sense of uncertainty and lowered morale. I had a very difficult time managing RBF in this context and I expect it would have been even more challenging after the institution moved to the 4-4 load.

ACTIONABLE STRATEGIES

This chapter illustrates the importance of building and maintaining "counter-spaces" of emotional support in dealing with RBF in historically White institutions (Yosso et al., 2009). I argue that these spaces and the emotional work that individuals invest in them should be valued and recognized formally by academic institutions in their policies, practices, and evaluations of academic production. This might entail a bigger discussion about the role of institutions of higher education in public policies and social responsibility (Aronowitz & Giroux, 2000), which is beyond the scope of this chapter. However, I do believe that there are at least three practical steps—all that speak to the power that "counterspaces" hold when it comes to reducing RBF—that academic institutions can take based on my experiences.

1. **Promotion of Physical and Virtual Spaces of (Informed) Academic Interaction**

Although having informal spaces of support and mentorship was helpful, to have them only as a marginalized practice and not properly recognized by institutions as a formal academic activity makes them easier for people to avoid, thereby giving preference to practices they know institutions will value for promotion and tenure. These spaces, formal and informal, should be promoted, recognized, and normalized by institutions to challenge hegemonic practices and policies that construct marginalized scholars who used these spaces as "others" in historically and contemporarily White institutions (Feagin, Vera, & Imani, 2014).

123

Institutions should also be knowledgeable and encourage flexibility when working with faculty dealing with immigration processes. The flexibility that my R1 university and my public regional university offered by opening virtual spaces such as classrooms for me when I was not allowed to be physically present and by working with me across borders largely reduced RBF.

2. Filling the Gap Between Research and Institutional Policies and Practices

Academic institutions need to periodically revise their policies so they are informed by research related to structural inequality in higher education. For example, as my experience illustrates, mentors who evaluated my teaching at my large R1 public university were aware of research on identity bias in relation to teaching evaluations and this research informed their evaluation of my work. This reduced RBF for me because I knew that I was evaluated as fairly as possible. Similar efforts should be taken in areas such as hiring practices, distribution of workload, and promotion and tenure policies. Particularly, mentoring programs for marginalized scholars should also be critically informed by research on the issues these scholars face and should include a training of mentors that is based on this literature.

3. De-Corporatizing Academic Institutions

Institutions should revise policies and practices that encourage and reinforce commodified time, toxic competition, isolation, and cheap racialized labor. As my experience in my public regional university illustrates, the corporatization of an academic institution increases faculty workloads, isolation, and leaves them with little time to dedicate to teaching improvement and supportive spaces. These practices leave faculty with a lack of guidance, support, and solidarity, exacerbating RBF. Next, I conclude by sharing research on racial and gender bias in teaching evaluations.

NOTE

1 Author Note: Thanks to Michelle L. Kelsey for her valuable feedback.

RESEARCH ON RACIAL AND GENDER BIAS IN TEACHING EVALUATIONS

Basow, S. A., Codos, S., & Martine, J. L. (2013). The effects of professors' race and gender on student evaluations and performance. *College Student Journal*, 47(2), 352–363.

Deo, M. E. (2015). A better tenure battle: Fighting bias in teaching evaluations. *Columbia Journal Gender and Law*, *31*(1), 7–43.

Martin, L. (2016). Gender, teaching evaluations, and professional success in political science. *PS, Political Science & Politics*, *49*(2), 313–319.

Rosen, A. S. (2018). Correlations, trends and potential biases among publicly accessible web-based student evaluations of teaching: A large-scale study of RateMyProfessors. com data. *Assessment & Evaluation in Higher Education*, *43*(1), 31–44.

Wallace, S., Lewis, A., & Allen, M. (2019). The state of the literature on student evaluations of teaching and an exploratory analysis of written comments: Who benefits most? *College Teaching*, *67*(1), 1–14.

REFERENCES

Aronowitz, S., & Giroux, H. A. (2000). The corporate university and the politics of education. *The Educational Forum*, *64*(4), 332–339.

Bobo, L. D. (2017). Racism in Trump's America: Reflections on culture, sociology, and the 2016 U.S. presidential election. *The British Journal of Sociology*, *68*, S85–S104.

Bynum, Y. P. (2015). The power of informal mentoring. *Education*, *136*(1), 69–73.

Case, A. D., & Hunter, C. D. (2012). Counterspaces: A unit of analysis for understanding the role of settings in marginalized individuals' adaptive responses to oppression. *American Journal of Community Psychology*, *50*(1–2), 257–270.

Center for the Study of Hate and Extremism. (2015). *Final U.S. status report hate crime analysis & forecast for 2016/2017*. Retrieved from https://csbs.csusb.edu/sites/csusb_csbs/files/Final%20Hate%20Crime%2017%20Status%20Report%20pdf.pdf

Chen, Y. W., & Lawless, B. (2018). "Oh my god! You have become so Americanized": Paradoxes of adaptation and strategic ambiguity among female immigrant faculty. *Journal of International and Intercultural Communication*, *11*(1), 1–20.

Collins, J. M. (2008). Coming to America: Challenges for faculty coming to United States' universities. *Journal of Geography in Higher Education*, *32*(2), 179–188.

Crenshaw, K. (1989). Demarginalizing the intersection of race and sex: A Black feminist critique of antidiscrimination doctrine, feminist theory and antiracist politics. *University of Chicago Legal Forum*, *1*, 139–167.

Crenshaw, K. (1991). Mapping the margins: Intersectionality, identity politics, and violence against women of color. *Stanford Law Review*, *43*(6), 1241–1299.

De la Luz Reyes, M., & Halcon, J. (1988). Racism in academia: The old wolf revisited. *Harvard Educational Review*, *58*(3), 299–315.

Domingue, A. D. (2015). "Our leaders are just we ourself": Black women college student leaders' experiences with oppression and sources of nourishment on a predominantly White college campus. *Equity & Excellence in Education*, *48*(3), 454–472.

Feagin, J. R., Vera, H., & Imani, N. (2014). *The agony of education: Black students at a White university*. New York: Routledge.

Finn, C., & Glaser, J. (2010). Voter affect and the 2008 U.S. presidential election: Hope and race mattered. *Analyses of Social Issues and Public Policy*, *10*(1), 262–275.

Giroux, H. A. (2009). Democracy's nemesis: The rise of the corporate university. *Cultural Studies Critical Methodologies*, *9*(5), 669–695.

Gonzales, L. D., & Ayers, D. F. (2018). The convergence of institutional logics on the community college sector and the normalization of emotional labor: A new theoretical approach for considering the community college faculty labor expectations. *The Review of Higher Education*, *41*(3), 455–478.

Guarino, C. M., & Borden, V. M. (2017). Faculty service loads and gender: Are women taking care of the academic family? *Research in Higher Education*, *58*(6), 672–694.

Hacker, K., Chu, J., Leung, C., Marra, R., Pirie, A., Brahimi, M., English, M., Beckman, J., Acevedo-Garcia, D., & Marlin, R. P. (2011). The impact of immigration and customs enforcement on immigrant health: Perceptions of immigrants in Everett, Massachussetts, USA. *Social Science & Medicine*, *73*(4), 586–594.

Jones, B., Hwang, E., & Bustamante, R. M. (2015). African American female professors' strategies for successful attainment of tenure and promotion at predominately White institutions: It can happen. *Education, Citizenship and Social Justice*, *10*(2), 133–151.

Leonardo, Z. (2009). *Race, whiteness, and education*. New York: Routledge.

Macedo, D., & Gounari, P. (Eds.). (2015). *Globalization of racism*. New York: Routledge.

Moattar, D. (2019, March 5). U.S. is stuck in the stone age and it is putting lives in danger. *The Nation*. Retrieved from https://www.thenation.com/article/us-immigration-is-stuck-in-the-stone-age-and-its-hurting-immigrants/

Moraga, C., & Anzaldúa, G. (Eds.). (1981). *This bridge called my Back: Writings by radical women of color*. Watertown, MA: Persephone Press.

Pérez Huber, L. (2010). Using Latina/o critical race theory (LatCrit) and racist nativism to explore intersectionality in the educational experiences of undocumented Chicana college students. *Educational Foundations*, *24*, 77–96.

Smith, W. A. (2008). Higher education: Racial battle fatigue. In R. T. Schaefer (Ed.), *Encyclopedia of race, ethnicity, and society* (Vol. 1, pp. 616–618). Thousand Oaks, CA: Sage Publications.

Solórzano, D., & Villalpando, O. (1998). Critical race theory, marginality, and the experience of minority students in higher education. In C. Torres, & T. Mitchell (Eds.), *Emerging issues in the sociology of education: Comparative perspectives* (pp. 211–224). Albany, NY: State University of New York Press.

Solórzano, D. G., & Yosso, T. J. (2002). Critical race methodology: Counter-storytelling as an analytical framework for education research. *Qualitative Inquiry*, *8*(1), 23–44.

Travel.State.Gov. (n.d.). *Exchange Visitor Visa*. Retrieved from https://travel.state.gov/content/travel/en/us-visas/study/exchange.html

Yosso, T., & Lopez, C. B. (2010). Counterspaces in a hostile place. In L. D. Patton (Ed.), *Culture centers in higher education: Perspectives on identity, theory, and practice* (pp. 83–104). Sterling, VA: Stylus Publishing.

Yosso, T., Smith, W., Ceja, M., & Solórzano, D. (2009). Critical race theory, racial microaggressions, and campus racial climate for Latina/o undergraduates. *Harvard Educational Review*, 79(4), 659–691.

Wood, J. L., Hilton, A. A., & Nevarez, C. (2015). Faculty of color and White faculty: An analysis of service in colleges of education in the Arizona public university system. *Journal of the Professoriate*, *8*(1), 85–109.

Chapter 10

At the Intersection of Gender and Race

Stories from the Academic Career of a Recovering Sociologist

Pamela Anne Quiroz

INTRODUCTION

Perhaps I should not have been surprised when at the conclusion of our tennis match my senior colleague began asking embarrassing questions about how to handle his wife's sexual dysfunction. After all, I had experienced a number of surprises since taking my "first real job" in an eastern public university whose mostly male faculty fancied themselves as displaced Ivy League professors. Life as a newly minted professor was not at all what I had anticipated, nor was it even as welcoming as the top-ranked university from which I had emerged—where one of my professors had likened the graduate student milieu to a "pure Hobbesian state." This job made me long for the world of brilliant if conservative White male professors who had mentored me and nurtured my regard for the discipline. In the pseudo liberal environment to which I had come, I became nostalgic about my graduate experience, where opinions and theories regarding "the great unwashed" were far more explicit, thus, rendering them more easily challenged if not less offensive.

As one of four junior faculty (all women) in the department, it did not take long to learn that my new department may have recognized the need to work its way into the twentieth century (even if it was at the end of the century) with a "buy one get one free academic" plan (one Latina and one African American woman), but certainly did not have to like it! Indeed, shortly after my arrival, the chair conveyed how close the decision was regarding my hire and joked that, after all, I really was not "ethnic enough."

I soon learned that insulting and officious comments made by socially distant colleagues would be part of the regular routine during my tenure at this university. For instance—the reception during which a prominent senior colleague spoke to me about his concern for his son, who was soon to graduate from a prestigious program in sociology— particularly now that all of the minorities and women were being *given* all of the jobs!

Or the other senior colleague who felt compelled to explain to me the difficulty of hiring a second Latino faculty member because there simply were so few "*really qualified ones* out there," completing this assessment with, "don't you agree?"

Or when the potential hire of a Latino job candidate resulted in the demand that all faculty members be granted access to the candidate's letters of reference. This suggestion had not been made for a recently hired White male colleague. It also established a precedent revising a long-standing hiring procedure that permitted only members of the department's personnel committee to read such letters. Nevertheless, the request was granted due largely to colleagues' astonishment that letters of support for this candidate were all from renowned colleagues in the discipline. [He was not hired].

None of these events prepared me however, for the colleague with whom I played tennis. Though he was regarded as a curmudgeon, we had established limited social exchange playing tennis followed by a brief discussion of work. My assumption was that our mutual regard and skill with the game, and the fact that we were in the same field of specialization is what made this collegial relationship possible. After engaging in this ritual for several months I was not prepared when he approached me with the news of his wife's problem. My response was sarcasm, "Since I don't have a wife I don't have to worry about it," yet as I attempted to leave the court he placed his hand on my arm and went on to explain that while he knew it was due to her condition [she had ovarian cancer] she didn't even "get wet." Again, I tried sarcasm, "I hear there are things you can purchase at the store." Then he came to the point of this conversation—he had determined that we should have an affair. As he elaborated in detail about where, how, when, etc., it became apparent that he had given this idea considerable thought. Finally, he announced that his wife had given him permission to attend to his needs elsewhere. At this point I told him not only how uncomfortable this situation made me but that I also considered his behavior unethical. I conveyed I did not have a desire to have an affair with him nor had I ever had such a desire. Finally, I reminded him that as the only colleague in my area of expertise he would undoubtedly be asked to serve on my tenure committee and he must therefore, know how inappropriate this made his suggestion. He simply shrugged his shoulders and waved his hand as if to say, "Don't let's bother with that insignificant nonsense when I have more important and self-serving interests." My response did nothing to allay his efforts and he telephoned a couple of days later at my home to reiterate his proposition and provide the details of a second plan he had derived. This continued for a few weeks.

In typical female fashion I engaged in self-flagellation, chastising myself for playing tennis with this colleague, examining what I did, said, wore, and could

129

have or *should* have done to avoid the situation. I had rarely fraternized with male colleagues out of learned habit and because the largely male environment did not encourage it.

Whether I was dodging the bullet of unmeritorious "minority hire" or the overtures of a colleague who convinced himself that a recently divorced 38-year-old must certainly be ready to rock, I alternated in what Donaldo Macedo calls the "dance with bigotry" and speaking truth to power (Macedo, 2000). When I did the dance, I told myself to bite my lip, always with the magic word in my thoughts: TENURE. When I could not keep silent and spoke truth to power I was warned by my department chair to be "well published or your A— is out of here," who also added that I wasn't ending up being "*one of the good ones.*"

The years of sexist and racist remarks had simply become too much to bear and my tennis playing colleague's overture was the last straw. I resigned my position and found a new one. However, as depressing as this decision was, it paled in comparison to my resulting disenchantment with the profession and my love of the discipline for which I once had an almost religious zeal. The effects were profound and remained with me for many years.

LIFE AFTER TENURE

Gender is injected into my racialized experiences in the academy because it would be disingenuous to state otherwise. The intersectionality of these master categories exacerbates the difficulties so many of us encounter in our profession so that cultural taxation is frequently accompanied by gender taxation and distinctions between the two are impossible. I wished I could say that once I achieved promotion I no longer had these types of experiences, and in truth, aging obviated sexual approaches by male colleagues but the character of racial microaggressions simply shifted to more subtle and seemingly empowering situations. As an Associate and Full Professor I received invitations to serve on multiple college and university committees and frequently became the Latina/o "voice," and sometimes the lone minority voice on these committees. Undoubtedly, many of these invitations were the result of an institutional mandate to have minority representation on committees but I participated in order to learn how universities operate and to inject my voice into the conversations. Too often however, I noted a polite pause in the conversation when I spoke, particularly when I spoke about racial inequities, as if a gentle wind had blown through the room, only to have colleagues return to discussion without acknowledging my voice. I engaged in self-recriminations and tried to modify my approach to be heard, only to learn from other minority faculty that these were common experiences we shared. As the sole or token representative(s) on university and professional committees or professional boards we tried to manage the fine art of educating without offending, broadening the conversation without overreaching or claiming to represent an entire community. I mentored colleagues and students even as I continued to encounter resistance to my efforts and authority. Regardless of professional accomplishments or opportunities that signaled empowerment, many of us continue to engage in this "dance with bigotry." The necessity of engaging in this dance at any level ultimately exacts a toll on our intellectual and physical well-being as academics (see Zambrana, 2018).

As a researcher I work to distill how race continues to be practiced in so-called diverse educational spaces. Race practices are the behaviors and interpretations associated with racial/ethnic groups and they are a central feature of the processes that occur in universities because they exist in our society. They shape interpretations of who belongs where, what categories mean, and what effect they have on people's opportunities. In contemporary mode it is the subtlety of race practices that defies description if not observation as race practices are almost certainly disputed as something other than what they are. And just as in other social spheres, the legitimacy of race practice is dependent upon who does the naming. Race practices occur in universities at many levels and in many spaces—in classrooms, faculty hiring committees and evaluations, the tenure and promotion process, and other committee meetings, and in everyday interactions between staff, students, administrators, and colleagues. These practices reveal the visible and invisible borders of race and help shape identities and careers.

ACTIONABLE STRATEGIES

Despite the clarion call of universities to address diversity, currently the academy can be characterized by the practice of recruiting a limited number of faculty of color on the basis of their difference, creating isolating or professionally subpar experiences for them, and expecting these faculty to validate the institution's commitment to inclusion and fairness without racial consideration. As law professor Catherine McKinnon once stated about sex equality, it is fundamentally undercut by the social and legal concepts of sex, inequality, and the law. In short, we create systems of hierarchy, then point to differences as the bases or legitimation of these systems. Once a system dictates needs, the outcome or solution for those needs result in writing the "Rubrics" that create the meaning behind the social system of hierarchy, or as McKinnon puts it, "Difference is the velvet glove on the iron fist of domination."

We must look beyond individualistic approaches to solve the problems of racism in academia. It is not enough to offer advice to individual faculty members about how to navigate the academy. Racism is a systemic issue and therefore must be addressed systemically. Of course we need to help develop professional networks and senior faculty members need to mentor junior colleagues. Faculty Development programs such as the National Center for Faculty Development and Diversity, are invaluable for individuals and institutions. Faculty members from underrepresented groups need to have a bill of rights, mentoring, professional development regarding how to obtain promotion, as well as assistance on how to address their professional and emotional well-being.

A truly progressive academic institution must also learn to combine administrative incentives with faculty governance to create an environment that recognizes and addresses the academic potential of their students and the academic value of colleagues from underrepresented groups. A first step is to examine some of the diversity initiatives of universities. It is rather obvious when a university's solution to issues of inequity and diversity is to hire a low-level or even temporary administrative staff person to oversee multiple initiatives, that the university is not serious about addressing these issues. Many universities hire a diversity administrator whose requirements are a bachelor's degree and a few years of experience as opposed to other administrative positions that require a Ph.D. These approaches to addressing issues of racism, equity, and diversity do not suggest a serious commitment.

Other universities author statements about their commitment to diversity and promote diversity through marketing initiatives in photographs or brochures without creating structures of opportunity and systems of accountability to measure their success. This too appears to be the window dressing that too many universities adopt. More recently, there are some institutions that demonstrate serious effort to develop a plan to assess, acknowledge, and modify existing inequities by creating structural incentives and pathways for changing the university's environment (akin to strategic initiatives). These are systemic and long-term initiatives. The process begins by acknowledging the university's history and current limitations and proceeds by tackling the difficult and complex questions that plague our society, and hence our universities. These questions involve not only race but also gender, class, sexuality, immigration, and disability. The process then moves to innovative strategies for change with ongoing assessment and modification. One of the unique features of John Hopkins University's efforts is a webpage with data to provide a public view of its progress (John Hopkins University's roadmap on diversity and inclusion, 2019).

As professors we are supposed to critically examine the flaws of a U.S. educational, economic, and political system that arguably exists absent of equality of opportunity, holds people accountable on the faulty presumption of "merit," and results in reproducing more inequity. We are also expected to promote efforts on the part of future scholars to invest in and modify this system, and thereby promote the university as a place that supports social justice. However, the experiences of too many underrepresented faculty often leave us feeling more like one of its sacrifices as opposed to its change agents. Much needs to be addressed if universities are to remain consonant with our proposed missions and if we have any hope to become places where faculty of color (and students) can thrive. Without such change, the changing demographics of our students will matter little and the potential, productivity, health, and well-being of faculty of color will continue to suffer.

REFERENCES

Johns Hopkins University's roadmap on diversity and inclusion. Retrieved from https://diversity.jhu.edu/wp-content/uploads/2019/04/Roadmap-Progress-Report-2019.pdf.

Macedo, D., & Bartoleme, L. L. (2000). *Dancing with bigotry: Beyond the politics of tolerance.* New York: Palgrave MacMillan.

Zambrana, R. E. (2018). *Toxic ivory towers: The consequences of work stress on underrepresented minority faculty.* New Brunswick, NJ: Rutgers University Press.

Part IV

The Politicized Experiences of Native Americans in U.S. Higher Education

Tribal College American Indian Faculty Perspectives on Sub-Oppression, Racial Microaggression

Shandin H. Pete and Salisha A. Old Bull

INTRODUCTION

Tribal College and University (TCU) settings are unique yet have many commonalities with other higher education institutions concerning Racial Battle Fatigue (RBF). The history of Indian Education in the United States is vast, but marked by periods of trauma and resiliency, including many stories of oppression of indigenous people. Education was first used as a tool for assimilation by the U.S. but eventually became a tool of empowerment for tribal nations (Deyhle & Swisher, 1997). One tool was the establishment of the TCUs during a time of cultural resurgence; they were established in 1973 (Pavel et al. 2001). The development of TCUs stemmed from a need to assist American Indian (AI) students in their unique learning styles and cultural backgrounds (Stein, 2009). Nearly 50 years has passed since their development, and AI college students' experiences have changed. Over this period of time some AIs pursued advanced degrees and transitioned into faculty positions, some within TCUs.

AI college graduates are consistently encouraged to return "home" to contribute to tribal progress for their people (Lowe, 2005). Finding employment in the modern tribal system that has adopted western ideas and values can provide discord with traditional-minded employees. Similarly, TCUs have followed a common western educational model. One purpose of Indian Education, and a focus of TCUs, is to address the issue of cultural uniqueness of its students. Developing a TCU to fit into a Western, non-Native model does not match AI cultural values and tends to view culture as barrier to success. Many tribes have not revised the Western model of education to fit culturally relevant structures. This exposes TCUs to the same educational barriers that exist in predominantly White institutions (PWI). TCUs mission and vision show their intent, but their student retention methods and program structures do not match. Supporting an educational system that struggles to view culture as a catalyst affects AI faculty who work within TCUs. This system creates a similar working environment to that AI faculty face at PWIs, where they are asked to conform to non-Native educational beliefs and become token representatives of their cultural background.

Many AI people describe the idea of "conforming," while maintaining traditional values, as "living in two worlds." Cleary and Peacock (1998) describe this phenomenon of "conformity" as "sub-oppression." According to Clearly and Peacock (1998), "Continued oppression eventually turns the oppressed against each other, and in these instances a twisted form of self-hate develops in the oppressed until eventually *they internalize their oppression and become the sub-oppressor*" (p. 63). Sub-oppression can be found in tribal higher educational systems, but many would deny that it is a form of oppression itself. Sub-oppression also means that RBF that can result when AI oppress other AIs. Described here is oppression that comes from AIs who have chosen to abandon parts of their cultural value systems. In the next section we share the RBF experiences of two TCU AI faculty members.

Salisha's Narrative: Story of an AI Woman Faculty Member at a TCU

When I first embarked on my journey toward higher education, I never thought that the crowning achievement in my career would take place at a TCU. I sacrificed my dream of becoming a professionally educated artist and instead focused on tribal government, politics, psychology, and education. I was determined to follow through with fostering American Indians, to work toward their personal educational endeavors. After obtaining two bachelor's degrees and two master's degrees, I thought this would qualify me for the world of tribal sovereignty and empowerment. I eventually returned home to Montana's Flathead Indian Reservation, landing an instructor position at the TCU, in a newly formed degree program in 2015. The program was new and found to be an area for opportunity, for professional growth within the tribe; according to the tribal members, shown through results of a reservation-wide survey on education. I felt as if it was the dream job for every AI woman seeking to contribute to higher education.

In the beginning, I was motivated to work in this position because of the program's infancy but, it was clear the program was so new there was no structure in place for any mandatory institutional processes. The program chair's inception was by default because he was the last faculty remaining in the department before its transition. My anticipation for this opportunity was a chance to contribute to TCU history, but I did not anticipate defeat and assumed that my cultural upbringing and consideration of a family-education model would give me a strong basis to move forward with the program's ideas and contributions. What followed in the next two years can be described as a series of hostile encounters and difference of opinions based on personal experiences. Here I will only high-light the worst occurrences of what I would categorize as being RBF.

A quirk to working at a TCU is that we are never referred to as "professor." My interpretation is that we all have obtained our doctoral degrees, which we may not have. It was my assumption that the word is one of prestige within a PWI. In either case, it was emphasized on our "contracts" that our job position was titled "instructor." Working at this TCU requires a minimum of a master's degree in any field of study. I was disappointed that once we hired new faculty in the department, most discussions and decisions were made behind closed doors, excluding our faculty group. We were rarely consulted and rarely had depart-ment meetings. Considering the TCU's unique student population and the diver-sity of faculty being a mixture of AIs and non-AI's, our input should have been included more often because of each of our educational experiences as AI faculty and former students. Again, I was wrong, and everything was looking like it would mirror the experiences that AI faculty describe who work at larger PWIs.

Within our program faculty group, we had varying levels of teaching experi-ence and education in higher academia. It came to be that when we would suggest program revision or updates, the response from the TCU's administration was that there would be no changes, for at least four years, and that our suggestions were viewed as stepping on the department chair's toes. Gradually, one person's (Instructor A) suggestions were deemed more valid over time. Eventually, the department chair constantly requested the rest of the group refer to Instructor A for all curriculum ideas and guidelines. It was confusing as to why the chair insisted on this referral process, but it got worse when he said that nobody else in the department was experienced enough to have individual thought on most curricular matters.

For me, this moment was the peak of the treatment I had begun experienc-ing, causing RBF. How could a department chair say that nobody but Instructor A was experienced enough to discuss matters of curriculum, regardless of our experiences that could help AI students? After a year of this treatment, I stood up for the experiences that I brought to the table. A heated argument ensued, during a rare department meeting, regarding a personnel action I had requested, authorized by the vice-president. It included adding a co-instructor (Instructor Z) to a course I was teaching for the first time. Prior to me, Instructor A taught this course and they were close colleagues of the department chair. It was a con-sensus, among our department faculty, that the collegiality between the two had a strong relationship to their common personal backgrounds. I observed that the department chair, although tribally enrolled, did not really spend much time on or commitment to tribal cultural practices and events; this was also true of Instructor A, who was not tribally enrolled, but they were both descendants of the tribe. These facts seemed to cause a common identity issue but it was a bonding topic. The opinion of the rest of the faculty group was that it was normal to see two coworkers cohere, over these types of commonalities. But on this day, the department chair interrogated why I had not consulted with Instructor A on this course, as opposed to requesting the co-instructor. I tried explaining that I wanted to take a fresh approach and stated that Instructor Z had strong insight and experience on the topic and that we would do well teaching the class together. He reacted by calling me unprofessional and stated that Instructor A was more experienced than both Instructor Z and I and that I should have sought advice from Instructor A. I anxiously defended myself and expressed that I felt he was not being fair about his accusation also assuming that Instructor A was the only member of the whole faculty group that was qualified. We were practically yelling and another faculty member interrupted to stop the argument.

Although it never went as far as addressing his observed favoritism of Instructor A, it was clear that this was the case. It was a moment of not addressing the underlying issue of his friendship with Instructor A, presumably based on their personal experiences of tribal identity; but the argument was leading there, had it not been interrupted. Later, the vice-president reprimanded me and validated the department chair, stating that I was being unprofessional, ignoring his part, by authorizing the personnel request. This would be the first of several reprimands stemming from the same underlying issue. My opinions were no longer valid, regardless of my representation of people who had strong ties to their cultural background. Over the next year I was urged by many faculty to file a harassment complaint; I never did. I felt the constant reprimands regarding my recommendations to positively implement program changes, to foster AI student achievement, were disregarded. However, many suggestions by faculty, who had minimal knowledge, or little in common, with AI student academic issues, were being ushered into TCU policy with no reservation. I felt the constant disregard of cultural commonality was causing me RBF, as I had no support in matters of diversity at this TCU.

Prior to taking a stand, my days were filled with severe stress resulting in several voluntary visits to a local psychiatrist. Time with my family was negatively impacted as most evenings were spent enduring anxiety and grief, anticipating each workday. The department chair was consistently implying that I was not qualified or educated enough to fulfill my job duties, despite the fact that the department chair is also an AI from the same tribe. We had four degrees, in similar fields and he was only a few years older than myself. Instructor A's educational experience was in an unrelated field; but Instructor A was pursing their Ph.D. at that time. The idea of continuously defending myself, my educational qualifications, and department contributions regarding the AI student population, struck a huge blow to my confidence and self-worth. I knew that I was not less qualified and the treatment and reactions of the department chair were not valid or deserved, but the daily negative affirmation was debilitating and there were many days that I would leave work in tears.

This treatment had been occurring for the better part of two years. I had concluded that due to my upbringing and the diversity of AI faculty in my department, my experiences were wholly unique. My colleagues were in fear of their association to the conflicts I was experiencing and their support was wavering. Even though the department chair and I were both AI, from the same tribe, we were the epitome of the internal diversity that can exist among AI faculty members. Our differences caused many adverse interactions, which resulted in a very hostile working environment. As an AI woman, holding strong to my traditional values, fighting stress and sorrow due to consistent microaggressions at work, I feel my story exemplifies RBF through comparing the differences in cultural identities that can exist within an AI cohort. After 3.5 years of no resolve, my solution was resignation and I now work back at a PWI serving socioeconomically disadvantaged students; not at home.

Shandin's Narrative: Story of an AI Male Faculty Member at a TCU

I am an AI male faculty member at a TCU where I have been working since 2008. I have a Doctorate of Education (Ed.D.) and a Master of Science (M.S.) in Geology.

Along my path—in 1999—as I was nearing completion of my bachelor's degree in Environmental Science at a TCU, one of my professors, who was a White Female, set me on a career trajectory to address a growing need for AI in graduate degrees in science fields. The professor suggested that I return to the TCU to add to the expertise and increase the representation of AI faculty. I took the professor's advice and after completing my master's degree I returned to the same TCU as an adjunct instructor; I eventually became a fulltime faculty member.

I had many mentors along the way who provided advice and encouragement. Many mentors embodied the characteristics needed to work with the population served by TCUs: Marginalized AI young adults. Marginalizing forces working against this population of students are apparent. The minoritization of my tribal people on the reservation is glaring, where the population of the reservation is comprised of just under 25% AI. Further, the enrolled members of the Confederated Salish and Kootenai Tribes (CSKT) represent only 17% of the reservation populace. The result of the population dynamics and intergenerational propagation of lost tribal identity and worldview is a tumultuous and conflict-laden relationship between tribal, inter-tribal, and non-Indian societies. This is also apparent within the educational arm of the CSKT.

The interactions that I have had with the administration of the TCU that I work for exemplifies these conflicts. While these interactions have been largely constructive, they are not without strife. One of the hallmarks of the communication

141

styles within the TCU system seems to be an imported, top-down, rigid system, modeled after corporate businesses. The free flow of ideas across the administration to faculty are limited to the whim of the individual leaders' own training and background, which in many cases are K–12 philosophies and standards; they are not traditional or tribally derived. When ideas or initiatives are challenged, silence is often the response while the ultimate no-action, in-action, or lamentation of ideas is the result. Largely, these responses are reflected in the cultural arena of the TCUs mission. The foreignness of culture to some of the Tribal members and the fragility of the ego to accept wrongness develops a strong barrier to cultural perpetuation. Misunderstanding and lack of knowledge of culture provide fuel to strengthening these barriers thus hindering progressive culture revitalization.

In some cases, I have experienced the cultural imposter. The imposter casts doubt about my own cultural knowledge, micro-invalidating my ideas as farcical. The imposter will not engage in a discussion to unify understandings nor to foster a relationship, for this may ultimately reveal their own lack of knowledge. Alternatively, the imposter seeks an audience of non-Native coworkers to validate their version of knowledge and propagate mistruths about our tribal people. I have experienced this from AI administrators and AI faculty. The repercussion of these interactions manifests in what feels like an ostracization from important efforts to promote the cultural mission of the TCU.

In one instance, I was invited to provide a traditional welcoming protocol for a conference on our campus. I opted to share a lost custom of greeting other tribes: A process of making peace that was a ritual performed when tribes met during their travels to hunting grounds or other business. I had previously arranged the details for the event and had already requested tribal community members to participate. As the event drew near, the coordinator received an email from our then-President, an enrolled member of the CSKT, seeking to change the welcoming event. The coordinator explained that the invitation was already confirmed. The President continued, asking the coordinator to "uninvite" me to the event. Ultimately, the President relented, allowing the event to proceed as planned. However successful the event turned out, damage to my confidence in the administration to carry out its cultural perpetuation mission and to further support cultural efforts was inflicted. It is difficult to understand the reason for this behavior yet I suspected that the President wished to include individuals she was personally aligned with or that were a part of her family.

In another instance, under a different presidential administration, I was invited to share my cultural knowledge at a college-wide training in replacement of a speaker that had canceled. I was asked to provide a cultural welcoming for returning and new college employees to campus. I had decided that the same traditional protocol for the conference was suitable to welcome new staff and faculty. On the day of the event, I was approached by the new college President, who was also an enrolled member of the CSKT, and asked if I would reconsider my presentation and opt not to share. I explained that following through with a request was a cultural norm that I was raised to understand as good manners. As such, I needed to follow through with the event. The President conceded, and again, the event proceeded as planned. In this case, a member of the board of directors for the college had pressured the President to make this request. The board member held a lower opinion of me and felt that I was not qualified to provide any college-related cultural services.

The expectation and understanding of what collegial is and what it is not at a TCU must be filtered through many lenses. At this TCU, AI comprise 25% of total faculty (SKC, 2019). This small group of AI faculty may share a quasi-unified understanding of a shared academic workspace, yet they vary in terms of socioeconomic and cultural upbringings, which causes divergence on some issues. The divergences can widen when the workspace is shared between many ethnic backgrounds. One of the more distinct areas in which this collegial relationship is tested is interdepartmentally, where faculty and the department head see academic leadership far differently. In these silent power struggles, AI faculty may be undermined by the department head. In functional cases, the administrative branch of the TCU seeks to balance these dysfunctions. However, when AI faculty are faced with pitting their value system against a majority non-AI value system at the departmental and administrative level, the faculty member has little recourse but to silently submit to the administration's requests.

Consequently, I have faced the subtle, passive-aggressive, microaggression that is the product of misunderstanding and a fear of my values. In some instances, I have been physiologically set apart from my colleagues. One example can be seen in my colleagues' bodily reactions to the foods I eat. In a conversation concerning a particular spicy food that both my colleagues and I consumed, a conclusion was made that his adverse reaction and my lack thereof was due to me having "… that Navajo stomach." Some cultures are accustomed to diets that others are not, yet the assumption rests in the misunderstanding that our reactions are likened to differences rather than similarities in our humanness.

Similarly, my practice of certain cultural pursuits is minimized to a primal characterization edging on animalistic behavior, with a lack of refinement or depth. In this case, I was asked of my summer availability for an ancillary academic activity. Before I could respond, my colleague surmised, "Oh right, you will be screaming your lungs out all summer at the powwows." Further, it is no surprise that when good weather is needed for an outdoor event the request is, "You better do a rain dance." Taking these opportunities to correct AI stereotypes is the usual approach; however, upon explaining that our tribes in the northern region of the U.S. do not perform such a dance, the ignorant response on this occasion was, "Oh … , better do a sun dance then."

Understanding that identity is often at the will of the individual there are a number of identity combinations that exist. There are faculty that claim AI

143

status, while lacking understanding of AI cultural morals and norms. There are also some faculty that meet the criteria for federal recognition despite knowing little of their ancestors' lifeways. Still, there are others that have heritage ties to the Native community but lack the criteria for federal recognition.

In many cases, the faculty at the TCU can often partake in the privileges of Whiteness, and also the surficial privileges of Indian-ness. In one instance, I challenged a faculty member's lack of decorum during a meeting. I was pushed back against when this faculty member explained his seemingly problematic behavior by saying: "I am rude!? It must be my American Indian side." The same faculty member, who is not a member of a federally recognized tribe, yet identifies openly as an AI, made a reference to various modes of communication as being "smoke signals." This faculty member has said to students, "I don't care how you get it to the instructor; email, write it down, send smoke signals ... I don't care." He also stated once in a faculty meeting, "They [students] can get a hold of us using many different ways; email, phone, text, or smoke signals."

The endurance of AI faculty and students in the face of these and undoubtedly other numerous examples of ignorance is a testament to the fortitude and resilience of the traditionally minded psyche. While at first it might seem unimaginable that at a TCU there would be prejudices, stereotypes, and outright racism directed toward AI there is space that is accommodated for and that persists. Admittedly, my own naivete about my fellow tribal peers has led to feelings of disappointment and defeatism. Yet, my passion to unify AI cultural values and belief keeps me in this space and strengthens my passion to be an agent of change. Driving this passion is also the acknowledgment that the "entirety" of the TCU reality is not characterized by these negative experiences. Some of the greatest inspiration and collegiality that I have received have come from my peers. I can also attribute much of my educational success to the support of the TCU and the academic freedom it offers.

ACTIONABLE STRATEGIES

Nation Building Approach to TCUs

Over the past 50 years, Native Nations have been breaking away from the cultural stereotypes assumed today by mainstream society. This change has been possible because of the development and revision of governmental and educational methods, transitioning toward self-determination and upholding tribal sovereignty (Cornell & Kalt, 2007). Culture is an immense piece of this changing climate, where success can be found by separating from the standard approach of operation (Boyer, 1995). This approach is described as a remnant of the boilerplate templates for policy changes of Indian affairs initiated by the federal government (Canby, 2004). The standard approach is summarized as follows: "Decision making is short term and nonstrategic; someone else sets the development agenda;

development is treated as primarily an economic problem; Indigenous culture is viewed as an obstacle to development; elected leadership serves primarily as a distributor of resources" (Cornell & Kalt, 2007, p. 8). After a history of assimilative U.S. Bureau of Indian Affairs policies, adjustments should be made to move toward a culturally relevant process. One suggestion is to use the Nation-building approach conceptualized by the University of Arizona's Native Nations Institute. This approach applies to a variety of tribal organizations, as a tool for success, while reclaiming tribal values (Cornell & Kalt, 2007).

The Nation-building approach is described as one that is "invented by Native nations" (Cornell and Kalt, 2007, p. 6). These changes are intended to focus on unique characteristics, such as cultural preservation. Applying the Nation-building approach to the Westernized system of higher education in TCUs can support the practice of culturally relevant pedagogies. This may allow TCUs to acknowledge their cultural significance and model what is expressed in their current missions and visions. The approach has a general set of principles that may apply to TCUs (Cornell & Kalt, 2007, p. 29).

Principle 1: Cultural Change Agents

Asserting decision-making power to cultural changing agents to build capable governance reflecting tribal value systems and incorporate culturally relevant ideas within the TCU is an important step to reducing RBF for AI faculty. Cultural change agents can be viewed as leaders in a nation's community. These agents are not always apparent and imposter agents who are self-serving or do not work toward positive change can be difficult to identify. True leaders of positive cultural change are not always degree holders or professional administrators within the tribe, but they are people who understand and practice tribal values. However, it is not uncommon for a person of this background to have a degree and be an AI faculty member. The advantage of TCUs within tribal nations is the accessibility to people with strong cultural backgrounds and knowledge, regardless of their educational and career achievements (Boyer, 1990; Grob, 2009). Heavily integrating cultural change agents would reinforce mission statements that include language, such as an intention to primarily serve AI students, and address their unique, cultural needs in higher education. For the AI professoriate, the idea of maintaining a continuous cultural change agent into all, or most, organizational decisions would support underlying issues that directly lead to RBF, which is generally a misunderstanding and lack of acknowledgment of cultural lifeways.

There is an expectation in today's American system of education to meet Western standards, or the standard approach, to higher education under the purview of fostering equal opportunity to support TCU stakeholders (Stein, 1992). After nearly 50 years of supporting AI students, TCUs are at flourishing levels of opportunity and stand at a crossroads to revise institutional governance.

Specifically, the governing process of TCUs would benefit most from a departure from the standard approach to higher education. Incorporating tribal value systems into all decision-making processes and mandating these values would serve a multifaceted purpose. Not only could this show support to the AI professoriate, it assists non-Native faculty in gaining a better understanding of the unique mission and vision of TCUs and shows action with implementation of traditional tribal governance. It is replacing the standard approach by creating a nation building inventive design for higher education.

Principle 2: Cultural Values for Strategic Orientation, Objectives, and Policies

Establishing a strategic orientation with objectives and policies to include cultural values within all levels of the TCU organization would provide a working environment that fosters growth for AI faculty and their cultural orientation. Providing a strategic orientation, with long-term foresight, can include culturally relevant objectives regarding the working environment. Like many universities and colleges, TCUs are not exempt from heavy dependence on temporary grant funding. In this sense, many decisions and planning are dependent on outside decision-makers, where goals and long-term vision are pushed to the curb. Stating cultural intentions within a mission statement is not enough to ensure commitment of the college to the AI faculty and student cohort. Actions are required and they must be consistent with stated intentions. Strategic orientation and culturally relevant objectives for annual programming is necessary to validate this language. Resolutely leading this process results in an emphasis on transparency and lends to fertility of cultural efforts at TCUs; it becomes more than words on a website.

Policies are a catalyst for shaping the structure of an organization. Policies will not support cultural congruence if TCUs are deliberately reflecting mainstream institutions and the "one size fits all" Western education model (Jorgensen, 2007). Western models for governing purposes do not factor in cultural values that are necessary for AI organizations. The replica of mainstream society's model of higher education applied to AI institutions will exhibit remnants of the assimilative purpose from past eras. Modern beliefs regarding Indian Education should specifically support, not seek to eradicate, the unique cultural heritage and histories of AI people. By clearly defining and utilizing culture as a method of implementation, TCUs can invent a culturally congruent set of policies that repurpose tribal philosophies, to guide action for higher education.

Principle 3: Diversity Training

Direct programming and project examples aimed at preventing or minimizing RBF for the AI professoriate could include mandatory diversity training. It would be an ethnocentric view to assume diversity training is irrelevant at minority-serving institutions because employees have sought a position within a TCU, with preexisting knowledge of diversity. But this would negate the phenomenon of RBF occurring at this type of institution and therefore deny these perspectives and personal experiences. Developing training aimed at addressing diversity within Indian Country as well as between ethnic groups can educate faculty, staff, and administrators, thereby debunking the assumption that minority-serving organizations lack racial prejudices. Education is one of the best practices to reducing prejudices.

Principle 4: Cultural Values as Foundations for Projects and Programs

Development of projects and program structures are critical to successful objectives being obtained. The TCU professoriate consistently seeks projects and program improvements. The driving force behind these projects should be to address the unique cultural aspects of AI students. A direct effect of prioritizing cultural value systems into all projects and programming will show commitment to visions and assist upholding Indian Education integrity. The AI professoriate, armed with cultural value integration experience, can use this to supplement the idea of multiculturalism, syncretism, and tolerance within modern Indian Education efforts. For career pursuits, the AI professoriate, within such a TCU, will have added diversity experience to their vitae and if choosing to explore mainstream university academia, will bring their unique professional experiences. The goal of strengthening the TCU in all aspects of programming and projects is at the forefront of most academic interests. Validating hypotheses regarding AI educational needs will create a supportive environment for the professoriate.

Implementing the chosen culturally relevant projects and structures is the final step in modeling the invented TCU nation-building approach to support the AI professoriate and overall vision. An individual experience of creating successful faculty groups that understand each other and the commitment toward cultural values is directly affected. Overarching support on all fronts and implementation will show the success of these processes and will in turn support any cultural idealism existent within the faculty cohort. It will exhibit tribal values to non-Native faculty and model how fostering them can lead to collegiality and extend into all arenas of TCUs.

Principle 5: Partnering with Tribal Governments to Campaign Cultural Values

Another project idea is for TCUs to work directly with tribal government systems to support a nationwide campaign on revitalization of tribal cultural values.

Values can be viewed as possessing varying degree of importance in today's society. Many AI people question their own tribal values and ties to their tribe as a defense mechanism to the historical trauma caused from the past. In some tribes, socioeconomic effects are daunting and flood the social work systems. Indian Country strives to support tribal sovereignty in revamping nation-building in this way. Partnering TCUs, professoriate, and Tribal Governments to address current issues within Indian Country to develop projects to revitalize cultural values could reinforce ideas from the 1970s, when TCUs were first established, to cause a second wave of cultural resurgence inundating the TCUs and their communities to unify tribal cultural values.

REFERENCES

Boyer, P. (1990). Building a tribal college: Six criteria for a college of quality. *Tribal College: Journal of American Indian Higher Education*, *2*(1), 13–17. Retrieved from https://tribalcollegejournal.org/building-tribal-college-criteria-college-quality/

Boyer, P. (1995). Tomorrow's Tribal College will redefine the culture of its tribe, and help shape national policy. *Tribal College*, *7*(1), 8–13.

Canby, W. C. (2004). *American Indian law in a Nutshell*. St. Paul, MN: West.

Cleary, L. M., & Peacock, T. D. (1998). *Collected wisdom: American Indian education*. Needham Heights, MA: Allyn & Bacon.

Cornell, S., & Kalt J. P. (2007). Two approaches to economic development on American Indian reservations: One works, the other doesn't. In M. Jorgensen (Ed.), *Rebuilding native nations: Strategies for governance and development* (pp. 3–33). Tucson, AZ: University of Arizona Press.

Deyhle, D., & Swisher, K. (1997). Research in American Indian and Alaska native education: From assimilation to self-determination. *Review of Research in Education*, *22*(1), 113–194.

Grob, A. (2009, November). Educational empowerment of native American students: A tribally controlled college leads the way. In M. B. Spencer (Ed.), *Images, imaginations, and beyond: Proceedings of the eighth native American symposium* (pp. 9–24). Southeastern Oklahoma State University. Retrieved from http://www.se.edu/nas/files/2013/03/NAS-2009-Proceedings-Introductory.pdf

Jorgensen, M. (Ed.). (2007). *Rebuilding native nations: Strategies for governance and development*. Tuscan, AZ: University of Arizona Press.

Lowe, S. C. (2005). This is who I am: Experiences of native American students. *New Directions for Student Services*, *2005*(109), 33–40.

Pavel, D. M., Inglebret, E., & Banks, S. R. (2001). Tribal colleges and universities in an era of dynamic development. *Peabody Journal of Education*, *76*(1), 50–72.

Salish Kootenai College. (2019). *Salish Kootenai College fact book*. Pablo, MT: SKC Office of Institutional Effectiveness.

Stein, W. J. (1992). *Tribally controlled colleges: Making good medicine*. New York: Peter Lang Publishing.

Stein, W. J. (2009). Tribal colleges and universities: Supporting the revitalization in Indian country. In L. S. Warner & G. E. Gipp (Eds.), *Tradition and culture in the millennium: Tribal colleges and universities* (pp. 17–34). Charlotte, NC: Information Age Publishing.

Chapter 12

Research and Resistance

Reasons for Indigenous Research
Methodologies

Dawn Quigley

INTRODUCTION

It all begins and ends with story.

(Kovach, 2009)

And so, here is mine.

Aaniin. Dawn Quigley nindizhinikaaz. Mikinaakwajiwing nindonjibaa. (Gloss: *Greetings, hello. My name is Dawn Quigley*).[1] I am from the Turtle Mountain Band of Ojibwe. As a Native person, I was taught to always share my name and who my people and land are, so this is why I begin my story this way. Dawn, my name, was given to me by my mother after she heard a relative share possible names for her next child. Mom loved the sound of that name and decided to also give it to me. Twenty-four years later, when I was working at a school in Minneapolis, Minnesota, an Ojibwe elder, Jim Clark, from the Mille Lacs reservation, said that he would call me Waaban (Gloss: *It is dawn / morning*) (*The Ojibwe People's Dictionary*, 2015). My Native American lineage comes from my mother's family and originates from the Pembina Band. I was raised by both my parents, a Native mother, and a father of Norwegian descent. Metaphorically, we had both fry bread and lefsa on our dinner table, and just as many varying points of view during discussions. I claim both of these heritages—Native and Norwegian—but identify closer with my Native side as these are the relatives with and places where I spent most of my childhood.

Research and resistance seemed to surround me. I was born in Madison, Wisconsin, in 1970, a few months before and a few steps away from the campus bombing, a protest against the University's research links to the U.S. military during the War in Vietnam (Vietnam and Opposition at Home, n.d.). The decade of the 1970s when I was born was also when the American Indian Movement (AIM), a Native rights and activist group, was formed in Minneapolis to transform policies and demand that the United States' government uphold and honor treaties and promises to support the self-determination of Native people (AIM Interpretive Center, n.d.). It was in my formative years when I realized I was an introverted activist. This method of resistance—introverted activism—was passed onto me from my mother who was quiet. When she and I watched the popular "John Wayne" cowboy movies of the time, she would cheer and root loudly for the Indians (who we knew would never win, but we yelled at the TV anyway). I was seven or eight years old before I realized *everyone* did not cheer for those TV Indians.

> I was excited to start my first research project! It was a great opportunity. Until it wasn't.

I began my Ph.D. program a few years ago. One of my main goals was to understand the research process: How do you interpret data? How does one set up and conduct research? How can a Native person learn to conduct research? These were the questions I hoped to answer in the program, so, during myinitialsemester when I was offered my first chance at being on a research team at the University of Minnesota, I was thrilled and nervous at the same time. Thrilled to begin unmasking the cloud of research elements; nervous to dive into something I didn't have any understanding of (with no research methods courses under my belt yet).

The focus of our research team (consisting of me and one other Ph.D. student) was how, or if, Minnesota teacher preparation programs were being successful in bringing in and graduating diverse teacher candidates. Multiple other universities and colleges were invited to join the project. This topic was right up my alley since I'm a Native woman who could share my own path to getting a teaching degree. However, as the project progressed, to me, it seemed as if no one actually wanted to *hear* my story. I found out later that I was asked to be on this project solely for the "diverse" appearance I would bring, as up until this point only white women had worked on the project. Thus, they apparently needed me as a "diverse" person. But it wasn't my voice or story the team wanted, it was the outward appearance of having a brown researcher on the team. I ended up having to tap into my Native community members to finish the project, as somehow along the way, the other MN teacher licensure programs (higher education institutions) changed their willingness to participate. They also decided not to allow their interviews to be used in the final conference presentation (here is where I first learned that some white scholars categorize themselves and others into "less evolved or more evolved anti-racist advocates"). They were fighting among themselves, and I was in the middle just trying to complete the project … to earn money … to pay my Ph.D. tuition … to learn how to become a Native scholar.

Throughout this project I ended up feeling like little more than a worker-body: I had to call my (white, Ph.D. student) colleague at a certain time to check in (it was always me having to call, not an equal back and forth), conducted 11 of the 12 interviews on my own (no help with this even though I was "co-PI"), wrote the interviews up, drafted the conference proposal, and finally, was accused by my co-PI of "sharing the findings with a 'rival' institution" before the final presentation of the findings. Soon after, my colleague apologized for this false allegation, but the damage was done. During this time my health started to decline in small ways: inability to sleep, developing high blood pressure and having to go on medication, fatigue working full and part-time jobs to pay for tuition, and mental doubts about my ability to continue the program.

In all of this, my most painful regret is that I had to tap into my Native community—relationships which have developed over decades—to finish this study since the other (mostly white) participants all dropped out. Yet, when it came down to responding to my questions, these Indian people came to my help to support me in my research. My Native friends, elders, and other Indian people in higher education allowed me to interview them, which ultimately filled the void of the participants who pulled out. However, I felt that *I* just contributed to the problem with Natives being the most researched people in the world (Smith, 2012).

This situation (i.e., culminating when I was accused of a breach of ethics) has been the only time I've cried in this program. I downright sobbed at being caught in the middle of a system which claimed to want to help diverse people yet was marginalizing and silencing me at the same time. Now I wonder if I was being led, by the Creator or universe, to use these tears to water a new field of agentic research methods; to use my weeping to weave a path to find safety and familiarity in Indigenous Methodologies (IM). During this time someone suggested I read Linda T. Smith's (2012) book *Decolonizing Methodologies*. Smith's (2012) book and ideas lit a spark in me and fanned the flaming desire to learn how to study in such a manner which honors and matches both my Native self and ways of knowing.

I didn't know how much I needed this book. Until I did.

SETTING UP METHODOLOGICAL UNDERSTANDINGS

It was this experience, an awakening of becoming a Native American researcher, which led me to take up research methods that deeply embody our indigenous epistemologies.

In my emerging understanding of Indigenous Methodologies, I have found a place to belong, a place to actively resist colonizing power structures, and a place to define a boundary in research. This chapter traces how I've tried to make sense of this paradigm. For this chapter, and my own research, I will situate my methodological focus within the Indigenous Research Methodologies (Chilisa, 2012; Kovach, 2009). Other terms used to describe this paradigm are Decolonizing Methodologies (Smith, 2012), Red Pedagogy, TribalCrit, along with others (Brayboy, 2006;

Grande, 2004). In order to better understand these terms, I will sort their genealogies as a way to show distinctions and connections threaded between them.

Smith, a Maori researcher, scholar, and activist, stated that at the time the first edition came out the term "'indigenous' was also a contentious and 'dirty' term in some contexts ... where in many countries indigenous is not a term that can be safely used" (p. xi) as it may be conflated with savagery or rebellion. Therefore, Smith (2012) chose not to use the "decolonizing" in the usual manner (which can be frozen in a definition of violence and corrupt elites), but rather to use it as a way of setting it inside an intellectual and transformative mission. Smith created the phrase and book title *Decolonizing Methodologies* (1999, p. xii) as a radically compassionate way to rethink and revolutionize the roles of knowledge, knowledge hierarchies, knowledge production, and how institutions of knowledge play into decolonizing and social transformation. The research paradigm continues to promote and support indigenous communities and their own unique challenges.

Smith's (2012) work inspired other shifts in indigenous research and knowledge. One term to emerge was *Indigenous Methodologies* (Chilisa, 2012; Denzin, Lincoln, & Smith, 2008; Kovach, 2009; Smith, 2005) which emphasizes the localized context of indigenous communities (i.e., *indigenous* is not to be understood as a pan-global group of people, but separate and distinctive communities). These unique indigenous populations must use their own epistemologies in researching and emancipating from the colonizers' point of view and marginalization (Chilisa, 2012; Kincheloe & Steinberg, 2008). For example, Maori researchers may focus on Whakapapa, or a specific worldview situated in their local place, language, time, political structures, and struggles while a First Nations Cree community would set research in a Nēhiyaw, or Cree, epistemology (Kovach, 2009). Linda Smith (2012) also asserts this need for site-specific indigenous research as each setting contains unique communities and needs.

Indigenous scholars continue to produce research frames such as Grande's (2004) *Red Pedagogy* which concentrates healing and restorative projects sustaining indigenous languages, cultural knowledge, and intellectual history. Like most indigenous scholars, Grande (2004) calls for a move from solely using critical pedagogy, to one which envisions ways to reimagine indigenous praxis. In this chapter I will expand on more indigenous research in both the Indigenous Methodologies and Indigenous Epistemology sections. To vary the wording, I will use all these terms interchangeably in this chapter.

Indigenous

For this chapter I will use my own current location of Minnesota, the United States, to position the site in the context of North America, and therefore will use the terms indigenous, Native, and Native Americans interchangeably. The term indigenous recognizes the stories, concerns, and struggles of globally colonized communities (Smith, 2012). Yet at the same time, the term does not allude to an essentializing of these diverse groups (Denzin, Lincoln, & Smith, 2008, p. 136). The term colonization can be understood as "European American thought, knowledge, and power structures [that] dominate present-day society in the United States" (Brayboy, 2005, p. 430).

INDIGENOUS EPISTEMOLOGIES

To appreciate why a scholar might set their work in an indigenous research framework, one needs to understand seeing epistemologies through a Native lens. Indigenous epistemologies and locations of knowledge greatly inform the decolonizing research framework and call for methods which mirror specific ways of knowing by a Native community and/or a Native researcher. Scholars of color and indigenous researchers continue to formulate and revise epistemologies which speak to their lived experiences and truths of existences. These ways of knowing must be "understood, respected and discussed just as ... [ones] produced by the dominant race are understood, respected and discussed" (Scheurich & Young, 1997, p. 11).

Decolonizing epistemology defines indigenous knowledge, locates where it originates, and who it encompasses (Chilisa, 2012; Kovach, 2009) all while being found in agency and relationships (Brayboy & Maughan, 2009; Martin, 2017; Richardson, 2000; Suina, 2017). Put another way, Indigenous Methodologies include a connection or relationship between knowledge and nature, Native scholar and the academy, knowledge and the Native community, researcher and Native communities, and/or between Native researcher and the dominant society. Due to indigenous epistemologies being a foundational component of IM, place matters (Richardson, 2000; Suina, 2017). In other words, regional context matters when implementing IM as an effort to move away from an essentialized conception of Native people. However, educational settings were, and still are, the site of Native people's assimilation and attempted decimation and therefore, must begin to be the site of indigenous self-determination and trauma healing (Grande, 2004; Kovach, 2009; McInnes, 2016; Richardson, 2012; Suina, 2017), beginning with acceptance of IM. Smith (2012, p. 214) says it best when she states, "there can be no ... social justice without ... cognitive justice."

Ways of knowing are central to indigenous epistemologies, and care must be given to honor and understand the difference between sacred knowledge given, and knowledge which has been given through a fully respectful and transparent protocol (Suina, 2017).

In decolonizing methodologies, there may be inner and outer locations of knowledge production, with a holistic and interactive connection between the two. Using multiple forms of indigenous knowledge, outside the usual Western literature, such as data gathering and analysis methods, is a way to decolonize the designation of knowledge and the West's fragmentation of body and mind (Chilisa, 2012; Kovach, 2009; Richardson, 2000; Smith, 2012; Suina, 2017). The outer way of knowing is based on a relational aspect to the ecological and human world such as learning from an elder, from a traditional story or song (Brayboy, 2006; Richardson, 2000; Suina, 2017), from insight in the natural world, from learning an indigenous language as culture is learned through it (Evans, 2009; Harrison, 2007), from a cultural artifact, or from interactive observations (Chilisa, 2012; Kovach, 2009; Smith, 2012). Inner ways of knowing can come from insight gained from a dream (and what one does with it) (Richardson, 2000), from intuition, or from a vision (Kovach, 2009; Smith, 2012).

INDIGENOUS METHODOLOGIES

Methodologies are the site where "ideology and epistemology meet research approach, design, methods and implementation ... of a study" (Ravitch & Carl, 2016, p. 6). In research, Methodologies (i.e., big M Methods as opposed to small m methods/techniques/procedures) are ways of doing research processes and approaches (Bloomberg & Volpe, 2016; Hermes, 1998; Miles et al., 2014; Smith, 2012). Methodology is a theoretical stance that guides research approaches, compared to the methods of gathering and interpreting data.

Indigenous Methodologies are a way to resist the educational research academy's use of hegemonic systems of knowledge and power (Kovach, 2009; Smith, 2012) which have primarily conducted research *on* Native American people as opposed to *with* Native communities. Also, much of the Western research focuses on both an exploitation of Native communities ((Chilisa, 2012; Hermes, 1998; Kovach, 2009; Smith, 2012; Suina, 2017) along with deficit views of indigenous peoples perpetuating centuries of colonial power (Martin, 2017; Richardson, 2012; Scheurich & Young, 1997; Suina, 2017).

Indigenous Methodologies offer a framework for research which privileges indigenous ontologies and epistemologies, but it is not a codified way of inquiry. Instead, Indigenous Methodologies seek to share knowledge by implementing overarching questions such as Smith (2012) does by asking:

Whose research is it? Who owns it? Whose interest does it serve? Who will benefit from it? Who has designed its question and framed its scope? Who will carry it out? Who will write it up? How will its results be disseminated?

(p. 10)

This paradigm, which I will place within a qualitative frame, can be implemented through such means as indigenous communities participatory action research along with Native scholars learning how to conduct Indigenous Methodologies in higher education and/or specialized indigenous research centers (Smith, 2012). Decolonizing research seeks to root out epistemic racism (Scheurich & Young,

1997) and allows each Native community to advance self-determination, resistance, and transformation (Brayboy, 2006; Smith, 2012) and to also integrate indigenous cultural knowledge into methodology (Kovach, 2009; Martin, 2017).

Indigenous Methodologies Situated in a Qualitative Framework

Qualitative research can be understood as a set of tools and techniques used to study and find ways of understanding a set of questions while implementing theory, evidence (i.e., data), and analysis (Kovach, 2009). It is also a paradigm which seeks to investigate the essence of a topic (Bloomberg & Volpe, 2016) in an exploratory, naturalistic, contextual, constructivist, and interpretive way (Kumar, 2014; Ravitch & Carl, 2016).

Because Indigenous Methodologies are an interpretive inquiry lens, some indigenous scholars have situated their work within a qualitative research frame as a way to intersect two paradigms which are complementary (Bishop, Berryman, Wearmouth, Peter, & Clapham, 2012; Brayboy and Maughan, 2009; Kovach, 2009, Martin, 2017 and others). Setting an Indigenous Methodologies study within a qualitative approach is acknowledging that research techniques gathered from Western methodologies can be implemented in ways which respect indigenous cultural traditions and ways of knowing (Brayboy, 2006; Chilisa, 2012; Kovach, 2009; Smith, 2012). However, Indigenous Methodologies are unique and distinct from Western qualitative frameworks as it seeks to reject commodifying, classifying, exploiting, and employing disrespectful practices to Native people and communities (Kovach, 2009; Smith, 2012). Indigenous Methodologies and the qualitative paradigm both contain elements of relationship and reciprocity with and between participants in addition to both frameworks needing to include "evidence of process and content" (Kovach, 2009, p. 32). Yet Indigenous Methodologies privileges indigenous ontologies and epistemologies and are upheld not as binary philosophies, but as a holistic way to approach research as a way toward self-determination and sovereignty (Richardson, 2000). Using a decolonizing framework has a goal of hope, but it also must be action oriented as a way to transform, for better, indigenous peoples' lives (Brayboy, 2006; Kovach, 2009; Smith, 2012).

By using Indigenous Methodologies, indigenous scholars can continue telling the narrative of how their work seeks to heal and support the sovereignty of our Native stories, land, and communities.

SITUATING INDIGENOUS METHODOLOGIES IN HIGHER EDUCATION

In creating an Indigenous Methodologies research framework, questions must be asked: *Why should Indigenous Methodologies be situated in colleges and universities?*

How do other Indigenous researcher practices inform my experience as a Native American researcher? How do indigenous researchers negotiate the academy? As I shared in my own story, at the beginning of this chapter, many Native emerging and early career researchers speak of getting hurt, burned, and "being done over" in studies (Smith, 2012, p. 11). Higher Education, or the Academy, maintains control over who has the power to define knowledge, gain access to it, and has the right to create it (Mihesuah & Wilson, 2004). Equity and diversity in research cannot simply be equated to racial equality. As stated before, research is one of the worst words in many Native communities (Smith, 2012), and therefore, it needs to be disrupted in an attempt to include other critical epistemologies and frameworks.

Every college and university in the United States sits on stolen Native land. The Academy must acknowledge this historical fact by supporting indigenous research frameworks as a way of decolonizing a site of modern-day knowledge gatekeepers (Mihesuah & Wilson, 2004). I was sitting at a conference, in a campus hotel, which sits on indigenous land, when I experienced what Indigenous scholars explained as silencing subjugated people as "Western societies reject the need to listen to marginalized people and take their knowledge seriously" (Kincheloe & Steinberg, 2008, p. 145). I include my story below, from my journal, to explain the attempts higher education makes to silence Indigenous people and why I will use Indigenous Methodologies in all of my future studies:

Dawn's Journal Entry—Fall 2015

Life imitating art, or my experience imitating the actual nexus of the problem of being Native in higher education. The conference was focused on: How do we diversify the teaching force? During this conference I found out, from others at my table, how they understood this issue.

She talked, and allocated all of the oxygen to three people: Her, herself, and she. When asked: "How do we diversify the profession of teaching?" she began a soliloquy that could have fanned the Nina, Pinta, and Santa Maria, with enough air left over to fuel the Hindenburg. Yet, in all seriousness, when I tried to interject (while she took a pause to breathe), as a Native person who *desperately* wants to seek out and welcome a diverse teaching force, I only got as far as, "Well, I think ..." *She/herself/her* cut me off continually (along with the other colleagues of color at the table) for the duration of the 30-minute session. Self-identified as a "six-foot tall Norwegian," she began talking about "in college she had an Indian roommate whom she interrogated to learn more about her Indianness." Yet the Native student walked away from her and closed the door saying, "You are being very rude."

I thought, now *that* was one smart Native woman.

But the irony was lost on She-Who-Does-Not-Stop-Talking: The White-policy-maker continued to "find the answers" for the diversity issue, yet she would not *listen to the questions* from an Indigenous person to begin with. It's like the doctor trying to diagnose the ailment, yet never giving the patient a chance to articulate the symptoms.

While *She/herself/her* tried to silence me during the power of policy debates and conversation, at lunch she finally turned and acknowledged me, asking, "So Dawn, are you from one of the MN Indian tribes?"

And I answered softly, looking down at my lunch plate, "No."

See, I responded not to her superficial query of: *Can you tell me of your tribal affiliation?* I answered "no" to her *intended* inferential question, which was: *Can I treat you as a curiosity, and not as one who has knowledge worth knowing?*

It was to this question that I said "no."

She did not want to hear my physical voice, as someone with a lived-experience of being a diverse person in education and higher education, someone who may just have strategies to *"Broaden the Diversity of Our Teaching Force."* I wanted to ask her, "If you were not ready to listen to my *physical* voice, *how* can you be ready to listen to our (collective diverse groups) voice of how to solve the problem?"

Freire (1993) stated that the person who claims devotion to a cause of social promotion, yet is not able to "enter into *communion* with the people, who he or she continues to regard as totally ignorant, is grievously self-deceived" (p. 61). Freire (1993) was able to articulate exactly what I was feeling in my journal story. This woman was an example of the "banking model" of knowing and teaching—a white person was filling me with her perceived knowledge. There was no room for using the "problem-posing" education model in order to create together what Freire (1993) identified as an "emergence of consciousness" (p. 81). According to James (2004), my experience is an example of how Natives in the academy find themselves in the "outsider" group along with being at the bottom of academia's hierarchical standing. Yet, in claiming my right of refusing to be used as a "curiosity" (Garroutte, 2003), or my ways of knowing not worthy, I am learning to navigate higher education. The number of Native American students who have earned doctoral degrees has remained consistently low—102 doctorates in 2012 (Patel, 2014); there simply are not enough of us in higher education. Native people make up 1.2% of the U.S. population, but in 2012 only earned 0.3% of doctorate degrees awarded (NCSES Survey of Earned Doctorates.) Therefore, we must all support, encourage, and mentor indigenous scholars (National Center for Education Statistics, American Institutes for Research, U.S. Department of Education, & Institute of Educational Science, 2017). According to Alfred (2004), as Indigenous scholars negotiate the academy, we have a responsibility to do "what we can where we can" (p. 88) as a way to guarantee the survival of our history, language, culture, and nations.

ACTIONABLE STRATEGIES

By incorporating Indigenous Methodologies in a study, Indigenous researchers can promote the interdisciplinary Native history, language, and culture to influence the education landscape in offering a new, transformative method of conducting research. Due to the low number of Native Americans in Ph.D. programs in higher education, the Academy must support and help to grow Natives in doctoral programs. In doing so, indigenous scholars foster a way for Indian people to take back control of the educational system which historically (and currently), abuses and marginalizes them beginning with the Indian Boarding School era up through today's inclusion of biased curriculum. How we frame story is critical, as it structures how our indigenous story is acknowledged, and ultimately how the story constructs the way we recognize the world (Langdon, 2009). It is a way to reclaim sovereignty (Smith, 2012) and to retell our story. As Native American researcher Kovach (2009) states, "our story is who we are" (p. 4) and we must inform the world of academia that an indigenous person's culture is critical to how we approach research.

Stories. It's always been about stories in my family. Hearing my grandfather's great booming voice telling tales is one of my earliest memories. When moushoom (Gloss: *Grandpa*) told stories, he used his hands with wild gestures and turned his voice into a great bird which we all followed to see where it landed. Some may not consider this art, or poetry, but to me I could see the birds soar as he spoke, emphasizing his words in Michif, the native language of the Turtle Mountain Ojibwe tribe. With rapt attention I could hear his voice, distressed at times, as he wrapped humor around his stories of growing up; other times, his voice held sadness edged with irony as he told us of being in the war and having to eat food made with rancid flour, flecked with bugs ("Extra protein!" he laughed).

Yet, as I aged, I began to ask my elders for more stories. A recurring theme emerged: The absolute sense of their voices and leadership being stripped with each generation further engrained in the assimilation techniques of the Native American boarding schools they attended. No voice in what they learned, no voice in being taken from their families, no voice in what, or when, they could eat, and of course, no voice in how they could read, learn, or pass on their Native culture, language, and history. In this, there were no dialogics (Freire, 1993) and no multiple perspectives were asked of them. There was a deafening "culture of silence" (Freire, 1993, p. 30) echoing in my family's' background story.

In my Native culture, it is the duty of Native adults to role model to our younger generations in speaking up when we detect negative views and misinformation being perpetuated. I believed that when I grew older I, too, could stand up to tell our own stories, and not step back to allow others to tell our stories for us. I hoped that I would be able to lead and honor all of my relatives who went before me; giving back and amplifying the voice which was taken from them.

Fulfilling this role, the role of continuing my grandfather's storytelling, I will study and support Indigenous Methodologies as a way to share research and stories which show how resilient and strong indigenous people have been, are, and will continue to be in the future.

To be an Indigenous scholar, we must be "warriors of truth" (Alfred, 2004) as we stay the course in our personal lives, but also in our research methods by engaging in educational activism through transformative praxis (Mihesuah & Wilson, 2004). We must resist the hegemonic structures of higher education where whispers of you *do not fit* echo the halls of universities (see Thompson, 2004). Yet, I say, we *do fit*. We *do belong* to this land and do not need invitations to the ground where our ancestors walked. Institutions of Higher Education are our inheritance and we who are indigenous researchers can do more from inside its walls than from outside as we work to join our Native ontologies to our academic training (Justice, 2004) as a way to serve Native communities. Inside academia, we can amplify our indigenous research agendas to increase the healing and voices of our people through implementing research methodologies which honor our ways of knowing (Kovach, 2009; Mihesuah & Wilson, 2004; Smith, 2012).

Some may ask "What can higher education leaders do?" Many times, Natives in the academy are the sole Indigenous person, thereby creating isolation. So, yes, hiring more Native academics would be a solution, yet, truly, the love and interest in becoming a scholar begins in K–12. If colleges of education head this and transform the teacher preparation programs to have culturally competent (white) teachers, young Native students might think about continuing on to earn a college degree, and beyond (Patel, 2014).

In addition to laying the foundation in K–12 schooling for Native Americans, Institutions of Higher Education must: recognize and prevent over-taxing emotional and cognitive labor of diverse faculty (e.g., asked to represent the diverse voice on multiple university committees) (Stevens & Dworkin, 2014). Also, the definition of "service" must be expanded to include Native American scholars' work and research in their own communities (i.e., away from campus) (Mihesuah & Wilson, 2004).

From the words of two Ojibwe language revivalists, Obizaan and Chato, Natives in the Academy can fight the colonial system by using these own weapons of research methods against them (personal communication, course discussion, October 18, 2017). In this way, research can be an attempt toward transformative action via self-determination and sovereignty of indigenous rights, stories, histories, healing, and knowledge.

NOTE

1 I, like many other Native writers, do not italicize our Indigenous words/language, since usually foreign words are italicized. Native American words are the first words on our land here. And so, I add the English word after and italicize it since English is actually the foreign language in the United States.

REFERENCES

AIM Interpretive Center. (n.d.). Retrieved from http://www.aim-ic.org/

Alfred, T. (2004). Warrior scholarship: Seeing the university as a ground of contention. In D. A. Mihesuah & A. C. Wilson (Eds.), *Indigenizing the academy: Transforming scholarship and empowering communities* (pp. 88–99). Lincoln, NE: University of Nebraska Press.

Bishop, R., Berryman, M., Wearmouth, J., Peter, M., & Clapham, S. (2012). Professional development, changes in teacher practice and improvements in Indigenous students' educational performance: A case study from New Zealand. *Teaching and Teacher Education, 28*(5), 694–705. doi:10.1016/j.tate.2012.02.002

Bloomberg, L. D., & Volpe, M. (2016). *Completing your qualitative dissertation: A road map from beginning to end* (3rd ed.). Thousand Oaks, CA: Sage Publications.

Brayboy, BM. J. (2005). Transformational resistance and social justice. *Anthropology & Education Quarterly, 36*(3), 193–211. doi:10.1525/aeq.2005.36.3.193

Brayboy, B. M. J. (2006). Toward a tribal critical race theory in education. *The Urban Review, 37*(5), 425–446. doi:10.1007/s11256-005-0018-y

Brayboy, B., & Maughan, E. (2009). Indigenous knowledges and the story of the bean. *Harvard Educational Review, 79*(1), 1–21. doi:10.1007/s13398-014-0173-7.2

Chilisa, B. (2012) *Indigenous research methodologies*. Thousand Oaks, CA: Sage Publications.

Denzin, N., Lincoln, Y., & Smith, L. (2008). *Handbook of critical and indigenous methodologies*. Los Angeles, CA: Sage Publications. doi:10.4135/9781483385686

Evans, N. (2009). *Dying words: Endangered languages and what they have to tell us*. Oxford, UK: Wiley-Blackwell. doi:10.1002/9781444310450

Freire, P. (1993). *Pedagogy of the oppressed*. New York: Continuum.

Garroutte, E. M. (2003). *Real Indians: Identity and the survival of native America*. Berkeley, CA: University of California Press.

Grande, S. (2004). *Red pedagogy: Native American social and political thought*. Lanham, MD: Rowman & Littlefield Publishers.

Harrison, KD. (2007). *When languages die: The extinction of the world's languages and the erosion of human knowledge*. New York: Oxford University Press.

Hermes, M. (1998). Research methods as a situated response: Towards a first nations' methodology. *International Journal of Qualitative Studies in Education, 11*(1), 155–168. doi:10.1080/095183998236944

161

James, K. (2004). Corrupt State University: The organizational psychology of native experience in higher education. In D. A. Mihesuah & A. C. Wilson (Eds.), *Indigenizing the academy: Transforming scholarship and empowering communities* (pp. 48–68). Lincoln, NE: University of Nebraska Press.

Justice, DH. (2004). Seeing (and reading) red: Indian outlaws in the Ivory Tower. In D. A. Mihesuah & A. C. Wilson (Eds.), *Indigenizing the academy: Transforming scholarship and empowering communities*. Lincoln, NE: University of Nebraska Press.

Kincheloe, J., & Steinberg, S. R. (2008). Indigenous knowledges in education: Complexities, dangers, and profound benefits. In N. K. Denzin, Y. S. Lincoln, & L. T. Smith (Eds.), *Handbook of critical and indigenous methodologies* (pp. 135–156). Los Angeles, CA: Sage Publications.

Kovach, M. (2009). *Indigenous methodologies: Characteristics, conversations and contexts.* Toronto: University of Toronto Press.

Kumar, R. (2014). *Research methodology: A step-by-step guide for beginners* (4th ed.). Thousand Oaks, CA: Sage Publications.

Langdon, J. (2009). *Indigenous knowledges, development and education*. Rotterdam, The Netherlands: Sense Publishers.

Martin, B. (2017). Methodology is content: Indigenous approaches to research and knowledge. *Educational Philosophy and Theory, 49*(14), 1392–1400. doi:10.1080/00131857.2017.1298034

McInnes, BD. (2016). Preparing teachers as allies in Indigenous education: Benefits of an American Indian content and pedagogy course. *Teaching Education, 28*(2), 145–161. doi:10.1080/10476210.2016.1224831

Mihesuah, D. A., & Wilson, A. C. (2004). *Indigenizing the academy: Transforming scholarship and empowering communities*. Lincoln, NE: University of Nebraska Press.

Miles, M. B., Huberman, A. M., & Saldaña, J. (2014). *Qualitative data analysis: A methods sourcebook*. Thousand Oaks, CA: Sage Publications.

National Center for Education Statistics, American Institutes for Research, U.S. Department of Education, & Institute of Educational Science. (2017). Status and trends in the education of racial and ethnic groups 2017. Retrieved from https://nces.ed.gov/pubs2017/2017051.pdf

NCSES Survey of Earned Doctorates – US National Science Foundation (NSF). (n.d.). Retrieved from https://www.nsf.gov/statistics/srvydoctorates/#tabs-1

Patel, V. (2014, May 27). Why so few American Indians earn Ph.D.'s, and what colleges can do about it. *The Chronicle of Higher Education*. Retrieved from https://www.chronicle.com/article/Why-So-Few-American-Indians/146715

Personal Communication, Course Discussion, October 18 (2017).

Ravitch, S. M., & Carl, N. M. (2016). *Qualitative research: Bridging the conceptual, theoretical, and methodological*. Thousand Oaks, CA: Sage Publications.

Richardson, T. (2000). Indigenous methodologies and educational research for meaningful change: Parsing postpositivist philosophy of science and mixed methods in collaborative research settings. *Journal of American Indian Education, 54*(1), 33–62.

Richardson, TA. (2012). Disrupting the coloniality of being: Toward de-colonial ontologies in philosophy of education. *Studies in Philosophy and Education*, *31*(6), 539–551. doi:10.1007/s11217-011-9284-1

Scheurich, J. J., & Young, M. D. (1997). Coloring epistemologies: Are our research epistemologies racially biased? *Educational Researcher*, *26*(4), 4–16. doi:10.3102/0013189X026004004

Smith, G. (2005). The problematic of Indigenous theorizing: A critical reflection. Paper presented at the American Educational Research Association (AERA) annual meeting. April 11–15, 2005, Montréal, Canada.

Smith, L. T. (2012). *Decolonizing methodologies: Research and indigenous peoples*. New York: Zed Books. Retrieved from https://nycstandswithstandingrock.files.wordpress.com/2016/10/linda-tuhiwai-smith-decolonizing-methodologies-research-and-indigenous-peoples.pdf

Kincheloe, J., & Steinberg, S. (2008). Indigenous knowledges in education: Complexities, dangers, and profound benefits. In N. K Denzin, Y. S. Lincoln, & L. T. Smith (Eds.), *Handbook of critical and indigenous methodologies* (pp. 135–156). Thousand Oaks, CA: Sage Publications. doi:10.4135/9781483385686.n7

Stevens, P., & Dworkin, A. G. (2014). *The Palgrave handbook of race and ethnic inequalities in education*. New York: Palgrave Macmillan.

Suina, M. (2017). Research is a pebble in my shoe: Considerations for research from a pueblo Indian standpoint. In E. S. Huaman & B. M. J. Brayboy (Eds.), *Indigenous innovations in higher education: Local knowledge and critical research* (pp. 83–100). Rotterdam, The Netherlands: Sense Publishers.

The Ojibwe People's Dictionary. (2015). Retrieved from http://ojibwe.lib.umn.edu/

Thompson, A. (2004). Gentlemanly orthodoxy: Critical race feminism, whiteness theory, and the *APA Manual*. *Educational Theory*, *54*(1), 27–57.

Vietnam and Opposition at Home | Turning Points in Wisconsin History | Wisconsin Historical Society. (n.d.). Retrieved from https://www.wisconsinhistory.org/turningpoints/tp-040/?action=more_essay

Chapter 13

Recommendations to Support Indigenous Faculty

Jameson D. Lopez

INTRODUCTION

Throughout my childhood my Dad always asked me, "JD, what do you want to be when you grow up?" I was not very good at school and I often skipped months out of the year by missing the bus and/or telling my parents I had a chronic stomach problem. In my naïvete, I thought maybe I would be a border patrol officer when I got older.

Our reservation is along the Colorado River on the California and Arizona state boundaries. It also happens to be a border crossing to Mexico and is one reason that we get lots of winter visitors who like to cross over to get their medicine filled and dental work done. But, most of the land is on the California side with a small land base in Arizona ... just enough for a casino. Due to the close proximity of Mexico, when I grew up, I would frequently see border patrol officers. To me, the border patrol officers "had it made." They had guns, they cruised around in a 4×4 truck, and chased people off their land that did not belong there. It sounded like a dream job for a Native person. But when I found out I could not deport White people, I changed my mind. I did not want to deport all White people, just the ones who were criminals. Needless to say, I quickly learned that being a border patrol officer was not compelling to me. When the idea of being a border patrol officer faded from my consciousness, I turned my eyes toward academia. Why?

My Dad was a Dean of Students, and my Mom was a faculty member at American Indian College. Every year we took both short and extended visits to reservations in the White Mountains, Pacific Northwest, Woodlands, Plains, and other locations. Watching my parents recruit, enroll, retain, and work with Native college students to earn their degree was always captivating to me. I liked hanging out with these Native college students.

Visiting and recruiting Native college students with my parents during my childhood years was a formative experience because many times we would visit in their living rooms and sometimes my parents would welcome in incoming and returning students at our house and on campus. At the beginning of the semester during the early 1990s, the campus had a large hill of green grass and immaculate trees on the west side of campus, where the Ramsey cafeteria is now. During each fall, the end of monsoon rains would plummet, and you could watch the rush of water combing through the green grass to a drainage area downhill east of the trees. The vast quantities of rain would cause three to four feet of stagnant water to form. My Dad was known because he would jump into the water and would convince other Native students to join in the fun, although many times they did not need much convincing. The flooded drainage area was later named as "Lake Lopez." Students would float in rafts, play volleyball, and wrestle. When your tribal college is severely underfunded, you quickly become creative when it comes to campus-wide activities. While those events often took my Dad away from me, along with the same Native students who visited our home, I understood as a child what my father was doing.

I remember that my Dad would sit with me and say, "JD, I hope you don't mind these students coming over, a lot of them never had role models, and it's important for your mom and me to be there for them." I had this understanding, from a very young age, that I would have to "share" my parents. Out of necessity, not out of abandonment. My Dad always took time to talk with his students. He never hesitated and would let me tag along as he walked with students to the gas station near the 6th Dr. house for drinks or an Icee. When I was little, my Dad explained to me why he helped students using a circle concept.

He said, "Some people's circles encompass just themselves, while others' encompass their families, and still others' have bigger circles that encompass a people. No circles are better than others, but they come with different responsibilities." I remembered this each time my Dad was taken away for work when I was a young boy, and I remember that when I'm called away from my children as a father. I hope my kids will understand the responsibility that comes with the faculty circle that I was given, and the Racial Battle Fatigue (RBF) that I endure.

Purpose of Chapter

In this chapter I speak about (1) my experiences with expected academic behavior stemming from institutional and tribal expectations to liberate, and (2) institutional abuse of Indigenous diversity and expectations for Indigenous faculty to assimilate which results in RBF. The chapter ends with ways to support the Indigeneity of Indigenous faculty and strategies to Indigenize the academy.

RACIAL BATTLE FATIGUE EXPERIENCES

I am an enrolled member of the Quechan nation located in Fort Yuma, California. Professionally, as an academic, I study Native American postsecondary education using Indigenous statistics and have expertise in the limitations of collecting and applying quantitative results to Indigenous populations. My research is informed by unique experiences, such as my 2010 deployment to Iraq as a platoon leader where I received a Bronze Star Medal for actions in a combat zone. I currently serve as an Assistant Professor in the Center for the Study of Higher Education at the University of Arizona, but my path to becoming an Assistant Professor was an adventure filled with my own experiences of RBF, like many other Native faculty who came before me.

Currently, Native Americans make up approximately 1.7 percent of people in the United States (Norris, Vines, & Hoeffel, 2012). The number of Native American faculty in the United States only accounts for 0.5 percent of the total faculty population (Chronicle of Higher Education, 2011). In fact, historically the number of Native American faculty has always been relatively low (Garcia, 2000). This becomes more evident when you look at the number of Native American Ph.D. graduates over the past ten years. In 2005, there were 139 Ph.D. graduates, and that number remained fairly stagnant over the next decade, with only 140 Native American Ph.D. graduates in 2015. Due to the low number of Native American faculty, senior Indigenous faculty have suggested some ideas for building, recruiting, and retaining Native American faculty. Pewewardy (2013) suggests that first and foremost Native American faculty should serve as role models and that "Indigenous students must see (witness) and interact with Indigenous faculty on campus to introduce them to the possibility of becoming future faculty members" (p. 141). Pewewardy (2013) gives five insights into the challenges of being a role model according to mainstream perspectives. I will mention three of them here.

First, it is difficult to be a faculty role model according to mainstream perspectives because we, Indigenous role models, are often expected to liberate our tribal people from social and psychological challenges. Second, institutions of higher education often encourage and want to take advantage of our diversity. This results in extra labor and burdens that other faculty are not expected to endure or offer: Native faculty advising and mentoring all Indigenous students, giving lectures, serving on diversity committees, and being available to Native students in ways that are not in line with other racial, ethnic, and cultural groups of students. Third, there is an institutional expectation that Indigenous faculty will assimilate into mainstream culture of the institution (at the same time as they serve as paragons of diversity). These three insights frame my RBF experiences.

EXPECTATION TO LIBERATE

Indigenous role models are often expected to liberate our tribal people from social and psychological challenges without taking care of our own health and well-being. The pressure stems from our own tribal communities when mainstream society manifests a deficit mentality that dominates the status of our nations. The expectation to liberate other fellow Native people is further perpetuated by institutions of higher education when we are expected to speak as the voice of our tribal communities. As if Native tribes are monolithic. When higher education looks to Indigenous faculty to be the sole voice of Indigenous nations, the responsibility to identify and solve problems rests on the shoulders of the Indigenous faculty. The expectations stemming from tribal communities and institutions of higher education apply pressure to Indigenous faculty to be "saviors." When pressured to become saviors, Indigenous faculty will often disregard their own self-care. This is especially true among Indigenous faculty working in underfunded institutions, and something that I experienced firsthand given that my parents were both faculty.

Each year, my family and I would take a family photo. There was a professional photographer who would come to my parent's work at American Indian College, and volunteer to take the faculty, staff, and administrator photos. If it was not free, we probably wouldn't have decent family photos because we could not afford those types of luxuries. I know there are some people who do not understand how I grew up below the poverty line because both my parents had graduate degrees. So, I will explain.

The college was, and still is, very small. There are less than 100 Native students from different nations across the United States, on a small ten-acre campus with more than enough facilities. The college was originally created to train Native pastors, because during the 1950s it was difficult to train Natives in mainstream seminaries. As the institute evolved, it expanded and began to offer a certified minister credential to become fully accredited and confer bachelor's degrees in elementary education, Christian ministry, and business. The college cannot survive on tuition from Native students alone. So, about half of the faculty, staff, and administrators' salaries are through raising their own support as U.S. missionaries. You must be a licensed minister and have the proper academic credentials to take this route. And this was the route my Dad took.

My Dad raised his support to work at American Indian College, and my Mom took a very modest salary to work as an elementary education faculty member. This fundraising model is not ideal. Faculty who raised their salaries went into various communities and asked for monthly donations. The monthly donations went into an account that was disseminated to the faculty member during the designated pay period. However, some donors often sent their monthly donations late or not at all resulting in extremely low wages. This is stressful. The actual salary is based off of pledges and it's up to the donors to send in the payments monthly. Not all of the donors send in their pledge money on time, and these uncertainties and irregularities resulted in my family being poor economically. However, in terms of knowledge, friendships, family, experience, traveling, wisdom, and living life, we were as wealthy as could be. My Dad was an administrator and taught

167

a few courses each semester. He started off as the Dean of Students, moved to Vice Presidency, and eventually Presidency. My mother taught five to six courses a semester and was the Elementary Education Department Chair for a while. Despite their heavy workloads and academic titles, we could not afford to take family pictures unless they were free.

That photographer would set up his lights and backdrop in the lounge of the girls' dormitory. My Mom and Dad would dress me up in my best "hand-me-downs," and would put in three flowers or hairspray and tell me, "do not touch your hair." We would wait in line for the other families to take their picture, and eventually it would be ours. We would sit and take a few photos and be done. … But every year, I would cross my eyes. For no particular reason. I would just cross my eyes because I thought it was funny. I guess it was because I liked to wreak havoc occasionally. My Dad would get upset and say, "JD, QUIT IT." He always did it calmly but loud and firm, because I knew he was trying to protect his reputation with his colleagues. Meaning I knew I was not going to get any corporal punishment from my Dad because he would not punish me that way in front of his coworkers. Which in my mind meant I could get away with it. So, I crossed my eyes again and again. Eventually that photographer would get a photo of me without crossed eyes. One year though, the frustration of my Dad, Mom, and sisters set in, and they were not amused. I was determined to cross my eyes in every picture, and I did, and the photographer kept insisting on taking another photo. Eventually my Dad said, "Forget it." He was done, and finally captured one of my favorite childhood family photos of my sisters and parents smiling while I was crossing my eyes. It was also the last time the photographer took our picture, but certainly not our last family photo.

Oftentimes, institutions do not understand that the expectation of Indigenous faculty to liberate comes at a price. It can be at the expense of the Indigenous faculty's finances or family. In the case of my own family, the cost to help liberate the social and psychological ills that faced our Indigenous community members came at the price of little things, such as family photos. Of course, this is a small example, and a relatively minor sacrifice. However, there is often an expectation for Indigenous faculty to sacrifice more than other faculty, because of the expectation that we will liberate our communities. The expectation to liberate becomes important to understanding our sacrifices to meet those commitments. The role of Indigenous faculty has a large circle, or large amount of responsibility to community, and most important in our circle is our families. The same holds true with my children: When I conduct my research, my family suffers in the sense that they miss my presence. And it was this way for me, when I was young, because both my parents served as busy faculty members. Our children and our families are not mutually exclusive. Our families are a part of this journey.

We were headed to the White Mountains to promote American Indian College on the Apache reservation. I was eight years old during that hot summer in June, so it was going to be nice to head to cooler-warm weather in Cedar Creek, Arizona. A place that I loved to visit as a kid because of the tarantulas, cliff jumping, and chance to chase cows. We jumped in our blue Astro van and cruised on Highway 60 from Phoenix to Globe, Arizona. A trip we had taken a million times before with my parents and sisters.

When we were little, my Dad never stopped unless we had been on the road for at least three hours. One trip, my sister Camie had to stick her butt out the window to pee because my Dad would not stop. I guess I was a little luckier, I got to pee in bottles. Besides our bodily relief being an issue, we always had an abundance of snacks for the road trips. We listened to the same cassette tapes and I remember drawing in my notepad to pass time during most of the trips. I collected Coke bottles and used my pocket knife to make gadgets and whatnots as well. My siblings and I never sat in our seats. We always had makeshift beds made of layered blankets that were laid between the rubber floors and the car seats. It's where we slept for our longer trips. It was a different time back then.

The trip to Cedar Creek was not a long one; it took us about four hours with a stop in Globe. After our stop, we headed through the beautiful windy Salt River Canyon. The drive through the canyon was filled with sheer cliffs, flowing waters, and on occasion, waterfalls would burst through the plateaus after heavy rains. My sister Camie and I crushed a family size box of Cheez-Its in the beginning half of our trip. About halfway through, just over the Salt River, I felt a stomachache coming. My stomach turned, and the Cheez-Its turned on me. I threw up on the rubber floor of our blue Astro van. There were not any pull-offs in the Canyon, so my Dad continued driving. My oldest sister, Joy, grabbed Camie, and yelled at her, "DON'T LOOK, DON'T LOOK!" But Camie looked, and she threw up also. Bits of Cheez-Its were sloshing back and forth on the floor as our van slowly climbed up the canyon. Finally, we pulled off to the side of the road, and my mom got a towel and cleaned as much as she could. My Dad was a little flustered, just because we always ran tight schedules during those trips. Once we finally got to Cedar Creek, my Dad asked his friend for a hose and sprayed the floor clean while my friends and I built a wikiup[1] in their yard.

This experience always reminds me of the obligations we have to our children to include them in our work as Indigenous faculty. This memory is not exactly a pleasant one, but it is forever etched in my mind because it highlights the obligations we have to our children in the work that we engage in. I feel that we are unable to fully engage in Indigenous communities without involving our children, or those closest to us, because they are a part of us as Indigenous faculty and researchers. Sometimes it distracts from the work we are doing, but we also have to maintain our families, and realize that we can not liberate a people if we are not looking after or including our families in the work that we do as faculty members. Our circles are vast as Indigenous faculty.

169

INSTITUTIONAL ABUSE OF OUR DIVERSITY
AS INDIGENOUS PEOPLE

Institutions often encourage and want to take advantage of our diversity, such as having Native faculty advise and mentor all Indigenous students, give lectures about Native issues, serve on a vast amount of diversity committees, and be available in ways that are not expected of non-Native faculty. I would like to first say that the Department and the Center that I serve in is overwhelmingly supportive and protective over my time as a junior faculty member. Nonetheless, there is always pressure from outside of my Department to give lectures across campus, serve on diversity committees, and start Indigenous initiatives normally reserved for tenured faculty. Higher education institutions need to realize that Native scholars approach our work holistically, and almost always our families are involved in our roles as faculty members. Unfortunately, and unrealistically, institutions of higher education tend to view Indigenous faculty as token Indians. The tokenism (appearance of showing diversity efforts for superficial reasons) can become a novelty and something I experienced throughout my higher education journey.

I took an opportunity during my undergraduate to go to a non-profit organization in Arkansas that often sent people to build community centers for some of the tribes in Arizona. One day I got a call inviting me to come speak to their organization, to talk about the work I was doing at the time. I remember thinking to myself, all these years they have been sending teams to help the "poor Indians." When they invited me to come speak, I told myself that now it is my turn to help them. I was also thinking that I may get a chance to take a picture as the sole Brown face among a bunch of White people. It would be a nice counterstory to always seeing a White face with a bunch of Indigenous kids. After I spoke to the mostly-White organization in the middle of nowhere in Arkansas, this little girl ran up to me and said in a thick southern accent:

"Hey sir, I just wanted to let you know that I told my mama that I'm coming to see you today. So, I jumped on that bus and came to see you."

I replied, "Well, nice to meet you."

And that little girl went on, "I told my mama that I have to make it, because there's gonna be a real Indian there. And I'm gonna shake his hand and touch his hair." She paused a few seconds and said in serious tone, "Sir, I was wondering if you'd shake my hand and let me touch your hair."

Not knowing what to do, I said, "Sure." So that little girl shook my hand and she touched my hair. ... That little girl was Hillary Rodham Clinton. Just kidding. It wasn't Hillary Clinton, but I'll never forget the time I went to visit the White people on their rez (a.k.a. Arkansas). I also remembered what it felt like to be treated as a novelty. Oftentimes, when Indigenous faculty are put on diversity committee, it feels like other committee members just want to shake our hands and touch our hair. Frequently, these committee members have little true interest in the ideas we have to improve the diversity of our institution; rather, they just want a token Indian on the committee. Furthermore, having a token Indian on a diversity committee is often a contradictory position because institutions simultaneously expect faculty members to assimilate. Foregoing this idea of having a diverse committee with faculty that can be representative of their respective identities.

EXPECTATION OF INDIGENOUS FACULTY TO CONTINUE TO ASSIMILATE

There is an expectation from institutions that Indigenous faculty will assimilate into mainstream institutional culture. It is especially true when it comes to academic writing (Lopez, 2015). I got my first glimpse of institutions trying to forcibly assimilate Indigenous faculty into institutional culture through a former faculty mentor of mine from a previous institution.

The words from that faculty's mouth were, "you're going to need my recommendation to get a job." He took a threatening tone and continued to berate my academic writing. The faculty member was notorious for bullying junior scholars, but I was in the Army for four years and knew how to talk to people like him. I straightened my back, lowered my voice an octave, and while looking him straight in the eye, I said: "I'm Native American, getting a Ph.D. with a Bronze Star Medal. I'm getting a job."

His face turned red and voice cracked. I knew then that I had made my point. He stumbled over his words and suggested that we not work together. I told him no, I had already spent a year at this point working on multiple projects with him, and that I was not going to let him steal my ideas without giving me credit for them. After tying up loose ends on a few projects, I parted ways with that faculty member.

When I ended my partnership with that faculty mentor it felt like a breakup. Except, instead of giving back old t-shirts and memorabilia, I was giving back books and promising not to distribute datasets. That's what happened; I had a breakup when that faculty mentor implied that I would not be able to get a job without their recommendation. I was not willing to conform to their writing style or their expectations for how I should present myself in academic spaces. However, at the same institution, I had a completely positive interaction with a different brilliant faculty member.

I'm normally awake by 4:30–5:00 AM, so my brilliant faculty mentor liked to schedule our weekly meetings around 6:00 AM. During my research meetings with her we mostly went over the research agenda, progress made on the projects, and she would ask how I was doing overall. One particular morning as we were walking into her office, she asked me, "JD, are you hungry?"

171

I answered, "Yes." I didn't eat breakfast, so I was a little hungry. She asked if I wanted a breakfast burrito, and I said, "Sure." Well at this point I'm thinking that maybe we would head out of the office to go grab something nearby, but we continued walking into the office. I thought maybe she had to grab something before we headed out, but then she reached into her bag and pulled out a big hot plate like she was Mary Poppins or something. Picture this: While she is doing all this she is talking to me about our research projects. I cannot focus at this point because I'm trying to figure out what's happening. And then, all of a sudden, she busts out some eggs from somewhere, and potatoes from somewhere else, and then some tortillas. She is not skipping a beat, and still talking about our research projects as she starts making breakfast burritos. I couldn't believe what was happening. My brilliant faculty mentor was making me a breakfast burrito in her office while talking about research projects.

My first thoughts were: (1) Is the smoke alarm going to go off? (2) Can we get in trouble for cooking in an office? (not that I cared) (3) This is going to be the best breakfast burrito of my life. When she finished cooking, we ate and talked more about the research.

I think about the experience I had with the mentor who said I would only get a job in higher education if I assimilated in ways he thought were needed, and my corresponding feelings that maybe academia was not a space for me. However, the moment this senior scholar busted out the hot plate to make breakfast burritos was the moment I knew I could belong in academia. I also learned that fateful morning that I could create space to support the scholars I mentor.

ACTIONABLE STRATEGIES

The following three recommendations to support Indigenous faculty stem from research, and my personal experiences with RBF. The recommendations are based on the expectations to liberate tribal communities, institutional abuse of our diversity as Indigenous people, and expectation of Indigenous faculty to assimilate.

1. Indigenous faculty need mechanisms whereby the academic institutions at which they work can learn more about Indigenous communities.
2. Indigenous faculty need institutions to take a holistic approach, whereby space to balance academic work with personal life is afforded, as the two are often braided.
3. Indigenous faculty need institutions to be considerate of the service obligations we have to our tribal communities.

The first and most basic step to supporting Indigenous faculty is to learn something about Indigenous people (Tippeconnic-Fox, 2005), and learning about

Indigenous communities at an institution is fairly easy. Utilize the institutional library, network with Indigenous faculty and students, utilize Indigenous support services or resources in Indigenous studies programs. The understanding of Indigenous folks is imperative to avoid reinforcing stereotypes, legitimizing Indigenous research, and understanding some of the political and historical contexts of Indigenous people. Non-Indigenous folks often have little understanding of Indigenous experiences outside of western movies on television and media coverage of mascots, pipelines, and protests. Limiting knowledge to these areas may reinforce stereotypical notions of Indigenous people. Furthermore, institutions should seek to understand the political and historical contexts of Indigenous people in their area. Understanding the political and historical contexts of Indigenous nations will help Institutions build partnerships with surrounding tribes and understand how their institution came to reside on Indigenous land.

The second recommendation is that Indigenous faculty need institutions to give us space to be holistic, as our academic work and personal life are often intertwined. The space to be holistic is integral (especially at non-Indigenous institutions) because Indigenous faculty feel isolation, lack of encouragement for research agenda, lack of mentorship, cultural discontinuity, and racism (Brayboy, Fann, Castagno & Solyom, 2012). The pressure to assimilate into mainstream academic norms becomes problematic as our work is embedded in our experiences as Indigenous people. If institutions care about supporting Indigenous faculty, they should read Indigenous faculty work and then cite the research. Citing research by Indigenous faculty further legitimizes our work and creates allies that build the capacity of Indigenous scholars' academic reach. Often, there is an expectation for new faculty to socialize with tenured faculty, but it is difficult for Indigenous faculty to model good collegial behavior and at the same time maintain our individuality, including our cultural traditions, because of the pressure to assimilate in academia. The presence of strong mentors who understand Indigenous communities and are willing to support Indigenous faculty research, tenure goals, and cultural values would likely reduce the amount of RBF Indigenous faculty encounter. As most Indigenous faculty experience racism while navigating graduate school, institutions that allow Indigenous faculty to be holistic allow them to seek support from our home communities, including other Indigenous faculty who can help us cope with inevitable racism and serve as mentors as we navigate the academic world.

The third and final recommendation is that Indigenous faculty need institutions to be considerate of the service obligations we have to our tribal communities. The need for universities to include Indigenous people in diversity discussions will not go away. For new faculty this is especially problematic as they embark on the tenure-track journey. Institutions hiring faculty should consider the service obligations they have to tribal communities. If institutions are requiring more faculty service on diversity committees, then the institutions should provide funding for research assistants, postdocs, course releases, and administrative support to participate in committee work that is not required of other faculty. Most of all, institutions of higher education must recognize that Indigenous faculty commitment to serving Indigenous communities meets the expectations of the academy. Additionally, Indigenous faculty commitment privileges the voices and viewpoint of our Indigenous communities and people (Brayboy et al., 2012). Supporting Indigenous faculty encourages faculty to maintain a connection to their community. Service to Indigenous communities is central to most Indigenous faculty research, but institutions often do not view that service as scholarly, which results in threatening the possibility of tenure (Brayboy et al., 2012). Finally, the purpose of most Indigenous faculty research is to improve our communities and make a positive impact on society. Making a positive impact is essential as past research on Indigenous communities by non-Indigenous faculty has hurt our communities (see Rainie, Schultz, Briggs, Riggs, & Palmanteer-Holder, 2017). Those institutions fostering these three practices will likely recruit and retain more Indigenous faculty who have experienced RBF in the past.

NOTE

1 A lodge consisting of a frame covered with matting or brush; used by nomadic American Indians in the southwestern United States.

REFERENCES

Brayboy, B., Fann, A., Castagno, A., & Solyom, J. (2012). *Postsecondary education for American Indian and Alaska natives: Higher education for nation building and self-determination*. San Francisco, CA: Wiley Subscription Services.

Chronicle of Higher Education. (2011). *Almanac of higher education*. Retrieved from http://chronicle.com/section/Almanac-of-Higher-Education/615/

Garcia, M. (2000). *Succeeding in an academic career: A guide for faculty of color*. Westport, CT: Greenwood.

Lopez, J. D. (2015). Native American identity and academics: Writing NDN in education. *Teachers College Record*. Retrieved from http://www.tcrecord.org/content.asp?contentid.18216 (Accessed on January 08, 2019).

Norris, T., Vines, P. L., & Hoeffel, E. M. (2012). *The American Indian and Alaska native population: 2010*. Washington, DC: U.S. Department of Commerce, Economics and Statistics Administration, U.S. Census Bureau.

Pewewardy, C. (2013). Fancy war dancing on academe's glass ceiling. In H. J. Shotton, S. C. Lowe, & S. J. Waterman (Eds.), *Beyond the asterisk: Understanding native students in higher education* (pp. 139–150). Sterling, VA: Stylus Publishing.

Rainie, S. C., Schultz, J. L., Briggs, E., Riggs, P., & Palmanteer-Holder, N. L. (2017). Data as a strategic resource: Self-determination, governance, and the data challenge for Indigenous nations in the United States. *The International Indigenous Policy Journal*, *8*(2), 1–29.

Tippeconnic Fox, M. J. (2005). Voices from within: Native American faculty and staff on campus. *New Directions for Student Services*, 2005(109), 49–59.

Part V

The Racialized Experiences of People of Color in Diversity-Related Faculty Fellow Positions and Non-Tenure-Track Positions in U.S. Higher Education

Chapter 14

The Convenient, Invisible, Token-Diversity Hire

A Black Woman's Experience in Academia

Paula R. Buchanan

THE *KNIGHT* FEDERAL COURT CASE AND THAT PESKY "BLINKING LIGHT" NEAR PIEDMONT, ALABAMA

"So, you're a *Knight* case hire then, right?" My mentor's question confused me. I had never heard of this *Knight* case and had no idea why my new job as an instructor at a predominantly White institution (PWI) in the University of Alabama's system had anything to do with it. After meeting with my mentor, I searched for and found some interesting facts about the *Knight* case.

"*Knight v. Alabama* was a federal court case that lasted almost 30 years, challenging numerous policies of the state's colleges and universities ... on the grounds that they were racially discriminatory" (Klass, 2014, p. 1). The U.S. Supreme Court found that Alabama's higher education policies fostered segregation (Hamill, 2008, p. 1), and after the second trial in the case occurred, "the district court ordered numerous changes to these policies and retained authority for ten years to supervise the state's progress" (Hamill, 2008, p. 1). That ten-year period ended right after I was hired as the *first*, and still the *only*, Black faculty member in the University's School of Business. I was their convenient, diversity-token hire whose existence as a Black faculty member "proved" that their specific university was racially diverse.

I had no idea that the *Knight* case had happened, and/or whether it had led to me getting hired in the first place. To make the situation even worse, I learned about the court case from a secondhand source instead of hearing this firsthand from my employer. I was not told about this issue during my university interviews. The people that interviewed me must have known about this case and my role in it, right? I had no idea, and did not feel comfortable bringing up the issue because the university was only a few minutes away from the blinking traffic light that led into Piedmont.

Piedmont, Alabama is a small, rural town that has a distinct reputation for Black people that know about it. My relatives that were from Alabama told me

179

to never go into Piedmont when I visited them. "Don't go past that blinking light into Piedmont," they would warn me. "They don't like Black people in Piedmont, so don't go there." Both of my grandmothers told me stories of Piedmont, a town whose White residents had proudly made and posted crude signs near the town's entrance that said things such as "Niggers Stay Out!" or "No Niggers Allowed."

My new work office was housed in the university's School of Business building, which was located toward the more remote, north side of campus within a few minutes of the "blinking light" that led into Piedmont. For me, that "blinking light" came to represent the fear, hatred, ignorance, discrimination, and racism that I have experienced throughout my life as a Black person.

JOUSTING WITH JANITORS AND OTHER INDIGNITIES: TWO PERSONAL STORIES

"How Did *You* Get This Office?"

As the convenient, diversity-hire faculty member in the School of Business in a university that was only a few minutes away from that "blinking light," I knew that I would have some interesting experiences getting to know fellow faculty members, staff, and students. While the university had an increasingly large number of Black students, especially in the School of Business, I was the *only* faculty member in the department that was Black, and the *only* employee that was Black. I was the proverbial Black unicorn.

I knew that my presence in the building where I worked would lead to various levels of microaggressions and some possible outright instances of discrimination and racism, but I was not prepared for an encounter that I had with the janitor that cleaned my office. At the time, I was teaching a weekly, three-hour evening course. While I did not feel safe or comfortable being so close to the town of Piedmont at night, I had to do my job.

Our building's janitors worked in the evenings, so I was also used to seeing them during my work hours. I knew that they had seen me walking around the building, but they probably thought I was a student. At the time, I looked and dressed like a student, wearing jeans, a golf shirt or blouse, and carried a large backpack to work every day. I was already in my office to prepare my evening class lecture when one of the janitors entered my office suite. No other faculty members that had offices in the suite were there since they mostly worked during the day and did not teach at night.

The janitor saw me exit my office and take out a key to lock the door behind me. Immediately, she confronted me in a hostile manner, locking eyes with me, and completely invading my personal space.

"How did *you* get this office?" she snarled at me.

The employee was an older, White female with an incredibly striking and scary look. She was scrawny, and had deep, furrowed lines and creases all over her face, suggesting that she had experienced hardships that made her look desiccated and decimated. She also smelled of cheap smoking tobacco. As someone with severe allergies, I am especially sensitive to the smell of tobacco products, and usually avoid interacting with anyone who smokes cigarettes. I noticed all of these details about the woman because she was right in my face, interrogating me to find out who I was, and questioning why I had keys to the office.

"I have keys because this is my office," I calmly told the woman, "because I'm Ms. Buchanan." To emphasize the point, I slowly turned part of my body toward my door to point out my name plate on the door. I kept the other part of my body facing the ornery janitor, just in case she decided to attack me. It was an incredibly tense moment, and I had only been working as an instructor for less than a year.

It was at this point that she exclaimed, yet again, "How did *you* get this office?"

"Dear lord," I thought to myself. "What is wrong with this woman? How dare she question my position! How insulting!" I had closed and locked my office door and started to move away from the woman because I had to go teach. I had answered her question, and now I had to work.

Unfortunately, the woman was not finished disrespecting me. She followed me, ranting, "Well, us maids, we ain't got no place to put our stuff, you know. So, since *you* have this office here, we gotta ask the bosses to set up the empty office across the hall from you so *we* can have a place to sit like you do." As she talked, she repeatedly coughed loudly, spewing her repugnant tobacco scent further in my direction.

"Unearned, White privilege gone amok," I thought as I walked away. "This foul-smelling female thinks that because a Black person has an office, that she should have one too." I walked up the stairs to my classroom. I taught the three-hour class as usual, and then immediately left the building to drive home away from the "blinking light," away from hostile people like her. As I drove, I contemplated ways to deal with this problematic encounter.

My first thought was to complain to the head of the Cleaning Services Department, my department head, and dean about what happened. But then I remembered where I was, and who I was. I was only a few minutes away from the "blinking light" and what it represented. I was a new hire who had recently started my job, and I was Black. If I complained, my new job opportunity could disappear. I did not want that. Furthermore, my mom and all her fellow sibling-educators would be so proud of my new career choice, keeping up the family tradition. I wanted to keep my job, so I said and did nothing about the possible racism battle that could have occurred if I had decided to complain.

I also found comfort in what my parents and family had often told me, that people like that janitor want to see a Black woman like me who had succeeded in life to eventually fail. "Don't give them that advantage over you," they would say. "You are better than they are because you *have* to be. Don't stoop to their level."

When I tell this story to Whites, they pooh-pooh my experience, saying that "I don't think that woman meant what you think she meant. You're making something out of nothing." My Black friends, especially those who work within academia, view the confrontational verbal joust with the janitor as insulting, and give me kudos for walking away from the situation.

A few weeks after the incident, I entered my locked office to prepare for that evening's class lecture to find the middle drawer of my desk and its contents strewn all over the floor. I had no idea what happened or who did it, but after the previous confrontation with the janitor, I decided to file a police report. While this might have seemed like an extreme action, I had to prevent whatever was going on from happening again.

I left my office desk as it was, took plenty of pictures, and called University Police to file a police report. I also emailed University Police, and included the head of the Cleaning Services Department on the email, to document that I had filed the police report. Cleaning Services called me the next morning to tell me that the janitor assigned to my office had accidentally "done something" that caused my desk drawer to come out of the desk and spill its contents on the floor.

I was livid, asking "how was I supposed to know what happened to my personal items? And the janitor did this, right? Can't she clean up the mess that she made? If this ever happens again, which hopefully it won't, I will file yet another police report if your staff refuses to fix any problems that their actions have created. Do you understand me?"

The Cleaning Services representative seemed to understand me, and told me that this will never happen again. And fortunately, it didn't. Unfortunately, there were other indignities that occurred over the years that made me feel, at times, that my working environment was not the safest space for me as a Black woman. Even more indignities would occur that reminded me of how close my work environment was to the "blinking light," and the fear that this one image could instill in Black people.

When a White Student Calls Her Black Instructor the "H" Word

Several years later after my jousts with janitors, there were faculty members in the School of Business who had never made eye contact with me, or even spoken to me since I was hired. I never knew if this was because I was Black, female, young, did not have a terminal degree, or some combination of all of those factors. But I did not care. To me, their decision to ignore me was *their* problem, not mine.

Instead of focusing on their racism, I focused more on the classroom and my students. I relished the fact that I sometimes had outstanding students in my classroom. One year, I had a group of students who all took my Principles of Management and my Organizational Behavior courses in the same academic year. They were so smart, witty, and such a joy to be around. They even poked fun at me (in a good-natured way) at the end of the Organizational Behavior course. Because I am incredibly short, it was difficult for me to reach the top of the white board to write on it, or to even pull down the cord for the overhead projector screen. This group of students pooled their money together to buy me a small step stool to use, and they all autographed it for me. It was such a sweet, sincere, and funny gesture that I laughed out loud when the students gave it to me. It was because of students like these that I could cope with students like Becky (not her real name).

Context to Becky's Use of the "H" Word

In 2008, Barack Hussein Obama was elected as our country's first Black president. Like almost every other Black person I know, I watched Obama's inauguration on television with sheer awe and amazement. But when his inauguration was over, reality began to sink in. I thought about the "blinking light," and I realized something that made me incredibly fearful. I thought, "there must be many White people out there that are very angry right now." And because I worked in a town—and at an extremely conservative, Fox News-watching PWI—that probably did not vote for Obama, they would be furious too. "Oh dear," I thought. "Because of institutionalized racism, Obama's election could be bad for people like me who are Black."

I was pondering this issue as I walked into work the next day. It was early in the morning, around 8:00 AM, but every Black student that I saw was so happy, joyful, and full of energy. They were ebullient in their walk and their talk. One student who was walking behind me whispered, "Obama!" repeatedly as he entered the building. I chose to keep walking and ignore this young Black man's glee, because I knew what the Obama election meant for people like me; Black people, that is.

It will get worse for us," I moaned to one of my colleagues who was a staff member in another building. She was one of the few Black women I knew on campus, and I really liked chatting with her because she had such a calming personality. She was one of my allies on campus. To protect my coworker's privacy, I'll call her Stacey.

"Oh, Paula," Stacey chimed in. "No need to be so negative. Be happy! We have a Black president."

"Yes, I'm glad he won," I responded. "But keep this in mind. Barack Obama and his family have a security detail for protection. We regular Black folks don't have that kind of security. Even Michelle Obama said that Barack, like any Black man, can just be shot or gunned down in the street."[1]

What I was trying to tell Stacey is that large parts of White America might be incredibly angry because a Black man was elected president. Furthermore, if they cannot

183

attack Obama, they will attack us. Shortly after having this discussion with Stacey, I had an interesting encounter in a class with a White, female student named Becky.

Becky

Becky was a student in a section of a Principles of Management course that I taught. While she seemed friendly enough, the best word to describe her as a student was "erratic." She was also extremely vocal, often asking multiple questions during class discussions, something that faculty usually encourage from students. However, most of her questions were wacky, off topic, and distracting. I would even see a few of her fellow classmates give her "stink eye" when she did this. Some of her classmates would just plain laugh at her. However, Becky continued to ask multiple questions.

One day after class, Becky approached me to dispute a low grade that she made on an assessment. After listening to Becky's complaint, I let her know that her grade for the assessment would *not* change.

You never knew how students will react when faculty say "no" to their "grade-grubbing" attempts. Some students would yell at me and send hostile emails. Some would even have their parents call me on their behalf to continue the dispute, something that I never understood, and was against the federal Family Educational Rights and Privacy Act (FERPA) law. I once saw a blond, ponytailed, female student verbally accost our dean to dispute a grade, right in the middle of the dean's front office. Since he was such a nice, soft-spoken, avuncular type of man, how could any student shriek and scream at a man like our dean?

While Becky did not shriek or scream at me, she did get so upset that she called me the "H" word. "You're such a Hitler," she said, right in front of a group of students. We were all shocked at what Becky, a White, female student called her Black, female instructor.

When this happened, I laughed it off and started to answer questions from other students. Becky reminded me of that "blinking light" again. I had more important things to do than deal with her hostility and racism. Of course, though, I remembered what Becky called me, just like I remember when the White, female janitor challenged my right to have my own work office.

Later, during the same week that Becky called me "Hitler," I was teaching the same Principles of Management class. As usual, Becky eventually asked a wacky question. It was at this point that I had finally had enough from her.

"Oh, Becky," I said in a slightly condescending tone, "the class and I know that you always ask some interesting questions. Right, class?" I took a long, pregnant pause in speaking to make sure that the entire class was focused on me and what I was saying.

"Class, I had an interesting chat with Becky yesterday. She didn't like the grade she earned on an assessment, and since I would not change the grade, do you know what Becky said to me?" The entire class was staring right at me, including Becky.

"Class, Becky called me Hitler! She called a Black person *Hitler*." Again, I paused long enough to ensure that each student had heard exactly what I said. I looked at the reaction across the room. Every student immediately turned around to stare at Becky's face, which was beet red with shock and embarrassment. All of the students stared at Becky with complete amazement. A few of them mumbled various expletives. For once in her life, Becky did not have anything to say.

"Okay, class," I said, "we've wasted enough time. Let's get back to work."

Internally, I giggled with glee at what I had done. I told the "blinking light," "you might have won some battles against me, but I *will* win the war. I may be tired and worn out from Racial Battle Fatigue after fighting and losing some of these battles, but I will be victorious. My family made me who I am: confident, smart, strong, and resilient. While fear, ignorance, and racism are strong, I am much, much stronger. Take that, you silly, little 'blinking light.'"

After class that day, some of the students walked up to my desk and apologized for Becky's actions. White students said, "We're not all like that Ms. Buchanan. I'm sorry Becky said that to you." Black students looked me in the eye, shook their heads in both disbelief and mutual understanding of what Becky had called me, and said, "Thank you, Ms. Buchanan." I took the many "thank you" responses from Black students as giving them the strength to also speak out against the "Beckys" of the world who have called *them* Hitler, or even worse.

ACTIONABLE STRATEGIES

I have shared only two of the many racially fatiguing indignities that I have experienced during my career as a Black female faculty member in academia. I omitted a discussion on my decision not to "codeswitch,"[2] or alter, my natural Black hair before my campus interviews began, which would have made me appear to be more of a convenient, non-threatening Black woman. I also regret that I did not have enough space to share the story of my student Kamala (not her real name), a former Black, female student from West Africa, who came to me after class in tears one day because one of her older, southern, White male professors would regularly make fun of her French-African accent *in front of her entire class*.

What happened to Kamala, and what has happened to me over the years in higher education, is not symptomatic of just one small, PWI university located in the deep south in Alabama. It is symptomatic of *all* colleges and universities across our nation. These stories can, and do, happen across all types and levels of academic institutions.

Unfortunately, I would need at least an entire book, not just a chapter, to fully share all of my incidents and indignities, and how they have led to my experiencing over a decade of Racial Battle Fatigue in academia. That said, my years of experience on the "battlefield" have armed me with some actionable steps and best practices that can help "C-Suite" academics (presidents, provosts, deans, etc.) create more inclusive working environments so that we all can work together to win the war against Racial Battle Fatigue and racism in academia.

Stop Saying, "Where Are the Black Faculty Candidates? We Cannot Find Them." Instead, Do Something About It

I often hear university leaders state that they cannot find Black faculty to hire. "We can't find them. If we cannot find them, then we cannot hire them. Where are they?"

We *do* exist, but administrators are not making enough of an effort to find us or they are choosing to overlook us (Gasman, 2016, p. 3). For example, if universities decide to recruit engineering faculty candidates at the National Society of Professional Engineers' Annual Conference, then they should also recruit at the National Society of Black Engineers' Annual Conference. For every professional, membership-based organization that is predominantly White, there is another professional organization that is predominantly Black. And all I had to do to find the Black Engineers' organization was to simply Google "Black engineers." It was that simple and easy. Hiring activities should also be expanded to include recruitment efforts at Historically Black Colleges and Universities (HBCUs), if they do not convenient for and useful to you.

Be Self-Aware

Presidents, provosts, deans, and department chairs must be self-aware when it comes to their universities and past experiences with diversity, equity, and inclusion (DEI) efforts. If the university has poor race relations, acknowledge that, and do so publicly. As my grandparents used to say, sunlight is the best disinfectant. Transparency about DEI efforts is the best policy, even if the university has a long way to go to achieve equity and inclusion.

Account for Implicit Biases

Part of being self-aware is understanding that individuals within academia have implicit biases. As universities decide to recruit more diverse faculty, they must acknowledge and account for segments of their White faculty and staff that have racist views toward Blacks and diverse groups that they view as "others" or "outsiders."

Create an Organizational Structure That Supports DEI at Every Level

It is important to hire more diverse staff at all levels of a university. Senior leadership must be diverse in order to start this process. In addition, DEI efforts must be documented in a transparent manner. For example, create and publicize your own DEI report card (Juárez, 2016, p. 310), building on lessons that you have learned in creating a more inclusive university environment.

Don't Burn Out Your Token Diversity Hires

Admit it: some academic C-Suite-ers reading this chapter have done exactly what the university at which I work has done. They have hired one Black faculty member. The "diversity unicorn" is invited to every diversity-related event. The diversity unicorn is in every university picture and video to represent its commitment to diversity, and is expected to mentor every Black student.

Don't burn us out by asking us to do too many things for too many people. Most of us will say "yes" to everything that you ask from us because we want to mentor students and help others, or we just want to keep our jobs. Fortunately, more of us now say "no" to place boundaries on what we will do outside of required job duties and responsibilities. Don't put all the pressure to promote university diversity on the diversity unicorn. Retention of diverse faculty can happen if you do not burn them out, and start to value them in equitable, sincere, and professional ways.

Ensure That We Are in the Room Where DEI Policies and Procedures Happen

If you want to more effectively improve DEI, you must also have diverse people in the rooms where these decisions are made. Not only is it important to have them present in the room, but it is even more imperative to empower them to speak their minds, and for you to listen to what they have to say. No group of ten or so White people at a university should determine the best practices to increase DEI. You must have multiple people of color in the room. Demonstrate your commitment to DEI through your university's policies and procedures, and have faculty of color in the room that aid in doing so.

Empower Us to Have a Collective Voice and Share It with Others

Empower faculty of color to speak truth to ignorance, fear, and racism when we need to do so. Give us an active voice and the agency to make universities more inclusive for diverse populations. Have ongoing, active discussions with faculty of color to get their perspectives. Empower them to feel comfortable to have a voice and share their stories of RBF to improve the quality, not just the quantity, of DEI initiatives in academia.

187

Create Safe Spaces for Us on Campus

Understand that people of color will want our own "safe spaces" separate from White colleagues so that we can share our experiences without experiencing any backlash or having to explain why. Make sure that your university policies and procedures support the creation of these groups. For example, some universities have safe space/zone programs to provide a network of safe space allies to support students that are LGBTQ (Lesbian, Gay, Bisexual, Transgender, Questioning). Consider having similar programs for students and faculty of color.

Invite the Entire Person to Your Academic Institution

As previously mentioned, I considered "code-switching" my natural, Black hair into a form that mimicked White standards of beauty to get a job as a faculty member. If I had decided to change who I am by changing my hair, I would not have brought my entire self to my job. Unfortunately, these are the issues that Black faculty must deal with if we decide to work for predominantly White institutions that want us to "just bring … the thing we ask you for, and leave the rest at home" (Brown, 2019, p. 2).

Empower us to be who we are instead of who you *think* we are, or who you *think* we must be. To increase equity and inclusion beyond the basic need for diversity, you must invite the entire, whole person to be a part of your team, not just the part of the person of color that is convenient for and useful to you.

Short-Term Sacrifices for Long-Term Gains and Increased DEI

The previous discussion of code-switching emphasizes the fact that as Black faculty, we are making ongoing personal and professional sacrifices to have the right and opportunity to work in academia. The "C-Suite" of academia must also make its own sacrifices to reach the long-term goal of increased DEI in higher education. If we, as faculty of color, must make sacrifices, so should you. If you want us to feel as if we are a part of your team, you must share in our sacrifices.

Learn from Other Universities and Leaders

While my experiences with RBF in academia showed me what was wrong, I wanted to find examples of what was *right* in academia to share with others who were dealing with similar indignities. I have compiled a database of these DEI programs that are shining examples of how DEI efforts can improve academic institutions. Some effective DEI programs are at the university-wide level. Some are managed through human resources. Others are at the departmental level. Nevertheless, they all are effective.[3]

In addition, learn from my example. Reach out to your fellow academics, both inside and outside of your institution, to find effective DEI initiatives. One of the major issues with academia is that we are incredibly siloed to the point that we don't interact with fellow academics outside of our own departments. We need to get out of those silos. Take advantage of the abundant resources that exist. Learn from each other. Find effective DEI efforts, and share them with others.

CONCLUSION

The stories that I have shared do not make me unique in academia. However, sharing my stories *does* make me and the other chapter authors unique in that we have found the strength to share our stories. Unfortunately, we often choose to not share our stories of RBF with people who can advocate on our behalf because we do not feel empowered to raise our voices to speak and share our facts and truths. We wonder if we will be reprimanded, ostracized, or even terminated. We fear that if we speak our respective truths out loud so that others can hear them, we will lose the jobs we have worked so hard to obtain, jobs that support ourselves, families, and other loved ones.

This fear makes it difficult to be honest and open in writing a chapter like this. Fear can make it hard to put proverbial pen to paper, but I am long overdue in sharing my stories of RBF with academia and the rest of the world.

Furthermore, it is important that leaders in higher education—C-Suite academics, the targeted audience for this entire book—understand the professional risks that all of us chapter authors take in telling our respective truths, in sharing our stories with the world. We chapter contributors have all agreed to take these risks because we must be heard to make academia and higher education more inclusive for all.

It is now time for C-Suite academics to take their own short-term risks for long-term gains. The C-Suite of academia must not only listen to stories that document the feelings "of invisibility and marginalization ..." (Hankins, 2016, p. 218) that faculty of color experience in academia, but also work to actively include us in a more inclusive future of higher education.

NOTES

1 This issue was discussed in a 2007 *60 Minutes* television interview with then-Senator Barack Obama and Michelle Obama.

2 Code-switching is defined as "the use of one dialect, register, accent, or language variety over another, depending on social or cultural context, to project a specific identity" (Lexico, 2019, p. 1).

3 I created this database of "DEI best practices" to conduct research. If you are interested in learning more about my database, contact me via my website at www.paularbuchanan.com.

REFERENCES

Brown, J. (Writer and Director). (2019, February 22). 'Moonlight' writer hopes audiences leave his new play 'full of questions.' *The PBS Newshour*. [Television Broadcast]. In J. Brown (Producer). Arlington, VA: Public Broadcasting Service.

Gasman, M. (2016, September 26). An Ivy League professor on why colleges don't hire more faculty of color: We don't want them. *Washington Post*. Retrieved March 01, 2019 from https://www.washingtonpost.com/news/grade-point/wp/2016/09/26/an-ivy-league-professor-on-why-colleges-dont-hire-more-faculty-of-color-we-dont-want-them/?utm_term=.d77e9cfb52eb.

Hamill, S. P. (2008, February 26). Knight v. State of Alabama. *Encyclopedia of Alabama*. Retrieved from http://www.encyclopediaofalabama.org/article/h-1480.

Hankins, R. (2016). Racial realism or foolish optimism: An African American Muslim woman in the field. In R. Hankins & M. Juárez (Eds.), *Where are all the librarians of color? The experiences of people of color in academia* (pp. 209–222). Sacramento, CA: Library Juice Press.

Juárez, M (2016). Making diversity work in academic libraries. In R. Hankins & M. Juárez (Eds.), *Where are all the librarians of color? The experiences of people of color in academia* (pp. 299–316). Sacramento, CA: Library Juice Press.

Klass, K. (2014, January 23). Historic ASU discrimination suit changed education in Alabama. *Montgomery Advisor*. Retrieved from https://www.montgomeryadvertiser.com/story/news/2014/01/24/historic-asu-discrimination-suit-changed-education-in-alabama/4813977.

Lexico Publishing Group. (2019). Retrieved from Online Dictionary https://www.dictionary.com/browse/code-switching.

Chapter 15

Experiencing Ellison's "Battle Royal" in Higher Education[1]

Martel A. Pipkins

APPLICATION 1: "TO WHOM IT MAY CONCERN, THE BATTLE ROYAL"

> On my graduation day I delivered an oration in which I showed that humility was the secret, indeed, the very essence of progress. It was a great success. Everyone praised me and I was invited to give the speech at a gathering of the town's leading white citizens. It was a triumph for our whole community. ... When I got there I discovered that it was on the occasion of a smoker, and I was told that since I was to be there anyway I might as well take part in the battle royal to be fought by some of my schoolmates as part of the entertainment. The battle royal came first.
>
> (Ralph Ellison, *Invisible Man*, 1952, p. 442)

After submitting my cover letter and application for a full-time position at the small state university and receiving a call back to interview, I, too, was filled with feelings of success. Success not just for me, but for our whole community. Not having a single Black or Brown teacher/professor during my entire PK–12 schooling, undergraduate, or master's degree, and only one in my very last semester of coursework as a doctoral student, this was a good day. Instead of the hotel ballroom, tuxedos, buffet foods, whiskey, and cigars in Ellison's story, and a physical fight to the death, we were in the university's conference room with faculty and administrators in their best JCPenney attire, picking around the dried-up fruit tray with their manila folders under their armpits. Forcing away graduate school-injected imposter's syndrome, I carried my journal in one hand, and a small cup of water in the other, both serving as security blankets accessorizing my invisibility. It was not long before Audre would walk in, increasing the total number of Black people in this near-capacity conference room to two. This university, meant to welcome new faculty to their academic homes, had an *invisible* underground, one which I would find myself in soon after Audre's departure from the university.

Audre and I got along well from the start—our forced falsettos fading instantly with "hey." We were both hired as non-tenure-track faculty. She was the vibrant Professor in the Psychology Department and I was the new *cool, young* Criminology Professor within the Sociology Department. Our first year went well. We both made a name for ourselves within our respective departments and throughout the wider university. After my first semester, as observed by my Department Chair, my courses reached their enrollment capacity within only a few days of registration opening. This remained the case throughout my time at the university. Audre and I found ourselves surrounded by students every day, especially Black and Brown students who had become unaccustomed to seeing Black and Brown faculty on campus. It is a common experience for Black scholars to pass up career opportunities if they notice there is already a Black faculty member in the prospective department: "They already have their token." "You know, two is too many." While Blacks and other oppressed groups already fight in the larger battle royal of capitalist labor, diversity fellowships works as microcosmic battle royals, pitting Scholars of Color against one another to fight for another one–six-year contract of racist hazing and silencing, often in the name of the university's first Black or Brown or Indigenous hire (my fellowship was named after educator and abolitionist Mary Miles Bibb).

The university-wide diversity fellowship, named after educator and abolitionist Mary Miles Bibb, the first Black female graduate of the university, was announced within a few months of joining the faculty body at the university. The supposed purpose of the two-year fellowship was to get new Ph.D.s of Color onto the tenure track. With both of us—Audre and I—meeting all the criteria, looking for tenure-track positions, and enjoying our first year there, our battle royal was set to begin. However, before the bell rang, another tenure-track position within the Sociology Department opened. Speaking with a colleague about applying for this position, she reminded me that as an internal applicant, I would be automatically granted an interview. After a slight hesitation, she *intoned*, "the Department Chair said that she wished you would *not* apply for it." I was perplexed, especially given the close bond I thought I had formed with the Chair. Later it became apparent that their intention was to secure me through the two-year university-wide, but department-situated, diversity fellowship position, and hire someone else, presumably a White scholar, for the tenure-track position. Believing in my better angel, and that the Chair must have had some other plan for me, given how she regularly assured me that the department wanted me there, I decided to not apply for the tenure-track position.

The next day, I reread an essay I was assigned as an undergraduate student, by Adalberto Aguirre, Jr. (2008) titled "Academic Storytelling: A Critical Race Theory Story of Affirmative Action"; then it dawned on me and I was able to situate my experience in the context of a "counterstory" (Aguirre, 2008) of how affirmative action is practiced in academia. One of the common practices, revealed in these affirmative action counterstories, is the unauthorized decision of departments to move a job applicant from one job pool (i.e., tenure-track opening) to another one (i.e., diversity position). Because the two application processes may be at different stages, sometimes this leaves no time for the department to consider the applicant for the position they actually applied for, as they feel the pressure of potentially losing other desirable applicants.

Reflecting on this essay, and my solidarity with Audre, I decided not to apply for the diversity fellowship position either. Later on, Audre learned that the clinical hours required for the completion of her doctoral program would not allow her to teach. She encouraged me to apply since she could not. Extremely fatigued at that point, I threw my hat into the diversity fellowship ring. Typing up another cover letter letter-writing apply for the position: To Whom It May Concern.

APPLICATION 2: "TO WHOM IT MAY CONCERN, KEEP THIS NIGGER-BOY RUNNING"[2]

Scholars and artists in popular culture have noted the long histories of white gluttony for Black culture and entertainment as well as Black bodies. This gluttony occurs simultaneously with rejection, dispossession, and erasure of the Black people that created it—a constant state of racist cognitive dissonance. My time and labor became another instance of indulging in Black commodification, while rejecting my Black personhood. I saw pieces of me scattered all over the place. After writing and being awarded several grants to develop innovative teaching and high impact practices for first-year programs at the university, I created a pedagogical package that included various teaching techniques, programming ideas, and activities. After presenting these at in-house conferences and workshops, several faculty approached me to learn more about my work and asked me about my creative processes.

For one activity in particular, I linked my Introduction to Criminology course to an Introduction to Sociology course taught by a colleague—the students from each class wrote a series of letters to one another. This letter-writing activity first came to mind when I came across letter correspondences between the founder of the first U.S. School of Sociology, W.E.B. Du Bois, and his German colleague, Max Weber. While lovingly asking about one another's family and personal life, they also conversed with each other intellectually by raising questions to one another that helped each scholar formulate their now classic works about race and social class, respectively. I dreamt of my own students engaging in such conversations with scholars across various disciplines. One of the people who approached me at this end of the year conference presentation was the former Department Chair who chaired upon my arrival and oversaw my initial hiring. He commented, "I had no idea you were doing all this, it's exactly what we need!"

193

The following year, the new Department Chair attempted to adopt this activity with an English professor. It was also the time that I was gearing up to apply for a tenure-track position in the same department; it would have been my fourth time applying in two-and-a-half years to this specific Sociology Department.

The continued theft of the fruits of my labor went beyond classroom activities. The self-study and five-year external review of the department was filled with my achievements, oftentimes without my name appearing at all when other faculty had been specifically named for the work mentioned. When asked to "describe the range of instructional methods used in the Sociology program, including any that are unusual or specialized," the first innovative form of pedagogy listed was the "Inside-Out Prison Exchange" program where

> each semester ten university students ("outsiders") join ten incarcerated individuals ("insiders") at a local prison for class once a week. The class meets for the entire semester, and is reading, writing, and discussion intensive. There is close collaboration between the university students and inside students throughout the semester. At the end of the semester, students in the class put on a final presentation, which prison and university administrators attend.
> (Department Self-Study, 2018 [internal document])

Although I am unnamed in the program's description—read: I am made invisible—I am the only faculty member in the department who is trained and certified and has taught an "Inside-Out" course. In the same section of the external review on innovative pedagogy, my grant-funded project entitled "Classrooms on the Move" was also listed, a project in which I explored the possibilities and meanings of teaching that occur physically beyond the classroom. This was one place I was actually named, but it also happened to involve another tenure-track faculty member I sought out for collaboration. The goal of "Classrooms on the Move" was to get students to closely explore and interrogate different settings in their immediate community (both on and off campus) as a way to foster their understanding of ways that the discipline can be defined and applied in action, cultivating students' identity as a sociologists and criminologists.

The problem I have described above is not about ownership over class activities and pedagogical techniques or even about being unnamed—being made invisible—in their reviews, but rather how this maintains my exploitation. The Sociology Department continues to utilize my intellectual property and leverage my achievements to gain greater merits both as individual faculty and as a department as a whole, while actively excluding me from full citizenship and the accompanying benefits, namely the job security that comes from earning tenure within a tenure-track position. I am but a denizen on indefinite probation.

In an attempt for me to internalize the idea that it was my performance that prevented my advancement to tenure-track, the Department Chair *suggested* that we have weekly meetings to make sure I was in the "best possible position if a tenure-track" line were to open. While this may appear to be mentoring, the reality is that it only created additional labor for me, took time away from me developing my craft and attending to students, and gave me anxiety from being surveilled, the hidden reason/function of these meetings in the first place. This was much obvious later as surveillance intensified. Up to this point, my student evaluations and teaching evaluations were all positive. At the time I had published a peer-reviewed article and had two other articles under review, along with several other creative pieces in development, had conducted several workshops for faculty and staff development, and had influenced other faculty as my work and/ or name appeared in external reviews, self-studies, and their self-evaluations for tenure.

Combining my love for storytelling and teaching created a knack for curriculum development. When walking or riding the bus, I would often get caught daydreaming about new classes to teach, mentally creating characters as I built the story-course from the start of the semester to finals week, searching my memory's history for books related to the title and picturing the characters watching related documentaries that would come to mind. "At least one new class each semester," I assured myself.

Given that research methods is an important facet of the undergraduate program, I turned one of those dreamt-up courses, "Images of Crime," into a one-time methods course that provided training on multimodal analysis, primarily text, discourse, and images, but also various modes of communication including film, sounds, toys, and other objects. While the new course did well, receiving great student feedback, it still came as a surprise when, as a member of the Department Curriculum Committee, I received the manila folder of new course requests to review including one titled "Media and Crime" that bore the same course description I created for *Images of Crime*, but with the Criminology Coordinator's name replacing mine. I convinced myself temporarily that in the end it was about the students and that as long as they could experience the course, it was a win. However, after thinking about my temporary or contingent fellowship status and the need to highlight achievements so I could obtain a tenure-track position, I presented the two course documents to several academics and non-academics within and outside the department, asking if they thought the two courses sounded like the same course or different courses.

After getting side-eyed or strange looks from them (for asking a seemingly obvious question) I still spent weeks mulling it over before finally deciding to speak with the Coordinator who proposed the course himself. Although I had been only one of four full-time Criminology faculty in the Sociology Department for nearly two years at that point, the Criminology Coordinator and I had never held a one-on-one conversation. Two of the other four Criminology faculty members' offices were directly across from mine, both of whom were "junior" tenure-track faculty members—one having arrived before and one hired after me. Being accustomed to exclusion in most spaces, I did not find myself too bothered seeing the Coordinator in their offices regularly, discussing research, department, and discipline-related things. However, my observations along with my status as a non-tenure-track "junior" faculty member made me more uncomfortable broaching the subject with the Coordinator. After explaining my concern about the course I created not being credited to me as it moved from the Department Committee to the University Curriculum Committee, the Coordinator dove into his White savior complex and responded by saying, "A few students in my class were talking about it [my course] and seemed to really like it, and I knew you had a lot on your plate, so I just did it for you." That being the very first time we had any conversation in all my time at the university, it was hard for me to believe that he knew or cared about what *was* or *was not* on my plate. I thanked him and left his office. The course was approved by the university as a permanent part of the curriculum and is currently being taught by a new White male faculty member. The names were never corrected.

Invisible.

APPLICATION 3: "TO WHOM IT MAY CONCERN, KEEP THIS NIGGER-BOY RUNNING"

The university policy restricts full-time temporary positions to two consecutive years, which includes the diversity fellowship I secured when I was found still standing after the battle royal or application number 2. Throughout my contracted time as a diversity fellow (including up until the time of writing this chapter), I inquired about my conversion into a tenure-track position—the supposed goal of the diversity fellowship to the Chair, the Dean, co-faculty members with pull, and the Vice President. Nearing the middle of my second and final eligible year, I still had not received any direct responses other than bits of what was later identified (but not confronted) as misinformation as I was told enrollment was too low to justify another line (although we are talking about the second-largest major on campus having only three tenure-track and two full-time temporary faculty at the time). In actuality, the only requirement needed for my conversion onto a tenure-track path was "full departmental support," support which some of the smiling faces had withheld for reasons that were never explained.

Failing to make a decision, the Sociology Department decided to ask the Union to request a policy change to amend the two-year limit for full-time temporary faculty. This was at a time the Union had been in the heat of a bad collective bargaining battle (at the time of this writing, all faculty and librarians are 746 days without a raise and 565 days without a contract). The two-year full-time temporary policy was changed to three years and my contingent contract was extended one year. If the policy change had not been approved, the only possibility of remaining at the university would be if I were demoted to an "adjunct" position. This was a possibility that several faculty in the department exaggerated as a considerable option for me, showing excitement about the possibility of me staying, but in a position empty of health benefits, job security, departmental influence/visibility, certain department/university opportunities in the form of professional development, and a pay cut that would repress my ability to remain fed and housed. I took their comments and attitudes as evidence that they did not really want me in their department. Or, at least, my integration was based on Black exploitation. Manning Marable (2015), discussing Black America, speaks of politicians, intellectuals, and civic leaders who condemned "the United States on the grounds that white society has systematically excluded blacks as a group from the material, cultural, and political gains achieved by other ethnic minorities" (p. 2). Continuing, Marable (2015) writes,

> Blacks occupy the lowest socioeconomic rung in the ladder of American upward mobility precisely because they have been 'integrated' all too well into the system. ... Capitalist development has occurred not in spite of the exclusion of Blacks, but because of the brutal exploitation of Blacks as workers and consumers.
>
> (p. 2)

I began to understand the smiling faces that created contradictions that did not become clear until much later. Yes, some may have wanted me there, but they wanted me there for their own university and departmental "development" in the currency of diversity, inclusion, and progress, that in which they had full control over, that is, making sure I remained the raw material that cultivated such development in Black Capital.

Another semester passes and I am in the second semester of my third year, facing the same reality of being invisible and looking in the mirror only to see that my contract will expire. Adding insult to injury, three new (all White) tenure-track faculty have been hired in the Sociology Department (in addition to a full-time spousal hire). It became clear that when the previous Department Chair said she "wished they had a job" for me at the university that yes, there were jobs opening here, but they were not for me. Inducing my Racial Battle Fatigue (RBF), I spent a few hours examining the CVs of the new hires. My CV outweighed theirs in teaching, research, and service—the three major fields of consideration for hiring. In the case of one of the new hires, my service and achievements from just my time at this university outweighed their entire vitae. There was no justifiable explanation as to why they were on the tenure-track and I was not—their Whiteness outweighed my accomplishments.

After a series (nearly ten) of hate crimes against Black students on campus, which got national news attention on news sites like *CBS NEWS*, followed by a

197

series of unfortunate responses by the university's administration and campus police, students and faculty began to be more critical of the lack of faculty of color on the university campus. This came to a head after the Director of the Center of Inclusion and Excellence resigned due to a hostile work environment, which involved her direct supervisor, the interim Chief Diversity and Inclusion Officer. University students confronted the President of the university after he unilaterally decided to bypass the national search and reappoint the sitting Interim, even after being provided with a lengthy testimony from the resigned Director of the hostile behavior of interim Chief Diversity and Inclusion Officer. Protesting students at the university demanded that he overturn his decision. While the students were meeting the President, another meeting organized by an English professor to discuss the racist hiring practices at the university was taking place, directly next door.

The hate crimes that occurred on campus increased the invisible (emotional) labor the very few faculty of color, including myself as one of two Black male professors (and only two Black women professors) in the entire university, were experiencing. Frightened and angry, Students of Color at the university dramatically increased the amount of time they spent in my office, as well as their general correspondence via email and phone. White faculty and administrators also increased their requests for me to participate in unpaid speaking engagements and workshops. The Sociology Department also participated in this racial/racist spotlighting, requesting me and another Faculty Member of Color to provide a training during the upcoming department meeting on how to talk about racism in the classroom.

APPLICATION 4: "FLASHLIGHTS OF INK"

The surveillance intensified once I refused to apply a fourth time for a tenure-track position that was seemingly created for me, but within a national search. This meant once again submitting the basic materials, calling on my references, and conducting a research talk and teaching demonstration, which I had no problem doing, but it was not the "conversion" promised. After reaching an all-time high level of RBF and making this decision, I moved out of my assigned office and worked from the campus coffee shop and held office hours in the Center for Inclusive Excellence housed two floors down. The decision not to apply put the department in a frenzy, forcing them to make a critical choice in a critical moment given the outrage from students at the lack of faculty of color, the chain of racist hate crimes and the poor subsequent administrative responses thereafter. There were three potential internal candidates who would, by policy, be guaranteed phone interviews (the White spousal hire, a Black woman, and a current Rescue Scholar).

As the students stood against the university administration, preparing a sit-in because of the overall campus climate, the administration got more directly involved in my fight as well. After taking a few sick days I was allotted, the Dean of the university emailed me one business day before *observing* each one of my courses. No explanation was provided, but I packed a box of tissues and headed to campus the next day. Meanwhile, the Chair emailed me suggesting that I take unpaid medical leave to maintain employment status. I found this extreme given I had only taken three to four total sick days in my three years there at that point, and that I was still actively advising students (and meeting them for serious matters and counsel relating to their own personal aftermaths of the hate crimes and other worries), working on research articles, and continuing to serve the university as a whole. Aside from that, there were only two weeks left of classes, so the lure of "maintaining my employment status" when I had already decided I would no longer remain at the university beyond those two weeks felt more threatening than caring and than accountability, especially since I had not gone over my allotted sick days/personal days. Given that the Chair of the department, whose duty it is to evaluate my courses had not yet done so, I initially assumed that the Dean's observation was for teaching evaluation. However, once the Dean finished up her last observation of my classes, the Chair emailed me saying she would also be observing all of my classes to do evaluations the following week, which was the very last week of the academic year. Though I felt the surveillance previously, before it was more like that lurking feeling of being followed in any store I walk into, but now I understood it very well that I was being surveilled. Not only that, but my teaching evaluations, which are filed into my record, would be treated unfairly given that they were taking place on the very last day of each class, when I would have no scheduled teaching and given my soon approaching departure from the university, would be celebrating the semester with my students with music, pizza, and reminiscence of the semester. Instead the Chair's flashlight of ink in the well-lit room hovered over us as like a police officer as we tried to say our goodbyes.

ACTIONABLE STRATEGIES

What my autoethnographic story captures is how un-democratic, un-meritocratic, and racist higher education is. I was selected a Diversity Fellow, yes, but it was a position that offers no job security (although it claimed to) and allowed my department and the university to use my labor and toss me to the side when my contract expired when necessary. And, also, to appear as though they are dedicated to diversity. I conclude my chapter by sharing recommendations for hiring diverse faculty. As I learned from reading Adalberto Aguirre, Jr.'s (2008) chapter, "Academic Storytelling: A Critical Race Theory Story of Affirmative Action," new practices must be developed and used within higher education in order to diversify faculty. Affirmative action has historically benefited Whites (see Katznelson, 2005). For this reason, universities must simply

199

be better. There are many strategies and recommendations for universities and their respective departments to do better and simply not be oppressive in their hiring practices, one being "Target of Opportunity Hiring" that one of my colleagues supports.

However, there are a ton of programs, policy initiatives, strategic plans, and books written on recommendations for policy and practice, many of those by higher education leaders, some by folks like the authors in this book you are reading who labor through this today and some who did so generations before us. Maybe this is a racially fatigued response, but it is simple: Be better. Stop doing all the shit you read in these chapters. You know you are doing it. In any other scenario, if a person or persons repeated the same negative behavior and truly did not know they were behaving negatively, your institutions would probably regard them as grossly incompetent individuals who leave much to be desired. Hire more than one person of color, especially Black and Brown women by removing the unwritten law of one-per-department. Your battles royal are tiresome. Much of this conclusion might be edited (out), as Collins (1989) warned us long ago that the academe gatekeepers do not allow such ways of speaking.

TO WHOM IT MAY CONCERN, BURNING BRIDGES TO THE RING

During this revision, my friend and I traded places. While he tends to emphasize the micro relations, my head stays flexing in the macro. Upon reading this he urged me to not burn any bridges and that being so specific about the positions can draw too limited a focus on those individual persons. Though, if the bridge is connected to a place of constant oppression and unrealized egos, I would rather swim in the bridge debris toward waves of change. It is my hope that readers understand that institutional racism is of utmost regard and that these individuals work at the institutional level, regenerating these forms of racism that impact me the individual and others like me, along with the larger institution. If RBF continues to push Scholars of Color away from professorships, that means less Black- and Brown-authored research and scholarship (legitimized research, anyway) and my son and other Black and Brown kids not having the opportunity to see people that look like them in educational and leadership roles.

As I continued to "stay on the market," applying for positions at other universities, which created a process of detachment from my current university (including applying for university-specific grants, building student and faculty relationships, new programming ideas, and spending less time in the office, etc.), I reached the limit of my RBF. Writing to one of my former professors, concerning letters of recommendation that were needed for the faculty positions I was applying for, I stopped "running," and *intoned* in an email message:

I am truly sorry for my lack of communication, I've been having the worst of it over here at my current institution regarding racist hiring practices. So much so that I believe I may have to exit academia as a whole. As of now, I will not be needing any more letters of recommendation for this endeavor. If that changes, which is very possible given my love for the classroom, I hope to count on your continued support, but I need to re-evaluate my path. In the meantime, I'll reflect on ways of building a larger, far reaching classroom. With the utmost appreciation,

Martel

Invisible. Again.

NOTES

1 The author would like to give a special thanks to Dr. Christopher Grice, Dr. Daisy Ball, and Ralph Ellison.
2 "Drawn from Ralph Ellison, *Invisible Man* (1952, p. 33).

REFERENCES

Adalberto, Jr., A. (2008). Academic storytelling: A critical race theory story of affirmative action. In A. Adalberto Jr. & D. V. Baker (Eds.), *Structured inequality in the United States: Critical discussions on the continuing significance of race, ethnicity, and gender* (pp. 74–86). Upper Saddle River, NJ: Prentice Hall.

Collins, P. H. (1989). The social construction of Black feminist thought. *Signs*, *14*(4), 745–773.

Ellison, R. (1952). *Invisible Man*. New York: Vintage International.

Katznelson, I. (2005). *When affirmative action was white: An untold history of racial inequality in twentieth-century America*. New York: W.W. Norton.

Marable, M. (2015). *How capitalism underdeveloped black America*. Chicago, IL: Haymarket Books.

Chapter 16

Ivory Tower Respectability and el Estado de Estar Harta

Sayil Camacho

INTRODUCTION

I left my second last name in Agua Blanca, *en medio del Barrio 5 y Tepeyac, donde la agua no está ni dulce ni blanca* (gloss: In the middle of the 5th Barrio and Tepeyac, where the water is neither sweet nor white). I know that when I pronounce my name in college corridors, I do not always enunciate the Mexican *a*. I may or may not tell you that I am a former undocumented person and that your assumptions about me do not affirm the multidimensionality of my identity. Even in this simple exchange, I have to navigate the contradictions of respectability. What is and what is not appropriate for me to name. And when I learned about the Latinx higher education pipeline and the dismal statistics that illustrate the unattainable nature of a graduate education, my experiences in college corridors—these premier research university corridors—began to make sense. I have borne witness to how we omit our workplace experiences within higher education and I do not want to cut my wrists and strip my soul for the White gaze either. My counternarrative is resuscitated here, on these pages, not for them but for you.[1] I see you. It has always been about you, especially during the dark times when I was not sure I would finish, walk across the stage, or sit at the table *después de tantas lágrimas y sacrificios* (gloss: After so many tears and sacrifices).

This counternarrative is not meant to essentialize the Latinx experience neither is it an exhaustive list of the challenges we encounter when we attempt to be part of the knowledge-production process. My narrative is not a place where grit is romanticized; this is not a coming-out-of-the-hood Disney story. This is my story. A story about a Latina[2] scholar activist who takes to task espoused institutional commitments of equity, diversity, and inclusion and eats resilience out of necessity. At this very moment, I am pursuing a tenure-track faculty job position during a time in which Latinxs make up the largest ethnic minority population in the United States (17.8%), but only 4% of university faculty are Latinx (U.S. Census Bureau, 2017; Saldaña, Castro-Villareal, & Sosa, 2013). This, too, is a gendered experience, as only 1% of full-time Latinx professors in premier research universities identify as female (Saldaña, Castro-Villareal, & Sosa, 2013; U.S. Department of Education, 2018). In enduring this experience, I almost allowed the politics of respectability and the state of being *harta* (gloss: Tired) to narrate my faculty job search process. But I am here now.

I am a *Cuāuhtli* (gloss: Eagle) and *Itzamna* (gloss: Creator Deity) rising because my heart cannot be still while they tear you apart in the name of trickle-down "progress." I will not be complicit to the status quo; to business as usual. We were meant to soar. I have called upon my ancestors and they have gifted me with these words. In asking for their guidance, I remembered that I was a warrior in a past life. A time when they slit our throats and shoved down seeds of respectability. This is my story, and it is a means to further interrogate White supremacy within the academy, particularly within premier research institutions that are leading by example. We see you.

This *platica* (gloss: Talk) would be remiss if I did not first honor Black feminist activists who came before me. Royalty that defined and defied the *politics of respectability*. Thank you for sharing your counternarratives and providing testament to the contradictions you were forced to navigate within and outside of your communities. Evelyn Brooks Higginbotham (1989, 1993)— thank you for demonstrating how the politics of respectability are in propriety of White supremacy and under the guise of what is and what is not proper. The cost of playing by their rules is our human dignity, our personhood, the silencing of our experiences, the complicated truth, and our shared and unshared pain.

The politics of respectability within higher education translates to what we already know to be true: Our places of learning do not allow for the full participation of self, and faculty can be both the gatekeepers of White supremacy and agents of change. In the company of Evelyn Brooks Higginbotham, I name the politics of respectability I encountered during my tenure-track faculty job search process, to first hold space for your Racial Battle Fatigue (RBF). If higher education faculty and administrators are reading this because they want to compel change, I hope they understand that their inability to implement equitable hiring policies and practices means that they are also in propriety of White supremacy. We know that these institutions were not built with our participation in mind. However, the sociopolitical history of higher education does not negate the responsibility that educators, university administrators, and policymakers espouse today. When they fail historically marginalized communities, they have also failed our shared humanity.

RACIAL BATTLE FATIGUE FROM THE FRONTLINES OF THE EDUCATIONAL PIPELINE

I was invited to give a talk at the Harvard Kennedy School and my mother could not have been prouder. She told me that everyone was praying for me, and that my aunt in Guadalajara was going to church precisely at the time of my talk *para prender la vela de cidro y hacerme una oración especial* (gloss: To light a citronella candle and say a special prayer). When I practiced my talk with my mentors, they told me that I needed to dig deeper and explain why I was there. I needed to tell my story and let people know what motivated me to do the work that I did. Though I understood the intention behind their words, I felt frustrated. I felt tired. I felt inadequate. How do you add intergenerational trauma and risks to your PowerPoint slides in a way that evokes change and not voyeurism? How do you speak about things that you had to do to survive without risking the perpetuation of negative stereotypes about you and/or your community? How do you simultaneously make room for *Latinx Joy* while standing in your truth? These are questions I still cannot answer. But to make room for the intersections of my story, I shared this at the start of my presentation:

> Recently, I had a conversation with my mother, and she told me that she did not think immigrating to the United States was worth her sacrifice and effort until she saw me walk across the stage and receive my doctorate degree. For most of my life, I knew my mother felt this way about living in the United States and that is a heavy burden for an immigrant mother and child to bear. I did not have the heart to tell her that universities in the United States, even fancy ones like Harvard, are places where immigrants can also experience workplace vulnerability, exploitation, and abuse. Nor did I tell her that earning a doctorate degree meant that I was safe from discrimination or had "made it." In this country, an immigrant, is an immigrant, is an immigrant.
>
> In this presentation, I will be speaking about the workplace experiences of postdoctoral scholars sponsored by temporary workplace visas and how their visa status compounds their workplace vulnerability, exploitation, and abuse at elite research institutions.

To start at the beginning means that I must first acknowledge the social contract my immigrant parents made when they entered this country. They would make sacrifices so their children could have a chance at a better life. They would set aside their unrealized dreams and ambitions and accept a lower station in life as immigrant workers so we could have an opportunity to realize our potential. In the same way that my parents applied a tireless work ethic to make ends meet for me and my four siblings, I applied myself in school. My American education gave me much needed structure, especially when I experienced negative health outcomes that are correlated with poverty; among these experiences were housing and food insecurity and substance abuse. By the time I was 18 years old we had relocated a total of ten times and even though that meant eight new schools during my K–12 journey, one thing remained constant—the profound love and appreciation I had for educators that provided comfort, security, and a place of belonging during times of uncertainty. Educators in different cities and districts encouraged me to imagine a fantastical future, one unconstrained by my socio-economic status.

Looking back, I knew then that I was one of the lucky ones. Attending low-income schools meant that alongside my peers, I experienced an education that oftentimes did not meet our needs, challenge our potential, and/or provide us with interventions necessary to promote our retention and success. Together, we walked a narrow mountainside trail—one misstep could send us tumbling into the abyss, never able to climb back up due to setbacks that were beyond our control. Socioeconomic status is unforgiving. When I received my college acceptance letters, I felt like I had just barely made it out alive.

LATINX EDUCATORS AND RBF WARRIORS

To understand the Latinx higher education pipeline in the United States, it is important to first recognize the disadvantages facing the Latinx population before we even set foot on a college campus. Latinxs are the largest minority group to not enroll in high school or complete a high school education (United States Census, 2017). Despite low high school enrollment and completion rates, Latinx higher education enrollment is currently at a record high of 47% (Pew Research Center, 2017). At the same time, retention and degree completion rates remain lower for Latinx students than for other ethnic groups (Pew Research Center, 2017). Specifically, only 23.2% of Latinx adults have earned an associate degree or higher compared to 41% of all adults (U.S. Census Bureau, 2019). When the data is further disaggregated by type of degree received, only 15% of Latinxs between the ages 25 and 29 years have earned a bachelor's degree (Krogstad, 2015; U.S. Census Bureau, 2017). Similarly, graduate or professional school enrollment is lowest for Latinxs (1.9%) compared to other minority groups (U.S. Census Bureau, 2017). Presently, Latinxs make up 8% of the graduate student population and 5.2% of master's degrees are awarded to Latinxs and 4.4% of doctoral recipients are Latinx (Kim, 2013).

To apply for a faculty position, a candidate must have a bachelor's degree, a master's degree, and a doctoral degree. Latinxs who wish to actualize teaching, research, and service in higher education have to first defy these odds, over and over again … to only experience labor segregation after completing their graduate education: 3% of Latino men and 2% of Latina women are full-time faculty in degree-granting institutions (U.S. Department of Education, 2018). Faculty participation also varies by academic rank and institution, whereby 2% of Latino men and 1% of Latina women hold the rank of full professor and 3% of Latinx men and women account for full-time assistant professors (U.S. Department of Education, 2018). In addition, 2.2% of Latinxs are full-time professors in public research universities and 2.1% of Latinxs are full-time professors in private research universities (Trower & Chait, 2002).

When Latinx faculty participation is further stratified by institution, elite research institutions have essentially told us that we can persist despite overwhelming obstacles, obtain our degrees, *y hasta pararnos de pestañas* (gloss: And even stand on our eyelashes [a colloquial saying of doing the impossible]), but we will not be part of the academic knowledge production process. The day I had to sit with this truth, pain and anxiety crippled me. My parents' unspoken fears were laid before me— fears that I would forget who I was and hope for too much. In being a first-generation college graduate, four-times overs, I have left so much behind. I remain haunted by anxiety. His fingers dig into my flesh while whispering, "They don't want you."

Today, I often wonder: how many people selected to interview at elite research institutions are people like me? How many of them look like me? How many of our faculty are survivors of the American education system? How many are free and reduced lunch and Pell Grant recipients? How many are faculty whose research is grounded in the experiences of injustice, faculty who translate research into pressing actionable policy changes for the betterment of society? How many faculty challenge the system beyond discussing the implications of their research? How many faculty share *el estado de estar hart@* (gloss: The state of being tired), are outraged by these statistics, and can be counted as allies on the other side of the glass ceiling?

It is not too often that we are able to celebrate a Latinx brother or sister securing a tenure-track faculty position at an elite research institution. What is more common is receiving confirmation that the search committee already had a candidate in mind and that our participation was solely to make the hiring pool appear to be diverse. During the Fall 2018 semester, I applied to 22 academic positions. The result of this endeavor was not a tenure-track position, but rather another postdoctorate appointment because the faculty job market was "*that* competitive" this time around. I do not remember a time in life when my academic dreams were *that* impossible. The majority of the positions I applied for specifically stated their respective postsecondary institutions were especially interested in hiring historically marginalized people who could support an increasingly diverse student population—my reason for being. Their silence is deafening.

THE STATE AND CONSEQUENCE OF RACIAL BATTLE FATIGUE

This is the part where I tell you, beautiful soul, that you can have all of the awards, accomplishments, grant funding, and publications in top-tier research journals, only to be turned away when it is your turn. They will see the potential in others before they see your accomplishments. You will be measured by a different set of expectations; expectations that permit the aforementioned statistics. This is also the part where I am supposed to tell you not to give up, but that would be irresponsible. The mind and body can only take so much pain. My own existence is still a process of rebuilding what has been fractured. One of my greatest fears is that there may come a time when I cannot put myself back together again. What I can tell you, is that you are not alone.

RBF requires an acknowledgment of paradox. It means accepting that the same educational system that was developed to support the actualization of personhood does not support our meaningful participation. RBF is accepting this truth but persisting for our students, community, and the unrealized dreams and sacrifices of people who were just as deserving of the education we had the privilege of receiving. RBF is lonely. RBF will haunt you long after you have given all of yourself to the academy. RBF will lie to you and tell you that you do not deserve a seat at the table, when you built your own table. RBF will lie to us and tell us there is not enough room at the table, when our eyes see nothing but seats, and much work to be done. RBF will not acknowledge that academic excellence necessitates diversity and your participation is paramount to our social progress as a nation.

During my tenure-track faculty job search, the Trump administration has waged war on my community. My students are worried about deportations, being separated from their families, how anti-immigrant state policies will affect them, and the future of their temporary legal statuses. This administration has bred bold, overt, and violent forms of racism. Educators at elite research institutions, faculty who have the ability to be beacons of hope and champions of change, know that the Trump presidency has been particularly defined by its human rights violations (Human Rights Watch, 2017). The Trump ideology echoes the words of colonizer John Winthrop's "City Upon a Hill," for he too seeks to build a wall on stolen land and claims predestination has to cast us away. Lest we forget that the same Puritan values that birthed racial and social hierarchies were foundational to establishing the first American college in 1636, Harvard College (Cohen & Kisker, 2010; Wilder, 2013). The Trump presidency is the consequence of an education system that has failed us all. It is important to include this in my counternarrative because my academic journey and faculty job search reflects the sociopolitical history of the United States. Tenure-track faculty positions are a matter of social justice and inextricably tied to our humanity and democracy.

With the preceding in mind, it is important to recognize that numerous research studies have been conducted on the topic of minority faculty participation and promotion. For decades, the implications of low representation of faculty of color and best policies and practices have been discussed at length (Turner & Gonzales, 2008). Related to the topic of minority faculty participation, research studies have also established the numerous ways in which minority faculty participation advances the mission and vision of higher education

(Tuner & Gonzales, 2008). Minority faculty participation translates into promoting inclusive learning environments, improved curricula and learning outcomes for students, and support for institutional commitments to diversity (Gasman, Abiola & Travers, 2015; Harper & Hurtado, 2007; Jayakumar, Howard, Allen, & Han, 2009; Piercy et al., 2005; Whittaker, Montgomery, & Acosta, 2015; Zambrana et al, 2015). No doubt, minority faculty participation within higher education is invaluable. However, in the same way that my humanity is not measured by my economic contribution to the United States, minority faculty participation should neither be bound nor justified by how we support Historically White Institutions (HWIs). We do not exist for you. Do not negate our humanity.

Marybeth Gasman, a leading expert on the topic of Minority Serving Institutions (MSIs), asked institutions and faculty search committees to consider the following: (1) how their use of the word "quality" is utilized to dismiss applicants of color, (2) how low numbers of applicants of color are used by the faculty search committees to justify and maintain the status quo, (3) how exceptions to hiring protocols are made for White applicants and not applicants of color, (4) how search committees espouse and inherently privilege some scholars over others and how this privileging perpetuates labor segregation, and (5) how search committees are unable to collaborate and recruit from MSIs (Gasman, 2016). When succinctly summarizing the institutional barriers that minority applicants experience, Gasman (2016) also echoed what I have experienced to be true, "The reason we don't have more faculty of color among college faculty is that we don't want them. We simply don't want them" (para. 5).

ACTIONABLE STRATEGIES

My counternarrative detailing the frontlines of RBF survival speak to how Latinxs are systemically marginalized from receiving a postsecondary education and how we are further segregated from working in elite research universities—educational spaces that we collectively recognize as knowledge-producing institutions. In order to combat long-standing educational discrimination and promote a diverse student-to-educator pipeline, additional interventions and resources need to be developed for historically marginalized populations. Though this is an important part of the conversation, my proposed policy and practice recommendations have been developed for faculty hiring and search committee members.

There are several reasons why I elected to develop recommendations for faculty hiring and search committee members. First, faculty hiring and search committee members are agents of change that can alleviate RBF at their respective institutions and immediately challenge current hiring practices. Second, my recommendations have been developed with best hiring policies and practices in mind and are also grounded in the experiences of my RBF survival, during my faculty job search. Without faculty hiring and search committee members realizing it, I have consistently interacted with them through the glass ceiling. It is my sincere hope that in naming what I have been taught to endure, I am further illustrating the consequence of inaction and the tremendous power of faculty hiring and search committee members.

The Labor of Student Activists

While in graduate school, I was part of a student activist collective named Call2Action. We formed in response to how White faculty were treating students of color at the University of California, Los Angeles (UCLA) Graduate School of Education & Information Studies. As a collective, we organized a series of community town hall meetings to discuss our concerns with faculty, staff, and students and were told that in leveraging our concerns, we were committing professional suicide. During one of our town hall meetings, a White, male, emeritus professor cornered my friend and colleague because he was upset students had spoken about the way they were treated in his class. The professor angrily placed his hands on my friend and shortly thereafter the professor was escorted out of the building by the Department Chair. Call2Action anticipated that the actions of the professor would be diminished by the department and we would be characterized as unreasonable and hostile. In addition to facilitating the town hall meeting, we collected statements from people who had witnessed the incident so that we could address this at the Graduate School of Education & Information Studies Race and Ethnic Committee meeting. Unfortunately, the majority of faculty were more interested in discussing the status of potential lawsuits against the university and professor as opposed to generating support for us and the aggrieved student.

This experience merits mention because it is illustrative of how student activists are oftentimes at the forefront of naming educational inequities. Historically, student activists have held postsecondary institutions accountable to their mission statements, advocating for affordable tuition, ethnic studies, increased minority student enrollment, and so forth (Altback & Cohen, 1990; Arthur, 2016; Joseph, 2013; Rhoads, 1998). Most recently, student activists have led changes to support undocumented students, institutionalize gender-neutral bathrooms and lactating rooms, and advance graduate student worker rights, among other social justice issues (Bousquet & Nelson, 2008; Brown & Nichols, 2013; Case, Kanenberg, Erich, & Tittsworth, 2012; Gonzales, 2008). While student activism has been central to equity, diversity, and inclusion efforts within higher education, the culture of elite research institutions discourages student activism. In my experience, particularly when graduate students participate in student activist efforts, their professional credibility is immediately at risk and it becomes that much harder to secure a tenure-track faculty job.

Faculty, and in this case faculty search committees, cannot, in good conscience, maintain a cool distance from students who have courageously come forward to testify how their places of learning have failed them. Faculty and faculty search committees must, first and foremost, recognize the unpaid campus climate labor that student activists have taken on and then seek to understand how their work informs their faculty search process. Faculty search committees need to establish collaborative partnerships with student activists who are arguably more attuned to campus climate and can support meaningful discussions about equity, diversity, and inclusion and the selection of faculty candidates.

Arriving to the Table

I am certain that elite research institutions are not telling their students that historically marginalized populations have no place in academia and/or that their institutions are purposefully turning away qualified candidates because they do not want to hire them. I am also certain that elite research institutions will not tell their historically marginalized graduate students that they are good enough to learn, work, and pay for an education at their respective institution but not good enough to teach at their graduate school. Therefore, similar institutional systems, structures, and interventions that have been enacted to increase minority student enrollment need to be established to create faculty of color access and retention pathways. #StayMadAbby[3]

Affirmative action for historically marginalized populations means that race should not only be a factor when considering faculty candidates, but the faculty selection process needs to allow the opportunity for applicants to provide testament to the overwhelming obstacles they had to overcome to be a candidate in the first place. Essay prompts, such as, "describe a time in your life you had to overcome an obstacle" are utilized to better understand historically marginalized students during their college application process and provides significant insight and context so that the totality of their accomplishments can be evaluated. When faculty search committees dismiss an applicant without fully understanding our academic journeys and the pathways we had to forge, the faculty search committee is participating in silencing and discounting experiences that are as valuable as the hard-earned accomplishments on our curriculum vitae.

Relatedly, faculty search committees need to ask themselves; "How are we supporting and preparing minority students for tenure-track faculty jobs?" "How are we allies on the other side of the glass ceiling?" "What systems and support programs have been developed for the access, retention, and tenure of faculty of color from graduate school to their full professorship status?" If institutions do not have said systems and processes, they need to hire members of historically marginalized populations to enact these changes at their institutions. Why? Because they have directly experienced these inequities.

210

White Logic and the Unearned Privileges of the Faculty Search Committee

During my first year as a graduate student, we were having a classroom discussion about minority faculty participation in higher education. I participated in the discussion and said something along the lines of it was shameful that UCLA had such low faculty of color participation when the institution was a public, land grant institution that served an increasingly diverse student population. The White professor became defensive and she dismissed my remarks by reminding me that compared to other UCLA departments, Graduate School of Education & Information Studies had more faculty of color. Note that utilizing systemic racism to measure the progress of basic diversity initiatives and recruitment efforts is White logic. Until there have been substantial changes to the diversity makeup of faculty and administrative leadership, any progress educators and policymakers think they have accomplished is not enough.

While some institutions have developed trainings for faculty search committees to better understand selection bias and to establish more inclusive hiring protocols, it is important that faculty search committees account for unearned privileges—how their status in society afforded them a place at the decision table—and intimately understand the ways in which they are not qualified to comprehend the experiences of historically marginalized populations. Then, and only after participating in critical self-reflection, should they recruit historically marginalized people that are members of their academic institutions to be part of the faculty search committee and hold an equal voice in the hiring process. A faculty search committee should never be a majority White, male, or abled space. When a historically marginalized applicant is turned away, the faculty search committee needs to be fully informed as to who they are turning away in their process and what that means for their institutional diversity efforts.

As a component of the critical self-reflection process for faculty search committees, such committees should account for all of the ways in which their respective departments did not follow hiring protocols in the past and which exceptions were made for whom. This is an important exercise because it will require the faculty search committee to understand how they have actively participated in maintaining the status quo, asking them to examine how White logic has permeated their process. The point of this exercise is to hold this reality into account when they invariably hold historically marginalized populations to different standards and processes.

Is Trump Business as Usual? Asking for a Friend

The Trump presidency has spurred higher education leadership to restate their commitments to supporting historically marginalized populations and the ways in which their institutions promote an inclusive learning environment. While these statements are a basic response to violent human rights violations, we are at a poignant time in history. How elite HWIs support and make good on their commitments to diversity will indicate our ability to undo the damage of the Trump presidency and address the long-standing racist structures and systems that poison our society and democracy.

With this in mind, I am compelled to also share that our meaningful participation will make people uncomfortable. Faculty search committees need to get used to that feeling. Historically marginalized leaders will seek to establish more inclusive learning environments and in doing this important work we will have to address systems, processes, and people who are not supportive of these efforts. As members of historically marginalized populations, we will be overburdened with this labor, and it will not always be in support of our tenure process. In fact, we will experience additional criticism and obstacles. When we accept faculty positions, we understand this unspoken contract. Critical self-reflection is uncomfortable; however, I can assure faculty and faculty search committees that the consequences of maintaining segregated labor practices will be much more damaging to them, their students, and our shared commitments to higher education.

NOTES

1 While the recommendations developed in this chapter are for university administrators and policymakers, in this chapter the author is in conversation with historically marginalized populations.
2 The author identifies as female, and utilizes Latina to describe herself.
3 This hashtag trended after the *Fisher v. University of Texas* (2013) affirmative action case, after Supreme Court Justice Antonin Scalia commented that Black students belong in slower track schools.

REFERENCES

Altbach, P. G., & Cohen, R. (1990). American student activism: The post-sixties transformation. *The Journal of Higher Education*, *61*(1), 32–49.

Arthur, M. M. L. (2016). *Student activism and curricular change in higher education*. New York: Routledge.

Bousquet, M., & Nelson, C. (2008). *How the university works: Higher education and the low-wage nation*. New York: New York University Press.

Brown, V., & Nichols, T. R. (2013). Pregnant and parenting students on campus: Policy and program implications for a growing population. *Educational Policy*, *27*(3), 499–530.

Case, K. A., Kanenberg, H., Erich, S. A., & Tittsworth, J. (2012). Transgender inclusion in university nondiscrimination statements: Challenging gender-conforming privilege through student activism. *Journal of Social Issues*, *68*(1), 145–161.

Cohen, A. M., & Kisker, C. B. (2010). *The shaping of American higher education: Emergence and growth of the contemporary system.* New York: John Wiley & Sons.

Gasman, M. (2016, September 26). An ivy league professor on why colleges don't hire more faculty of color: 'We don't want them.' *The Washington Post.* Retrieved from https://www.washingtonpost.com/news/grade-point/wp/2016/09/26/an-ivy-league-professor-on-why-colleges-dont-hire-more-faculty-of-color-we-don t-want-them/?utm_term=.1da72555fcaa

Gasman, M., Abiola, U., & Travers, C. (2015). Diversity and senior leadership at elite institutions of higher education. *Journal of Diversity in Higher Education, 8*(1), 1–14.

Gonzales, R. G. (2008). Left out but not shut down: Political activism and the undocumented student movement. *Northwestern Journal of Law & Social Policy, 3*(2), 219–239. Retrieved from https://scholarlycommons.law.northwestern.edu/cgi/viewcontent.cgi?referer=https://www.google.com/&httpsredir=1&article=10 26&context=njlsp

Harper, S. R., & Hurtado, S. (2007). Nine themes in campus racial climates and implications for institutional transformation. *New Directions for Student Services,* 2007(120), 7–24.

Higginbotham, E. B. (1989). Beyond the sound of silence: Afro-American women in history. *Gender & History, 1*(1), 50–67.

Higginbotham, E. B. (1993). *Righteous discontent: The women's movement in the Black Baptist Church, 1880–1920.* Cambridge, MA: Harvard University Press.

Human Rights Watch (2017). United States events of 2017. Retrieved from https://ww w.hrw.org/world-report/2018/country-chapters/united-states#

Kim, Y. M. (2013). Minorities in higher education: 26th status report. Retrieved from http://diversity .ucsc.edu/resources/images/ace_report.pdf

Jayakumar, U. M., Howard, T. C., Allen, W. R., & Han, J. C. (2009). Racial privilege in the professoriate: An exploration of campus climate, retention, and satisfaction. *The Journal of Higher Education, 80*(5), 538–563.

Joseph, P. E. (2013). Black Studies, student activism, and the Black power movement. In P. E. Joseph (Ed.), *The Black power movement: Rethinking the Civil Rights–Black power era* (pp. 273–300). New York: Routledge.

Krogstad, J. M. (2015). *5 facts about Latinos and education.* Washington, DC: Pew Hispanic Center.

Pew Research. (2017). Hispanic dropout rates his new low college enrollment at new high. Retrieved from http://www.pewresearch.org/fact-tank/2017/09/29/hi spanic-dropout-rate-hits-new-low-college-enrollment-at-new-high/

Piercy, F., Giddings, V., Allen, K., Dixon, B., Meszaros, P., & Joest, K. (2005). Improving campus climate to support faculty diversity and retention: A pilot program for new faculty. *Innovative Higher Education, 30*(1), 53–66.

Rhoads, R. A. (1998). *Freedom's web: Student activism in an age of cultural diversity.* Baltimore, MD: Johns Hopkins University Press.

Saldaña, L. P., Castro-Villarreal, F., & Sosa, E. (2013). "Testimonios" of Latina junior faculty: Bridging academia, family, and community lives in the academy. *Educational Foundations*, *27*(1/2), 31–48.

Trower, C. A., & Chait, R. P. (2002). Faculty diversity too little for too long. *Harvard Magazine*. Retrieved from http://harvardmagazine.com/2002/03/faculty-diversity.html

Turner, C. S. V., González, J. C., & Wood, J. L. (2008). Faculty of color in academe: What 20 years of literature tells us. *Journal of Diversity in Higher Education*, *1*(3), 139.

United States Census Bureau. (2017, August). School enrollment of the Hispanic population: Two decades of growth. Retrieved from https://www.census.gov/newsroom/blogs/random-samplings/2017/08/school_enrollmentof.html

United States Census Bureau. (August 2017). Annual estimates of the resident population by sex, race and Hispanic origin for the United States and Counties. Retrieved from https://www.census.gov/newsroom/press-kits/2017/estimates-characteristics.html

United States Census Bureau. (2019, February). Educational attainment in the united states. Retrieved from https://www.census.gov/data/tables/2018/demo/education-attainment/cps-detailed-tables.html

U.S. Department of Education, National Center for Education Statistics (2018). *The condition of education 2018* (NCES 2018-144), Characteristics of Postsecondary Faculty. Retrieved from https://nces.ed.gov/programs/coe/indicator_csc.asp

Whittaker, J. A., Montgomery, B. L., & Acosta, V. G. M. (2015). Retention of underrepresented minority faculty: Strategic initiatives for institutional value proposition based on perspectives from a range of academic institutions. *Journal of Undergraduate Neuroscience Education*, *13*(3), A136.

Wilder, C.S. (2013). *Ebony & Ivy: Race, slavery, and the troubled history of America's universities*. New York: Bloomsbury Press.

Zambrana, R. E., Ray, R., Espino, M. M., Castro, C., Douthirt Cohen, B., & Eliason, J. (2015). "Don't leave us behind": The importance of mentoring for underrepresented minority faculty. *American Educational Research Journal*, *52*(1), 40–72.

Afterword

Paying Professional Taxes – Academic Labor Cost for Faculty of Color and Indigenous Faculty

Noelle W. Arnold

When asked to write this afterword, I was not sure what I would discuss. The editors requested that I conclude the book by offering an institutional perspective, but not necessarily sharing personal experiences with Racial Battle Fatigue (RBF).

As an Associate Dean at The Ohio State University, my position deals with issues of diversity, equity, and inclusion. I have far too many professional stories that illustrate that while institutions of higher education indicate they want diversity, equity, and social justice, these institutions are not discourse-neutral. These processes and discourses are a part of the larger institutional frame and "serve to entrap (certain) individuals in certain representations, roles, contracts, hierarchies and other hegemonic processes" (Arnold & Crawford, 2014, p. 2).

After reflecting on the chapters in this book, a salient theme emerged for me: Working in academia is "costly" and "taxing" for faculty of color and indigenous faculty. In this afterword I discuss some of the costs or taxes while outlining several of the precursors to RBF. For faculty, there are material costs and taxes for being non-White and doing critical research, teaching, and service. However, as this book illustrates, there are also emotional and physical ones as well. In the Academy, "costs" are incurred in a variety of forms depending on the price faculty are willing to pay to gain status, security, and a sense of belonging in their workplace (Fenton et al., 2012). Academics receive salaries for their work, but they must also pay taxes on the "real currency" of institutional frames. These currencies lie in courses taught, committee contributions engaged, and most importantly, research completed and published. Like a proverbial "pound of flesh," certain faculty meet with inequitable professional demands, sanctions, and penalties. For instance, faculty experience marginalization by virtue of their gender, race, differing abilities, and/or pedagogical stance.

As the chapters in this important book show, despite an increased number of faculty of color in positions of authority, discrimination continues to manifest itself through devaluation and an institutional culture of lip service to equality rather than a "real" one. An ironic thing is that diversity efforts may exacerbate rather than ameliorate inequality (Iverson, 2007) if postsecondary institutions have not modified policies and procedures nor prepared the institutional culture and climate to support them. Despite espousing programs and initiatives to create greater diversity on campus, flagship, and research-extensive research institutions can contribute to inequities in higher education (Gerald & Haycock, 2006).

The inclusion of marginalized groups only appears to signal an increase in organizational diversity and increasing professional access for marginalized people. Though the number of diverse faculty is growing (Walesby, 2013), university structures, policies, and procedures have not grown in parallel to support them. Indeed, in Chapter 4, Section 4.1, Shandin H. Pete and Salisha A. Old Bull state that institutions often have "traditions in their mission statements yet struggle with implementing them." Faculty of color remain vulnerable to continued tokenization and outdated attitudes that often create disparities (Ortega-Liston & Soto, 2014). In Chapter 5, Section 5.1, Paula R. Buchanan discusses how the tokenization of faculty of color is often a way for institutions to "prove" that their university system is racially diverse. Buchanan recommends more diverse people should "be in the rooms where diversity decisions are made."

While some intensive policy and structural interventions (e.g., Civil Rights, Title IX, and Affirmative Action) have intended to rectify and prevent exclusionary practices, inequalities persist in higher education (Turner, 2002). For example, fewer faculty of color are in Associate Professor ranks; they are often paid less and are unable to persist in the professoriate for lack of success in securing tenure and the not-so-blind journal review processes (Smith, Turner, Osei-Kofi, & Richards, 2004). Further, institutional efforts to recruit, hire, and retain faculty of color may also be limited (Fenelon, 2003), and university diversity missions may be only partially implemented (Griffin, Bennett, & Harris, 2013; Stanley, 2007). Sometimes a single person of color represents the diversity of an organization (Park, 2013; Huo & Molina, 2006). As an Associate Dean, this is unacceptable to me. The result is that in many Historically and Predominantly White institutions (H/PWIs), faculty of color are still treated in stereotypical and racist ways (Feagin, 2010; Frazier, 2011). This too is unacceptable.

RACIAL BATTLE FATIGUE

Smith, Allen, and Danley (2007) describe Racial Battle Fatigue as "social-psychological stress responses (e.g., frustration, anger, exhaustion, physical avoidance, psychological or emotional withdrawal, escapism, acceptance of racist attributions)" (p. 552) associated with being a person of color and the repeated target of racism. The accumulative encumbrance and consequences of racism can result in "public health and mental illness" (Pierce, 1970, p. 266). RBF can manifest itself broadly in physical symptoms by increasing a stress-induced body response state resulting in "weakened immunity and increased sickness, tension headaches, trembling and jumpiness, chronic pain in healed injuries, elevated blood pressure, and a pounding heartbeat" (Smith et al., 2007, p. 301). The racism that non-White faculty experience literally makes them sick. Presidents, Provosts, Deans, and Department Chairs need to reduce the RBF that their non-White faculty experience. Feagin (2010, 2013) states that "inclinations to discriminatory action" make up the White Racial Frame (WRF), which in turn re/produces oppressive conditions in institutions that cause distress, leading to RBF and a kind of "psychological warfare." In H/PWI professional contexts, RBF can result in "strained relations with white colleagues; [experiencing] constantly having one's credentials questioned; an unwieldy workload; job insecurity; lack of respect from white colleagues; and cultural, social and professional alienation" (Fields, 2007, p. 1). RBF is taxing physically and emotionally for diverse faculty members.

Academic Labor and Currency

In some cases, there are penalties and forfeitures when certain taxes are not paid. Academics' emotional and physical well-being is bound to be affected by decisions made about their lives in the academy. Stephen Ball (2003) discusses policy in higher education as influenced by the "the markets" and "managerialism." This performativity is

> a culture and a mode of regulation that employs judgements, comparisons and displays as means of incentive, control, attrition and change—based on rewards and sanctions (both material and symbolic). The performances serve as measures of productivity or output, or displays of "quality," or "moments" of promotion or inspection. As such they stand for, encapsulate or represent the worth, quality or value of an individual within a field of judgement. The issue of who controls the field of judgement is crucial.
>
> (Ball, 2003, p. 216)

The currency of academia is thusly commoditized by tenure and promotion systems, target-settings, and output comparisons. These systems lead to "security seeking tactics and existential anxiety" (Ball, 2003, p. 216) such as RBF. It is important to consider that academic labor is not merely an essence of a thing. Academic labor is an articulation of active processes that normally go unspoken (Winn, 2015). Adrianna Kezar (2004) concludes, "The costs appear to outweigh the benefits" (p. 454). What does this mean for the leaders of these institutions?

Racial Opportunity Cost

Racial Opportunity Cost or ROC (Chambers et al., 2014) describes the price African American and Latinx students pay to pursue educational success in a predominantly White school terrain. Chambers et al. (2014) write, "Racial opportunity cost diverges from its traditional application in that it can examine the costs to individual students of color as a result of the press of larger contextual factors" (p. 466). Although ROC describes the experiences of P–12 students, ROC is effective at detailing the racialized experiences of other underrepresented groups due to the utility of its *four assertions*.

The *first assertion* is that the dominant society places expectations on students of color. In applying this to faculty of color in higher education, expectations often shift for those of color in academia (Matthew, 2016). The *second assertion* of ROC is the intersection of other identities for students that affect success. For instance, in Chapter 3, Section 3.1, Mildred Boveda reminds us that identities intersect and these intersections often become salient in academia's processes (Perna, 2001, 2005; Turner, Gonzalez & Wood, 2008. The *third assertion* is that academic persistence in relationship to the institutional climates influence student success. For many faculty of color, this persistence often translates into extra work and overwork when other faculty are insulated from the same (Eagan Jr. & Garvey, 2015; Jones, Hwang, & Bustamante, 2015). Lastly, the *fourth assertion* of ROC addresses the mental and emotional cost students of color pay when navigating a White-normed formal education system. In higher education, faculty of color endure mental and emotional cost in a WRF (Feagin, 2013). The WRF mostly provides the context within which faculty of color must operate (Guarino & Borden, 2017).

The ROC construct can offer insight into standard operating procedures at the institutional level, and assist in examining how decision-makers often function not as autonomous actors, but are primarily guided by the systemic influences of a larger context (March, 1994). The ROC construct provides the analytic lens to view the far-too-common experiences of faculty of color and indigenous faculty.

THE WHITE RACIAL FRAME

Scholars have postulated that faculty of color represented on campuses still operate within a hegemonic system of White supremacy (Andersen, Taylor, & Logion, 2014; DeCuir & Dixson, 2004; Feagin, 2013) that offers furtive and overt advantages to Whites over people of color (Watson, 2013; Winkle-Wagner, 2009). Feagin (2010) coined the idea of the White Racial Frame (WRF), which includes Whiteness, White privilege, and institutionalized racism. The WRF perpetuates disproportionate power, as Whiteness "has become … 'common sense,' [which] includes important racial stereotypes, understandings, images, and inclinations to act … [That prevail] because whites have long had the power and the resources to impose this reality" (Feagin & Cobas, 2008, p. 39). This framing maintains systemic racism in the United States and its institutions and among institutional agents (Feagin, 2013, p. 1). With the WRF as the "norm," faculty of color are often represented as disadvantaged in these institutions from the start (Iverson, 2007). I would argue that many university processes operate based on rules of Whiteness.

In the next section, I reflect on the costs for faculty of color in academia and taxes incurred as themes in the chapters of this book.

Credibility Tax

The credibility tax has to do with the new knowledge faculty of color bring to the university and faculty themselves. Questions about these faculty may be: "Are they themselves seen as credible, and is what they have to share credible?" In Chapter 1, Section 1.1, Robin R. Ford reminds us of the minefield of tenure and promotion and "What is and is not valuable in these categories depends very much on who is serving on the committees and what they value."

In universities, some forms of research are valued and celebrated more than others, especially research that conforms to dominant ideologies (Bonilla-Silva, 2001). For example, in Chapter 4, Section 4.2, Dawn Quigley discusses the resistance encountered in response to indigenous scholarship. Mental models of the dominant culture that justify systems and rules in educational research in such a way that make these models the standard for "good" research and complicates research by faculty of color (Stanley, 2007) regulate research. Research-intensive Institutions (R1s), like The Ohio State University where I work, expect faculty members to seek out perceived top-tier journals that privilege empirical, scientific, and "objective research." This coded-language discursively culls qualitative research and scholarship on topics like race, ethnicity, and gender (Fenelon, 2003; Tillman, 2002).

Many scholars of color write on issues mirroring their own societal status; publishing in "objective" journals is often untenable (Allen, Epps, Guillory, Suh, & Bonous-Hammarth, 2000). Given White racial frames, "the general perception is that minority-related topics do not constitute academic scholarship ... and that they are inappropriate and narrow in scope" (Reyes & Halcon, 1988, p. 307). Confounding the issue further, when faculty of color do publish in preferred, top-tier journals, they can still experience "racial separatism" (Steward, 2006, p. 45). In this case, the work of faculty of color are then considered outside of the mainstream for their professions and isolated as unique but not "standard" for the field.

Leading Edge Tax

Leading edge taxes are imposed on individuals when raising new inquiry and perspectives for groups not previously represented, such as feminists or faculty of color. Blazing new trails often creates certain inequities (Bankier, 1985). While obvious to faculty of color, "Marginality is often neither observable nor acknowledged by others within the academy" (Thompson & Dey, 1998, p. 325). Faculty of color in particular are entrapped as they face extra scrutiny, stereotypes about their abilities, and expectations that they act "nice" in the wake of discrimination and adversity. Even though marginality is sometimes unobservable in a WRF, inequity remains obvious to faculty of color. In Chapter 1, Section 1.2, Robert Palmer notes that there are "stereotypical assumptions about him (and other Black men) simply because of the color of skin."

Faculty are told they can achieve the same rewards as their White colleagues if they adapt, try harder, or take leading edge work and make it more "mainstream." Faculty of color, such as Sayil Camacho in Chapter 5, Section 5.3, are told to be flexible and adaptive while White colleagues may even be explicitly told institutional practices should accommodate them.

Leading edge work can often come with inequitable material realities like inequality in pay and other rewards (Acker, 2006) (e.g., holding leadership positions, holding an endowed chair or distinguished professorship). In Chapter 5, Section 5.2, Martel Pipkins discusses his time in an adjunct position "empty of health benefits, job security, departmental influence/visibility, certain department/university opportunities in the form of professional development, and a pay cut that would repress my ability to remain fed and housed." These inequities constitute another form of racial microaggressions and reinforce a type of economic or opportunity ceiling (Fuller, 2014) for faculty of color.

Group Status Tax

Tierney and Bensimon (1996) described the price faculty are willing to pay in order to be accepted. Their term "smile work" (p. 83) aptly describes how marginalized faculty try to navigate institutional patterns in academia. Being "nice" is a pervasive mediator for faculty of color in professional communities, demonstrating how professional taxes intersect along lines of race and gender. In Chapter 1, Section 1.3, Cleveland Hayes reminds us that colleges are often "spaces that uphold and maintain White supremacy."

Niceness is problematic, and it creates a pitfall for those of color. The persistence of niceness as a discourse functions as a gendered and raced mental habit that remains firmly entrenched. It is a recurring frame through which Whiteness is normalized, "constituting a tenuous sense of belonging and rightful presence" (Butler, Laclau, & Zizek, 2000, p. 14). In Chapter 2, Section 2.1, Andrew Cho and Sopang "Pang" Men discussed how prolonged silence in the institution is often stereotyped as being timid or indicative of the quiet Asian male stereotype. These silences are often another way that White voice is reaffirmed and upheld and other voices subsumed in the larger discourse. Cho (Burmese) and

Pang (Cambodian) encourage the full support of upper administration to counter these silences.

Group taxes can also come in the form of professional station or regard or *place* in an organization (Cresswell, 2014). Group tax is the "result of processes and practices" (Cresswell, 2014, p. 2). Places and spaces hold certain norms, mores, formal, and informal ways of operating that materially and subjectively influence certain individuals, from their sense of being to the entitlements they receive. In Chapter 2, Section 2.2, Anita Chikkatur reminds us that many in the "White environment often reify the Whiteness of the space." To counter RBF, Chikkatur proposes developing networks in which people understand that "academia is a racialized, gendered, and classed space."

The social "geographies" of a group affect and manipulate one's sense of position and behavior in an environment. Changes in expected positioning is a form of "being out of place." Potentially viewed as out-of-place or out of their expected position, faculty of color can experience aspects of RBF by feeling isolated, feared, unheard, outnumbered, and/or feeling an out-of-place-ness (Pittman, 2012). In Chapter 2, Section 2.3, Takumi C. Sato discusses being "(1) ignored, (2) pacified, and/or (3) deflected." In Chapter 4, Section 4.2, Dawn Quigley discussed countering naysayers and "resisting the hegemonic structures of higher education where whispers of you do not fit echo the halls of universities (see Thompson, 2004)."

Sociologist Nirmal Puwar (2004) discusses elite professions to demonstrate how institutional spaces and places can contain certain "embodiments" or behaviors, exerting influence over how people physically conduct themselves. People with power or prestige in elite professions like academia regulate others along lines like gender and race. They set the conditions, policies, and processes that decide who is in, out, fit, or unfit for a place. Even institutions, like universities, that postulate objectivity and universality, privilege Whiteness and function within the White racial frame (Watson, 2013). Bias on the part of the establishment often becomes a convenient apologetic for racial taxation (Amparo Alves, 2009).

Retaliation Tax

Retaliation tax is the formal and informal attacking and mobbing of faculty who may just not be willing to "play the game" to get where they want to go in the university. Attributing excessive weight to areas such as teaching and evaluations becomes a form of retaliation. The rigor and empiricism of research, and the expertise and competency of the Black professor, are most often questioned if they teach about and research issues of race, racism, sexism, LBGTQI phobias, or analyze other discursive practices (Smith & Hawkins, 2011). Evaluations for faculty who teach and research such issues are weighted more heavily. Service is also a form of retaliation imposed upon faculty of color. Research indicates faculty of color generally devote more time to service than White faculty (Frazier, 2011). Leaders who are reading this book ought to know this and take it into consideration when reviewing tenure and promotion files.

In Chapter 3, Section 3.2, Nadia Martínez-Carrillo discusses how universities "increasingly commodify time, and encourage toxic competition and isolation." In Chapter 3, Section 3.3, Pamela Anne Quiroz echoes this by saying that the "institution structures isolation and division among its faculty of color." More troubling than the trends of faculty of color bearing the weight of service at H/PWIs is the heuristic expectation they do so while their White peers are free to engage in research without retaliation (Wood, Hilton, & Nevarez, 2015). In Chapter 4, Section 4.3, Jameson D. Lopez warns how "institutions often encourage and take advantage of our diversity." In this case, faculty of color end up advising and mentoring all students of color or serve in many ways that are not expected for White scholars.

DIGNITY

Many in higher education live, learn, and work in spaces and places in which they experience multiple assaults to their sense of dignity (Witherspoon & Taylor, 2010). In addition to the recommendations from the contributors in each of their chapters, I offer an essential recommendation, particularly to those of us who work in areas of diversity, equity, and inclusion. Dignity is essential to authentic inclusion. Inclusion is produced by treating others as human beings, no matter their state, condition, or behavior. Irby and Drame (2016) assert that intentional efforts must be made "to understand and eliminate all subjective experiences and conditions of oppression, humiliation, and degradation" (p. 7). The authors in this book remind us that although inherent dignity is inviolable and cannot be stripped, a person's sense of dignity can. In their work to develop inclusive cultures, leaders must address forces that dehumanize at personal, systemic, and institutional levels. The editors remind inclusive higher education leaders and influencers that RBF can be eliminated if they make changes to their colleges/universities, irrespective of the institution's research status or type.

The inclusive educational leader creates purposeful inclusion by being deeply mindful of others' identities, fostering understanding, respect, and dignity, and working to build a sense of mutual responsibility for and commitment to cultivating an inclusive, supportive, and rigorous educational experience for each student.

This kind of work requires a common framework for understanding dignity, as it is difficult to determine what threatens dignity, and, conversely, how to honor commitments to protect and promote it, if one does not understand or value it.

CONCLUSION

Place is being rediscovered as a potentially powerful yet unexplored concept in leadership (Smith, 1991). As makers of place, inclusive leaders must attend to (a) spatial practices, (b) representations of space, and (c) representational spaces—"the conceived, the perceived and the lived, respectively" (Baker & Foote, 2006, p. 93). They must apply the knowledge and skills they have developed to build inclusive, safe, healthy, caring, responsive, and respectful cultures, places where students, faculty, staff, and community members feel respected, welcome, and validated.

We must incorporate dignity as an explicit value and goal. Grace and Gravestock (2009) wrote, "we believe that working inclusively is not quite the same as 'dealing with' diverse student groups'" (p. 2). The inclusive educational leader creates purposeful inclusion by being deeply mindful of others' identities, fostering understanding, respect, and dignity, and working to build a sense of mutual responsibility for and commitment to cultivating an inclusive, supportive, and rigorous educational experience for each student. After reading this book, it became apparent to me that there are academic labor costs for faculty of color and indigenous faculty. Higher education leaders need to stop collecting these professional taxes. They can begin by showing dignity toward their non-White colleagues.

REFERENCES

Acker, J. (2006). Inequality regimes: Gender, class, and race in organizations. *Gender & Society, 20*(4), 441–464.

Allen, W. R., Epps, E. G., Guillory, E. A., Suh, S. A., & Bonous-Hammarth, M. (2000). The Black academic: Faculty status among African Americans in U.S. higher education. *The Journal of Negro Education, 69*(1/2), 112–127.

Amparo Alves, J. (2009). Narratives of violence: The White imagiNation and the making of Black masculinity in City of God. *Universidade Federal de Goiás, 12*(2), 301–310.

Andersen, M., Taylor, H., & Logio, K. (2014). *Sociology: The essentials* (8th ed.). Independence, KY: Cengage Learning.

Arnold, N. W., & Crawford, E. R. (2014). Metaphors of leadership and spatialized practice. *International Journal of Leadership in Education, 17*(3), 257–285.

Baker, M., & Foote, M. (2006). Changing spaces: Urban school interrelationships and the impact of standards-based reform. *Educational Administration Quarterly, 42*(1), 90–123.

Ball, S. J. (2003). *Class strategies and the education market: The middle classes and social advantage*. Abingdon, UK: Routledge.

Bankier, J. K. (1985). Equality, affirmative action, and the charter: Reconciling inconsistent sections. *Canadian Journal of Women & the Law, 1*(1), 134–152.

Bonilla-Silva, E. (2001). *White supremacy and racism in the post-civil rights era.* Boulder, CO: Lynne Rienner Publishers.

Butler, J., Laclau, E., & Žižek, S. (2000). *Contingency, hegemony, universality: Contemporary dialogues on the left.* Brooklyn, NY: Verso.

Chambers, T. V., Huggins, K. S., Locke, L. A., & Fowler, R. M. (2014). Between a "ROC" and a school place: The role of racial opportunity cost in the educational experiences of academically successful students of color. *Educational Studies, 50*(5), 464–497.

Cresswell, T. (2014). *Place: An introduction.* Hoboken, NJ: John Wiley & Sons.

DeCuir, J. T., & Dixson, A. D. (2004). "So when it comes out, they aren't that surprised that it is there": Using critical race theory as a tool of analysis of race and racism in education. *Educational Researcher, 33*(5), 26–31.

Eagan, M. K., Jr. & Garvey, J. C. (2015). Stressing out: Connecting race, gender, and stress with faculty productivity. *The Journal of Higher Education, 86*(6), 923–954.

Feagin, J. R. (2010). *Racist America: Roots, current realities, and future reparations.* Abingdon, UK: Routledge.

Feagin, J. R. (2013). *The White racial frame: Centuries of racial framing and counter-framing.* Abingdon, UK: Routledge.

Feagin, J. R., & Cobas, J. A. (2008). Latinos/as and white racial frame: The procrustean bed of assimilation. *Sociological Inquiry, 78*(1), 39–53.

Fenelon, J. (2003). Race, research, and tenure: Institutional credibility and the incorporation of African, Latino, and American Indian faculty. *Journal of Black Studies, 34*(1), 87–100.

Fenton, N. E., Shields, C., McGinn, M. K., & Manley-Casimir, M. (2012). Exploring emotional experiences of belonging. *Workplace, 19*, 40–52.

Fields, C. D. (2007). A morale dilemma. *Diverse Issues in Higher Education, 13*(17), 22.

Frazier, K. N. (2011). Academic bullying: A barrier to tenure and promotion for African-American faculty. *Florida Journal of Educational Administration & Policy, 5*(1), 1–13.

Fuller, D. (2014, August 18). Despite academic achievement, pay gaps likely continue between the races. *University of Cincinnati News.* Retrieved from http://www.uc.edu/news/NR.aspx?id=20131

Gerald, D., & Haycock, K. (2006). *Engines of inequality: Diminishing equity in the nation's premier public universities.* Washington, DC: Education Trust.

Grace, S., & Gravestock, P. (2009). *Inclusion and diversity: Meeting the needs of all students.* Abingdon, UK: Routledge.

Griffin, K. A., Bennett, J. C., & Harris, J. (2013). Marginalizing merit?: Gender differences in Black faculty D/discourses on tenure, advancement, and professional success. *The Review of Higher Education, 36*(4), 489–512.

Guarino, C. M., & Borden, V. M. (2017). Faculty service loads and gender: Are women taking care of the academic family?. *Research in Higher Education, 58*(6), 672–694.

Huo, Y. J., & Molina, L.E. (2006). Is pluralism a viable model of diversity? The benefits and limits of subgroup respect. *Group Processes and Intergroup Relations, 9*(3), 359–376.

Irby, D. J., & Drame, E. R. (2016). Introduction. Black bridges, troubled waters, and the search for solid ground: The people, the problems, and educational justice. In E. R. Drame, & D. J. Irby (Eds.), *Black participatory research* (pp. 1–19). New York: Palgrave Macmillan.

Iverson, S. V. (2007). Camouflaging power and privilege: A critical race analysis of university diversity policies. *Educational Administration Quarterly, 43*(5), 586–611. doi :10.1177/0013161x07307794

Jones, B., Hwang, E., & Bustamante, R. M. (2015). African American female professors' strategies for successful attainment of tenure and promotion at predominately White institutions: It can happen. *Education, Citizenship and Social Justice, 10*(2), 133–151.

Kezar, A. J. (2004). Obtaining integrity? Reviewing and examining the charter between higher education and society. *The Review of Higher Education, 27*(4), 429–459.

March, J. G. (1994). *A primer on decision making.* New York: Free Press.

Matthew, P. A. (Ed.). (2016). *Written/unwritten: Diversity and the hidden truths of tenure.* Chapel Hill, NC: University of North Carolina Press.

Ortega-Liston, R., & Rodriguez Soto, I. (2014). Challenges, choices, and decisions of women in higher education: A discourse on the future of Hispanic, Black, and Asian members of the professoriate. *Journal of Hispanic Higher Education, 13*(4), 285–302.

Park, J. J. (2013). *When diversity drops: Race, religion, and affirmative action in higher education.* New Brunswick, NJ: Rutgers University Press.

Perna, L. W. (2001). Sex and race differences in faculty tenure and promotion. *Research in Higher Education, 42*(5), 541–567.

Perna, L. W. (2005). The benefits of higher education: Sex, racial/ethnic, and socioeconomic group differences. *The Review of Higher Education, 29*(1), 23–52.

Pierce, C. M. (1970). Black psychiatry one year after Miami. *Journal of the National Medical Association, 62*(6), 471–473.

Pittman, C. T. (2012). Racial microaggressions: The narratives of African American faculty at a predominantly White university. *The Journal of Negro Education, 81*(1), 82–92.

Puwar, N. (2004). *Space invaders: Race, gender and bodies out of place.* New York: Berg.

Reyes. M., & Halcon, J. J. (1988). Racism in academia: The old wolf revisited. *Harvard Educational Review, 58*(3), 299–314.

Smith, P. (1991). Positioning recreational sport in higher education. In R. L. Boucher & W. J. Weese (Eds.), *Management of recreational sport in higher education* (pp. 5–12). Carmel, IN: Wm. C. Brown & Benchmark.

Smith, B. P., & Hawkins, B. J. (2011). Examining student evaluations of Black college faculty: Does race matter? *Journal of Negro Education, 80*(2), 149–162.

Smith, W. A., Allen, W. R., & Danley, L. L. (2007). "Assume the position … you fit the description": Campus racial climate and the psychoeducational experiences and racial battle fatigue among African American male college Students. *American Behavioral Scientist, 51*(4), 551–578.

Smith, D. G., Turner, C. S. V., Osei-Kofi, N., & Richards, S. (2004). Interrupting the usual: Successful strategies for hiring faculty of color. *The Journal of Higher Education, 75*(2), 133–160.

Stanley, C. A. (2007). When counter narratives meet master narratives in the journal editorial-review process. *Educational Researcher, 36*(14), 14–24.

Steward, D. (2006). Review of scholarship on the status of African American faculty members in English. *ADE Bulletin, 140*, 45–60.

Tillman, L. C. (2002). Culturally sensitive research approaches: An African-American perspective. *Educational Researcher, 31*(9), 3–12.

Tierney, W. G., & Bensimon, E. M. (1996). *Promotion and tenure: Community and socialization in academe.* Albany, NY: State University of New York Press.

Thompson, E. A. (2004). *The soundscape of modernity: Architectural acoustics and the culture of listening in America, 1900–1933.* Cambridge, MA: MIT Press.

Thompson, C. J., & Dey, E. L. (1998). Pushed to the margins: Sources of stress for African American college and university faculty. *The Journal of Higher Education, 69*(3), 324–345.

Turner, C. S. V., Gonzalez, J. C., & Wood, J. L. (2008). Faculty of color in academe: What 20 years of literature tells us. *Journal of Diversity in Higher Education, 1*(3), 139–168.

Turner, C. S. V. (2002). Women of color in academe: Living with multiple marginality. *The Journal of Higher Education, 73*(1), 74–93.

Walesby, A. (2013, November 5). Future hiring trends in higher education: What institutions can do to thrive and succeed in challenging times? *Higher Ed Jobs Career Tools.* Retrieved from https://www.higheredjobs.com/articles/articleDisplay.cfm?ID=466

Watson, V. T. (2013). *The souls of White folks: African American writers theorize Whiteness.* Jackson, MO: University Press of Mississippi.

Winkle-Wagner, R. (2009). *The unchosen me: Race, gender, and identity among Black women in college.* Baltimore, MD: The Johns Hopkins University Press.

Winn, J. (2015). Writing about academic labor. *Workplace, 25*, 1–15.

Witherspoon, N., & Taylor, D. L. (2010). Spiritual weapons: Black female principals and religio-spirituality. *Journal of Educational Administration and History*, *42*(2), 133–158.

Wood, J. L., Hilton, A. A., & Nevarez, C. (2015). Faculty of color and White faculty: An analysis of service in the Arizona public university system. *The Journal of the Professoriate*, *8*(1), 85–109.

Index